*Once upon a time, I saw a line.
I saw the paper pull the ink from the brush
and the brush, one hair at a time,
relinquish the ink, allowing it to become
a line, to settle into its destiny.*

DRAWING THE LINE

Susan Gardner

RED MOUNTAIN PRESS

2011

For RDR

ONE · *Tepoztlán* 6

TWO · *New York: Our Pasts as Prologue* 37

THREE · *Incidents of Change* 80

FOUR · *Korea* 114

FIVE · *Annandale* 152

SIX · *Japan* 158

SEVEN · *Fairfax* 184

EIGHT · *Mexico* 191

NINE · *Detours* 200

TEN · *Santa Fe* 210

ELEVEN · *Turnaround* 217

TWELVE · *In Transit* 260

Afterword 266

ONE

Tepoztlán

MOUNTAINS ENCIRCLE MEXICO CITY. On clear days the snowy peak of La Malinche is visible in most of the city. It is named for the noble, enslaved woman who became the wife of Hernán Cortés, conqueror of the Aztecs. Its high beauty is a beacon as you enter the long highway south to Acapulco.

I drove alone. The road climbed over the mountains toward Cuernavaca. At the busy rest stop at Tres Marias pass I took a break. This spot on the flank of the sierra is known for the rock formation that reminds people of three women, three Marias, with their heads covered by shawls. Behind the several roadside restaurants and souvenir shops, the sierra was visible on every side across a wide valley. The piney air smelled of chile, toasting tortillas, gasoline, and wildflowers. An hour later, I came to the turn-off for Tepoztlán and drove the few miles down into the village.

The name Tepoztlán means "place where there is copper." It also means "place of the Tepozteco," the spirit being who later in his life was transformed into Quetzalcoatl, the Plumed Serpent. In the cool early afternoon, it was beautiful. Because of its energetic, traditional celebration of Carnival, the village was well known, but a bit off the main highway and somewhat inconvenient to get to. Not many foreigners lived there yet. Mostly they were Germans who were older than I was. Many more were going to arrive soon.

After wandering around for a few minutes, I found a two-storey, bright white, concrete hotel, still in the last stages of construction. I went up the three concrete steps and checked in. Tepoztlán had one old, atmospheric, somewhat moldy hotel—which I didn't know about yet—and the wacky, brand-new hotel where I planned to stay for a few days. The hotel had only one phone for all the guests to use, right next to the reception desk. Any and all conversations were held under the inquisitive clerk's direct supervision. It was a fair introduction to the little town that was about to become the nearest thing I had ever had to a home.

This hotel lobby was not grand. Perhaps in other circumstances it might not have qualified for the status of lobby. The space was smaller than the small rooms, furnished with just a stiff settee not quite sufficient for two people to sit comfortably. Five feet from the clerk at the reception desk, a tiny, round telephone table held the only phone on the premises.

I walked out to the *zócalo*, the main plaza, and found the café. Two or three other customers were already eating, and the owner wasn't sure if they had enough food left to serve me. They hadn't been prepared for this rush of weekday business. They put together a country dinner, with plenty of handmade tortillas, chile stew, and a homemade flan. I took a leisurely *paseo* and crossed the zócalo again. Every shop was closed for dinner and the siesta. I took their example and returned to the hotel for a siesta with a good book.

The lobby was empty except for the clerk. My steps on the tile floor were the only sound until the clerk said, "Señora," and handed me a fistful of message slips. They were all from Edwin. The clerk placed the call to Mexico City on the lobby phone. Under his watchful ear, I replied as Edwin quizzed me about where I had been, why had it taken so long to have lunch, why hadn't I called him at once when I arrived.

Through the "friend of a friend" chain, I found a guesthouse for rent. It was tiny and Spartan in its furnishings but luxurious in charm. A wealth of fuchsia bougainvillea fell over the stone wall. A blue gate opened just barely wide enough to pull my car off the street. The owner, a German woman named Paula, had lived in Mexico for many years. She built the guesthouse, which was separated from her own home by a seven-foot-high stone wall. She gave me a key to the street gate. In order to close the gate again, I had to pull up so that the bumper touched the wall to Paula's garden. The car was bigger than my lawn.

In typical Mexican style, the front of the house was mostly glass, small paned, floor-to-ceiling windows and wide double doors with lapis lazuli blue frames. When you looked from inside, the glass was filled with the lavish bougainvillea cascading over the walls.

The casita had a small room that served for sitting with guests, eating, and cooking. A narrow, turning staircase led up to a big bedroom and bath with a splendid terrace upstairs. At the bottom of the staircase was a phone extension from the main house. There was a small cistern which would tide me over during the dry season when the village water supply was empty.

The zócalo of Tepoztlán was one block long on each side, and around it was one each of most things needed: one café (the only restaurant outside of the hotels), one bar (several more around the village), one pharmacy, one commodities store (through the social security system only), one clothing store (for tourists and weekenders), one stationary store (with school supplies, needles, and thread, etc.), one tobacco store (with newspapers, magazines, and gossip.) The town hall offices were there on the zócalo, open part-time. The mayor's job was part time, too. The largest building was the *ex-paroquia*, the grounds and buildings of a sixteenth-century abbey. The building had been home to the Dominicans for centuries before sheltering Zapata's troops, then the Federales, then Zapatistas again, during the Revolution of 1910.

The busiest building was the tortillería, where the corn brought by customers was ground. Tortillas were also made and sold there. Every day around one o'clock a long line formed as people waited to buy fresh tortillas for the midday dinner. The toasty corn smell permeated the whole block, awakening appetites and stimulating gossip. While the customers were in line, they brought each other up to date. It was a more current source of information than any radio "drive time" news could have been.

Of course, everyone knew that real, homemade tortillas were better, ground by hand on the stone *metate*, patted by hands, slapped onto a hot *comal* for a few seconds. The first time I ate such a tortilla I was captivated by its taste and smell and texture. In the countryside there were still many women who made their tortillas from scratch. But even in a rural village like Tepoztlán, many people bought their tortillas from the little mill. There were no tortillas yet in plastic packages. For those you had to go to Cuernavaca or Mexico City.

Tepoztlán had two market days. On Wednesdays, the market was small enough that I soon knew my favorites: fruit and vegetable vendors, the stands with chicken and pork, the woman who sold raisins and nuts. Jícama with a sprinkle of red pepper was sold by the slice. Over by the café a few people sold nuts, rice, beans, and dried fruits.

Sundays the zócalo overflowed with about twice as many food vendors, flower stalls with girls sitting by mountains of the white callas called *alcatraz*, clothing of every description—undershirts, hand-embroidered blouses, socks, cotton farm pants, baby clothes, and *huaraches* (woven Mexican sandals). Many craftspeople set up at the Sunday market. Some came from as far away as Guerrero and Oaxaca. They brought painted papier-mâché birds and bowls, paintings of the stories of their village life on *amate* bark paper, tiny buildings carved delicately from tree bark. Every sort of plate, bowl, water jug, *cazuela* (an open casserole pot) was brought to the market. Tourists from Mexico City and Cuernavaca, and people with weekend houses, came on Sundays to cruise through the market and have lunch at one of the outdoor Sunday cafés. On Sunday, almost the whole zócalo was covered with a sea of white umbrellas and shade tarps over the vendors.

The busy activity of the weekend market was entirely absent from weekday life in Tepoztlán. I lived by the sun, rising near dawn, walking in the early morning, returning for breakfast and studio work, cooking a very simple midday meal. I took the siesta seriously, reading and resting. I learned to play the recorder, sitting on my little veranda in sight of the mountains. Afternoons I returned to work and kept on through the evening. When people got together for a meal at midday, everyone understood that the time was to be around two o'clock. In the evening, the time was set for "when the sky turns red" at sunset. I liked to walk to most places.

Occasionally I went to Cuernavaca for the museums or to exchange the propane gas tanks used for cooking and hot water. Cuernavaca had some wonderful restaurants in old former haciendas. It was a treat to eat in one or another and while away a long, quiet afternoon under the massive, old trees. Except on the hottest summer days a breeze stirred the leaves, and the shadows were caught in reflections on the surface of the sweet black coffee.

People didn't have phones, at least most didn't, and so they walked to each other's homes, calling at the gate or pulling a bell cord, if there was one. I arrived in Tepoztlán a stranger, with an introduction to just one, somewhat reclusive person, a Swiss artist, Roger. Soon enough, people greeted me in the zócalo, the tortillería, and the Wednesday market. A few weeks after I moved to Tepoz (as it is called), there was a wedding a few houses away. I was in my tiny garden, enjoying the music, when someone banged on my gate. *Come to the fiesta!* I was late! *Nevermind changing clothes, just come!* I met the neighbors, ate, and danced under the jacaranda trees. It was mellow evening by the time I came back through my blue gate.

My little guesthouse was a charming haven and, in sight of the sierra, I recovered from the stresses of Mexico City. Daniel came out weekends, sometimes with his friend Michael. We had fun there, exploring the village and a bit of the surrounding countryside. Sometimes Dan wanted to stay over at Michael's house in the city to attend some school event or just for a sleepover. I missed him those weekends but knew it was good for my son to have some autonomy at fourteen.

Edwin called me often. He required an explanation if I was not there to receive the call. He often phoned late at night, but he came from Mexico City rarely. One Saturday night, though, he came with the two boys for dinner. Afterward, we drove to Cuernavaca for ice cream. When we came back, there was a big note on my door. My landlady, Paula, had taken a message inviting me to supper and a movie with a group of friends at someone's house. (Tepoz had movies only once or twice a year in a community center, and videos were still far in the future.) Edwin grabbed the paper off the door. He imagined I was having an affair with the man who called to leave the message. He berated me in front of the boys, who quietly went inside to occupy themselves with a card game.

BOUNDARIES • *A couple of weeks later Daniel was to stay at Michael's.* Edwin came to Tepoz by himself. I was uneasy. Edwin had never learned to drive and hired a car and driver for the hour's trip. He sent the driver back and settled in for a domestic evening. It was awful. I was uncomfortable when he climbed in bed next to me. We had been married for nineteen years and still had not worked out where the boundaries were drawn. I did not want to sleep in the same bed with him or have any other intimacy. He would not accept a refusal. It was a quiet struggle with unhappy results.

The next morning Edwin behaved as if nothing particularly notable had occurred. He made coffee in my kitchen and eventually his driver returned to take him back to the city.

I decided to seek a divorce. You hear a lot about Mexican "quickie" divorces, but at that time it was difficult to arrange custody and foreign property issues. I called a lawyer I knew in Virginia, where I was a legal resident, made an appointment, bought a ticket with my own check, and went to untangle my life. I stayed with Myrt. We had known each other since our friendship began fifteen years before in Korea. We sat on her porch and talked. She was very shocked that I was seeking a divorce. I had not told any of my friends of my difficulties.

I saw the attorney, Jason, the next day. I tried to get through the process without too many grim details. Jason explained the divorce laws in Virginia at that time. Regardless of the cause, I had left the family home and could lose all rights to financial assets, no matter what I had contributed. Due to the State Department's past prohibition on wives earning money, I was considered not to have made an economic contribution. Nothing we had as husband and wife was attributed to me. Virginia had a one-year waiting period between the conclusion of a separation agreement and the granting of a divorce. During that time we were required to seek some sort of counseling and show an effort to reconcile our differences. The terms of the separation agreement were the basis of the divorce and could not easily be changed. This was the time to consider all the circumstances. Jason questioned me gently but persistently. The story spilled out. The years of jealousy, infidelity, rough treatment, and sexual incompatibility filled the sunny office. I had never told all this to anyone, ever. It took time and tears to get it said. Jason drew up the separation agreement as I wished, the grounds being the innocuous "irreconcilable differences," and no details. He said that Edwin would get a lawyer, there would be some discussion, but in the end he would sign the papers. Edwin asked me to meet him, alone, and Jason advised a discreet but public place and a time limit. We met for an hour, during which Edwin begged me to not go forward with the divorce. Afterward, he signed the agreement, and Jason filed it with the county.

When I returned to Mexico, Edwin and I did try counseling, as required. I drove into Mexico City from Tepoztlán for these meetings. The first sessions were all about my defects, which are varied and many. Edwin explained to the therapist that if only I could improve in a few areas he would not become so agitated and angry. He would be the loving husband he wanted to be. In fact, most of the times he had slapped or pushed me were really for my own good, to shock me out of my erroneous thinking and bad behavior. The subject came up of our last night together in Tepoztlán. Edwin seemed amazed, as if he just then realized what he had done. The time was up and the therapist walked him to the door, came back, and asked me why I wanted to be in this marriage. She indicated that maybe the time for counseling had passed. I didn't go back again.

CLOSE TO PARADISE • *From the time I first arrived in Tepoztlán I had been* meeting people. I had begun to have Sunday dinner with a circle of writers and artists. Usually we were about eight or ten at the table, sometimes a few more when another guest or two joined the regulars. We arrived around one or one-thirty, and each of us contributed something toward dinner. The women did most of the cooking. A few of the men cooked and washed up, too. The conversation ranged from the most ordinary everyday topics to the political news to the latest art exhibitions in the city. We played ping-pong or cutthroat dominoes. We had long leisurely dinners, with a lot of food and wine. After dinner, with the inevitable little cups of "Mexican dynamite" coffee, someone pulled out a manuscript and read an excerpt from a new work. The talk lasted into the evening: a new play to dissect, a concert to look forward to, a politician to criticize, a love affair beginning or ending. Daniel came along once in a while, if he stayed late enough on Sunday. Usually he went back to Mexico City around noon or one o'clock, to avoid the heavy Sunday-evening traffic jam at the highway tollbooth.

My little guesthouse wasn't working out so well. The owner didn't provide water, as she was required to do, and was regularly listening in on phone calls. Weekender friends said to stay in their house while I looked for something better and more permanent. I slept at Pancho and Silvia's old house and looked for a home.

My first acquaintance in the village was Roger. He was a well-known painter, both modest and arrogant, reaching for a kind of abstract figuration in his painting that later he also realized in large-scale sculptures. Roger had lived in Mexico for about twenty-five years by then, in Tepoztlán for about a third of that time. He was divorced, with two children who were sometimes with him. We had many midday dinners, rainy evenings listening to music, excursions to Cuernavaca for errands and ice cream and to see the Diego Rivera murals at the Palace of Cortés. In his own Swiss way, Roger was at least as earnest as I was. On a rainy summer evening he told me the story of Trotsky's murder fifty years before. People were still arguing about it in the 1980s. Around that time, I met and came to admire Trotsky's granddaughter, who is a wonderful Mexican poet. Roger and I liked each other, hovered at the edge of something else, and remained friends as long as I stayed in Tepoz.

Although a very private person, Roger seemed to know everything that was going on. Tepoz was the sort of place where word of mouth was the fastest and most accurate way to find out anything. He called an acquaintance, Margot, and made an appointment for me to see her house. The next day, I drove through the iron gate, over a little stone bridge, along a mossy cobblestone driveway between ten-foot high walls of bougainvillea, and stopped in paradise.

Margot's husband met me in front of the veranda. I would have taken the house without even going inside, but we went through the formalities —he was descended from Germans, after all—and in a few minutes we agreed to terms. I moved immediately. Margot came to show me around. She introduced me to the caretaker, Octavio. I was grateful beyond imagining that this beautiful spot was mine to occupy.

In Tepoztlán, everyone knew where you lived if you had a phone, because the phones stayed with the house. My number was 005. It was almost impossible to get a new residential phone. Besides the new hotel, the only other phone service was at the one-booth phone kiosk near the main plaza, open weekdays when someone was available. When I rented my house, I also requested a box at the post office and received mail there in Box 35, unless it was something the postmaster deemed important, in which case he waved to me, checked the address (or return address), and handed it over the counter with a friendly comment.

The house was just the right size. As you approached, there was an open patio in front with a view to the mountains on three sides. A deep veranda spanned the front of the house and covered the front door. Inside, the central room, the *sala*, had a brick ceiling sixteen feet high in the center and an arched fireplace, big enough to sit in. It took huge logs from old dead trees cut down around the property. It provided the only heat on chilly winter evenings. This room accommodated some chairs and a small sofa, a dining table and chairs, a rocking chair next to the fireplace, and my studio space. The kitchen was very roomy and well equipped, intended for much more cooking than I ever did, except on a few Sundays. To the left was a bedroom with a double bed and bureau, a bathroom with a deep old-fashioned tub, and, miracle of miracles, enough hot water for a comfortable soak with a good book. The house had been built with a huge cistern underneath, and it collected enough rainwater off the roof to supply the house through the driest spring.

To the right of the sala was another bedroom with twin beds and another bath. The whole house was white plaster inside and out, under a terracotta tile roof. When you looked out the kitchen window in the winter, the fifteen-foot-high stone wall was completely covered with orange, red, and yellow-pink bougainvillea. In early spring, the colored bracts fell to the ground, and the walkways and driveway were covered in brilliant splotches for weeks.

The veranda was very deep and furnished with a sofa and four large armchairs, tables, and plants. *Golondrinas* (swallows), nested in the corners of the veranda roof from early spring to fall, and produced an abundance of chicks. Every day, as afternoon turned to evening, they all swooped out from under the eaves and turned in wide circles over the grass with the low sun reflecting on their wings, making graceful patterns in the air, as if they were saying goodnight to one another.

The garden was like a movie set or a novelist's dream of Mexico. From the veranda and patio you stepped onto a lawn of Bermuda grass, cut and groomed by Octavio. There were beautiful leafy trees that budded out as they shed their old leaves so that the branches were never completely bare. The garden had a few banana trees with their long hanging leaves brushing a distinctive steady sound when the wind blew. The garden was filled with plants I had associated only with florists or pictures in books. The birds-of-paradise stood three and four feet tall, stiff stems holding blossoms that did look like birds. There were ginger plants, callas in tropical colors, flowering vines creeping over every stone wall, dark pink roses with small flat flowers and a deep perfume. Through a gate in the north wall, there was an orchard with twenty avocado trees. In the corner was a vine-covered bower with a bench five feet long. The shade was so thick that in the summer it was like a cave. Broken sun glinted through the heavy foliage. I loved to read there. Often the book stayed open and unread on my lap while I dreamed away an afternoon's siesta.

From the main garden there was a path to the lower garden. It had once been planted, but was now mostly wild and overgrown. At the bottom of the steep rock steps, I found an unused, derelict, and romantic fountain, a semicircle about fifteen feet in diameter, with a verdigris-bronze head on the wall that no longer spouted water except in the rainy season. The path continued as a dirt track, some places no longer wide enough for two people to pass, with odds and ends of things: a ten-foot-high ceramic pot on a pedestal, a few little stone animals and mythological figures from the Tepozteco's story on ledges, traces of plantings visible in the wild overgrowth, an occasional slab, artfully artless, suggesting a place to rest.

At the bottom of the second garden, you finally came to the river. It had water in it only during and just after the rainy season. Many tall leafy trees lined the banks on both sides, and from time to time, low accumulations of stones made shallow rapids. The sounds of the water, the leaves, and the birds were a steady background when I walked there. Once in a while I encountered someone on horseback or a farmer who had brought his animals to drink. Occasionally an especially energetic tourist wandered along the riverbed and wound up in my garden. Mostly it was a solitary, nearly silent Eden.

This river in my garden is featured in the story of the Tepozteco. He was the offspring of a woman and the wind. Her father threatened to kill the infant, and his mother wrapped him in maguey leaves, and put him in a basket on the riverbank. He was saved and grew up, through an exciting childhood and several metamorphoses, to be the Tepozteco. Depending on who does the telling, he is or is not the Quetzalcoatl, the Plumed Serpent, whose story is told throughout Latin America. And the stories all started in the river at the bottom of my garden.

Like most houses in Tepoztlán, the *adobes*, the earthen bricks, used to build my house had been dug right there and, as in many weekend houses, the excavation site had been turned into a swimming pool. There was not enough water to fill the pool in the dry season. Once the rain came again it was filled from late July until the winter. I bought a badminton set and Daniel and I played often. We had a game where the object was to keep the birdie in motion, and a few times we reached our goal of a hundred times over the net. The house came with a ping-pong table and paddles, from when Margot's daughters were young. Daniel coached me enough so that we could have a game. When it was my turn for the Sunday dinner, my poet friends used it, too. Someone would bring a guitar and play under the trees while we were making dinner. It sounds very idyllic and it was.

My life took on a rhythm in Tepoz that was exactly what I needed. I worked with purpose and pleasure. It was a time of intense growth and experimentation. I did a lot of papermaking right there on the veranda. The physical process is both arduous and sensual. It has a distinctive, woodsy smell and watery sound as the slurry swirls and waves in the vat. Fifteen years before in Korea, I had become acquainted with the process and products of handmade paper. In Japan I saw the process and used many different kinds of papers in my work. When I began to make my own paper, it was in the context of this past experience. Once I began to use my own papers for painting, the subtle distinctions took on even more importance for me. It spurred me to try many new creative avenues. I made unusual sheets for my painting and for several years did relief sculpture.

I went several times to San Pablito de Pahuatlán, a small Nahuatl village that had made amate bark paper since before Aztec times. The complicated rural route took several hours from Mexico City. On one trek with city friends, about an hour from the village, butterflies began to appear. They descended from the tree branches, first by the hundreds and then thousands. By chance we had entered the world of the monarch butterfly. Some hung so thickly from the trees that they appeared at first to be some sort of strange, wonderfully colored foliage. We slowed the car and finally came to a standstill as the huge flight surrounded the car. We got out, waving our arms and scarves. We passed through their territory at a slow walk. Eventually, we could get back in the car and resume the drive to San Pablito.

In pre-Columbian times, San Pablito's papers had been used for medicines and as tribute to the Aztecs as well as for drawing stories and records. The village culture was changing rapidly. The one man who knew how to do arithmetic became the de facto leader once the papermakers decided to sell their papers for money instead of barter. He and I met often the last year I was in Mexico, and we struck a deal. I showed him how to make the papers acid-free so that they could be used for modern artist prints, and he gave me a supply of the fiber, *amatl*, for my own use. A couple of years later, it was this fiber that I gave to the Library of Congress when I consulted with them on the repair of a precious Mexican colonial document.

Again through a friend of a friend, I met people with a ceramics studio in Cuernavaca, and in 1984 and 1985, I made some pieces there, creating my own glazes for my largely hand-built work. Daniel was doing a project for a science fair and formulated a number of natural glazes, showing the reactions of different combinations of elements — feldspar, ash, quartzite, and metals — in the firing. It was very helpful to me to have his experiments. I had a good time, and the work turned out well.

CLEAR LINE OF SIGHT • *Mostly I painted. For the first time in my life, I used each day as I chose.* For so long, I had struggled to guard a few hours for studio work. In Tepoztlán, the imperatives of other times and other roles were pushed aside. I was free to think and work with all my attention. Although five years had gone by since I left Japan, I had practiced when I could and had not forgotten everything. I used my large Japanese brushes on various papers and made much calligraphy at this time. I put canvas on the easel and made larger images with Chinese colors, attaching amate paper in low relief, glazing it with delicate metallic, water-like colors. I used my Chinese and Japanese inks, colors, and brushes on primed canvas. One of these works is titled *Manzanas de Amadeus/Amadeus' Apples*. It is three blue apples set in a straight line, clear and unadorned. *Manzanas* is an important turning point in my painting. I looked for the attributes that make an apple an apple — and the way the light can alter shape and color and intensify them. I learned more from this painting than any other I have made.

For the first time, I undertook the human figure. I drew and painted my own hands, then Octavio's hands. I received a commission from the Instituto Nacional de Bellas Artes, the National Fine Arts Institute, to do the drawings for a magazine, *Pauta*, using the music staff as the theme. In 1984, I was commissioned to make twenty-four images relating to music for *Dialogos*, the arts magazine of El Colegio de México. I went to the studio of a choreographer friend and asked to watch the rehearsal, to see the repetition, and learn what happens when dancers dance. At home at night, I danced in front of my windows, reflecting my moving figure like black mirrors. I studied the human form from inside my own muscles. Outdoors I worked with black ink, painting the mountain landscape visible from the patio. I signed my work with my name stamps or painted a script version of it, and felt that, as my long-ago Korean teacher had expected, the name had come to represent me. Invitations for solo exhibitions and participation in good events began to come regularly.

The work with oils gradually became more abstract and so did the calligraphy. A line can have many qualities, revealing the character and personality of the artist. The painted line defined the space — that was really the subject matter. A line gives shape and dimension to the air and light. We can make a reality of our choosing. Making art is a powerful and addictive preoccupation.

From childhood, I had kept a journal of sorts, with long periods of absence and bursts of fidelity. Many of the entries were drawings in addition to or instead of words. I continued the habit off and on through my college years, but all that material was thrown away sometime when Mother was clearing out debris. I had kept on intermittently through the peripatetic decades, but in Tepoztlán, I became a faithful recorder again. In two books, I kept drawings, small watercolors, and poems in English and Spanish.

My Spanish language competence was growing but by no means was fully mature. I constantly heard myself make mistakes, speaking awkwardly or with oddities picked up from not understanding all I read or heard. My ten weeks of lessons had gone only so far. Because I lived life mostly in Spanish, I became fluent while having some very odd gaps. The first novel I read in Spanish was *Cien años de soledad*, *One Hundred Years of Solitude*, by Gabriel Garcia Marquez. I read it when I first arrived in

Mexico City, and it took me a very long time, with the help of a fat dictionary and much puzzling, to finish it. I read poets like Villarrutia, Neruda, Borges, and old ones like Halevy. Tomás Segovia was a guest at my house for Sunday dinner and gave me his lovely book, *Partición*. I was inspired to read the rest of his work. Tomás is about fifteen years older than I am. He was born in Valencia, Spain, at the southern edge of Catalunya, and went to Mexico as a young man in flight from Franco. *Partición* was, I think, the first book he did with Catalá and Spanish on facing pages. He was very charming and erudite at the same time.

I also liked the poetry of Veronica Velkov, then a very young woman with great talent and finesse. She is Leon Trotsky's granddaughter and was very determinedly non-political, in itself a political position in the Mexico City literary world.

From my days in Japan, I had some of my journals, with poems in Japanese that I had composed while studying calligraphy. In Tepoz, I wrote literally hundreds of poems in my journal, sometimes with small watercolor or ink drawings on the page, as was my old habit. I thought out paintings and aesthetic puzzlements. I kept recipes for ceramic glazes and papermaking. Parts of the journal are safely between the covers of a nice black book; some are on envelopes, leftover stationary, sketchpads, whatever was at hand. I took very few photographs in those years, but my brush and pen recorded most of what I saw. It doesn't matter to me which tools I use, only that I use them.

Pancho and Silvia had become comfortable friends whom I saw often on the weekends. Pancho was working on the Mexican dictionary project at El Colegio de Mexico and was a writer himself. He walked in one day when I was writing on the veranda, asked to see, and without waiting, took a look. He thought the abundance of short poems made a single book-length work and suggested that he present it at El Colegio for publication. He thought it could be published as a limited edition, on my handmade paper, with handset type. I had not ever thought of myself as a poet — that exalted term — and did not consider the work ready for publication.

CARMEN AND OCTAVIO • *I had wonderful good fortune in the people I met in Tepoztlán. The caretaker of my house, who worked for the owner,* was also my neighbor. He and his family lived in a small house on the same property. Octavio and his wife, Carmen, had met when they were teenagers. He told me that he had loved her from the first, but he was very poor and thought she would never even notice him. Her parents were members of an *ejido*, one of the cooperative farms founded at the time of the Revolution. Membership was hereditary. Her parents worked the farm with many other families, and they lived in a little house of their own nearby. Octavio felt great affection and responsibility toward his wife's family, and as they grew older, took on their share of the work at the farm. Although Carmen had a brother and sister, neither of them wanted to carry on with the ejido. In the mid-1980s, Carmen's parents were in the process of adopting Octavio, then about forty, as their legal son so that he could inherit their right to be a member of the farm. Everyone seemed to think this was a right and just idea as Octavio had worked at the farm for about twenty years by then. The adoption and other paperwork were accomplished. During the legal process, Octavio asked me to help him read a letter. He told me this story with his voice so low I had to lean toward him to hear the words.

They were a beautiful family. After almost two decades together, Carmen and Octavio were tender and caring. Their three children were all thoughtful, bright youngsters. Unlike most Mexican parents, neither of them had ever hit the children. Wrongdoing brought teaching rather than punishment. When I met them, Miguel was seventeen and in high school, just a little older than Daniel. The twins, Maura and Mauricia, were fourteen and in middle school. Miguel was headed for university to become a lawyer. Maura was a gentle girl, and after high school she expected to marry and be a homebody. Mauricia loved science and wanted to go to university to study biology. Carmen was doubtful but not opposed. Octavio was adamant that this course was entirely unsuitable for her. He said no, but for months his decision sat in the middle of the room with them, stubbornly unresolved.

Like most people in Tepoztlán, Carmen and Octavio had a regular daily routine. The children all came back from school around one-thirty. They ate dinner together, and then in the quiet afternoon, the kids did their homework while Carmen and Octavio took their chairs outside with a little table and a pile of magazines, along with pencils and a workbook.

For an hour or so, they practiced reading and writing. They had decided to learn to read well enough to read a book, and at this point they were up to stories in popular magazines. They worked hard. Penmanship was especially tough. Octavio had gone to school through the third grade, and Carmen had finished elementary school. After the hour of practice reading, they went back to the hard, strenuous work they did all day. Study was their siesta. Occasionally one or the other came over to discuss a tricky phrase, but mostly they coached each other toward their goal.

One night Mauricia came running over to my house and breathlessly told me to come with her. Maura had been washing the dog and was stung by a scorpion. Scorpion stings are poisonous and often fatal. The body reacts to the poison almost immediately. It is painful and blood pressure can spike dangerously. The throat becomes sore and swollen, and the person will die of suffocation if the throat closes entirely. In Mexico, about two thousand people die every year from scorpion stings. The pharmacy in Tepoz usually had the anti-venom, but at that moment it was out of stock.

The six of us climbed in my car to find an all night drugstore in Cuernavaca, normally a half-hour drive away. I drove faster than I ever have, hoping all the way that I wouldn't hit a cow warming itself on the pavement for the night. I got to the city in about fifteen minutes. The first open pharmacist didn't have anti-venom either but called around and found someone who did. Meanwhile, Maura could hardly speak, her neck looked twice its normal size, and her face was getting very puffy and swollen. Her leg above the sting was swollen and tender and more so every minute. I drove the little distance at the highest speed that allowed us to turn the corners. At the pharmacy they were waiting for us. Octavio and Carmen half carried Maura into the pharmacy, and in another minute she was injected with the anti-venom. She began to improve at once. The pharmacist had Maura wait for fifteen minutes to be sure she was recovering, and then sent her home to rest. He thought maybe she could stay home from school for a day to recuperate.

From that night on, I had a new bedtime routine. *El alacrán*, the scorpion, loves to snuggle into your bedding or shoes, someplace warm and cozy. Each night I folded back the blankets and sheets and plumped the pillows energetically. In the morning, I made it a habit to shake my shoes before I put them on. More than once, I saw scorpions hop away from all this activity. Later on I saw platoons of black ants carrying off a scorpion as their prize of war.

The spring weather grew hot and dry. The girls' school year was ending, and it was time to decide about Mauricia's future. If she were to have a chance for university, she needed to go to Cuernavaca with Miguel to a high school that had a college preparatory program. Mauricia cried and insisted and cried some more. Carmen came to my house to talk it over. By this time, we knew each other well. Of course, I could easily understand Mauricia's urgent desire, but few girls from Tepoztlán had gone to university. The ones who left never came back home. Carmen wanted to find a way to help Octavio change his mind. She asked me to talk to him.

He and I talked on the veranda. He said he could not bear to think that he would lose her. She would go to university, meet a well-spoken man of education, and he, Octavio, would feel ashamed. After all, he could hardly read. When she married, he and Carmen would not know their grandchildren. We talked about Mauricia's temperament and character, her determination and aspirations, what a loving daughter she was, and how she had promised not to disobey him. If he forbade it, she would not study science. I wondered if a compromise was going to be found. He talked about how proud he was of all three of his children.

Octavio left without telling me what he was thinking. The next day Carmen came over. Mauricia was going to high school in Cuernavaca. She was going to study nursing, which required a great deal of science, and yet caring for other people was a feminine occupation. She could even come back to Tepoztlán when she finished the course and be a nurse right there in the village. Possibly. In any event, when Octavio considered her temperament, he decided it might be impossible to find a husband for her among the people they knew, since everyone was aware of how stubborn she was. If she was going to be an old maid anyway, she needed to be able to support herself.

Middle school graduation came along. The girls invited me to attend the performance in honor of mothers. The students danced traditional dances from the regions of Mexico, gave their mothers handmade fans, and passed around sandy cookies and reddish punch. Apparently, school punch and cookies is a thoroughly international convention. I think the punches I had in Japan and in Virginia were from the same recipe.

ANTHROPOLOGY • *Since the 1920s anthropologists had visited Tepoztlán*, written about it, gotten grants to spend the winter there, and earned Ph.D.s for their research there. The town is on the flank of the mountain range, *la falda de la sierra*, beautiful, near enough Mexico City to be accessible and rural enough to be interesting. It had become famous from the books written about it. Periodically another credentialed or aspiring anthropologist arrived to poke around, notebook in hand. In 1984 one arrived from UCLA and rented two rooms over someone's store. The anthropologist was going to use this research for her dissertation. She began her project. And every day she put on her beautiful, figure-hugging spandex and ran around the village for exercise. No one in Tepoztlán had ever seen clothes like hers. Neither had I, outside of a dance studio. This clothing and behavior made for lively conversation.

The anthropologist's research was on the social and family structure of the village and how it related to the formal and informal governance. She wanted to know how everyone was related to everyone else, who was who in the pecking order, and so on. She spoke utilitarian Spanish, but people found it hard to understand her and vice versa.

The Tepoztecans had their own theories about anthropologists. 1. The researchers don't go away without their research. 2. They write articles and books for their own purposes and not for the benefit of the people in the village, the *pueblo*, and were often lacking in respect. 3. They like good stories and expected to hear them.

I learned all this one day when a few people came to see me. They explained these facts of life and said that they wanted me to act as their translator. I had met the anthropologist once or twice, and they said it would make things go more smoothly if I participated in her interviews. It was true that by then my Spanish was better, but nevertheless their request seemed strange. The anthropologist was delighted to have my participation, she said, and we commenced the interviews.

The role of a translator is to faithfully reproduce the meaning of what is spoken and not to add or subtract any information. The text should be modified as little as possible. The words that go in your ears should come out of your mouth without a detour through your independent knowledge. The translator is not telling the story, just reproducing the story told by another person. Cortés' wife, La Malinche, is the most renowned translator in Mexico. Her words were the Spaniards' window into the mystifying world they found in the high air of Mexico.

I asked the questions and spoke the answers of the Tepoztecans. They looked straight at the anthropologist and gave answers they knew I recognized as fairy tales. They felt that this invasion of their privacy was out of bounds, and the only way to bring it to a close was to give her enough stories so that she would go away and write her book. Indeed in a few weeks she was gone. No one ever talked to me directly about it, but every now and again one of the participants saw me in the market, patted my arm, and told me what a good translator I was.

SECURITY • *All the time I lived in Tepoz I kept my curtains open and rarely* locked my house unless I went away from the village. It wasn't necessary to hide anything. One day someone went in my house. Nothing was stolen, but whoever it was had looked through my drawers and closet. I mentioned it to Octavio so that we could be a little more alert. He agreed that this was not good and said he had an idea who it might have been. Someone had recently rented a house in the village, and it was believed the guy smoked pot. In those days Tepoztecans did not approve of using drugs at all, and were very suspicious of people from the city who did. Tepoz had no police because the village believed that the police brought crime with them. If there were incidents, the villagers knew how to deal with them.

The next afternoon, Octavio knocked on my door after lunch. The neighbors didn't like the idea of someone in my house, and the men had organized a response. First, they had tied strings around the perimeter of the garden and hung the tops of metal cans together so that if anyone walked into the strings he would make noise. Second, the neighbor men planned to take turns sleeping in the garden for a while. If the intruder came back they knew how to deal with him. I mustn't worry. Everything would be fine. No one was going to bother me again. And no one ever did.

Soon after I moved to this house, I met Carmen's mother, Doña Elvira. She was about sixty-five or seventy in the mid-1980s. She was born and had always lived in Tepoztlán, as her parents and grandparents had. She often dressed in traditional white cotton clothes, wore her hair in long gray braids that came over the front of her shoulders. She was literally shoeless and had never worn shoes or huaraches. Doña Elvira lived in her own house about a mile away along the road toward Amatlán. I walked this road many times on my morning rambles and made some drawings of things that caught my eye. One was a little house with its back to the road and yellow-flowered vines over the veranda facing the mountain. This turned out to be Doña Elvira's house. She was a truly great cook. She ground the corn on her own stone metate and patted the tortillas with her brown, knobby-knuckled hands. With a final slap, the tortillas were on the comal, the earthenware griddle, and then off again in seconds. Miguel liked to sit near her and listen to her stories or tell her about his day while the pile of yellow tortillas filled the white cotton towel in the tortilla basket. The gentle slapping sound was the prelude to the meal.

Carmen worried that I didn't eat well, and around two o'clock one of the girls often brought a few of their grandmother's tortillas for my dinner. Eventually, Carmen began to teach me to cook. I had fed a family and hosted innumerable guests for almost 20 years but had little incentive at this point to fuss much over food. Carmen taught me to make *posole* (corn and chicken stew), and *mole* (a sauce of ground spices, vegetables, and chocolate), and squash-blossom soup, which is one of the great things to eat in this world. Once in a while I went and sat on a stone near Doña Elvira as she was making the tortillas and listened as she told her stories while the girls helped their mother with dinner. Many days I went home with a "care package" for my dinner. The warm tortillas and a good book were all I needed to make scrambled eggs into a feast.

QUINCEAÑERA • *When the girls turned fifteen it was time for their quinceañera,* a major fiesta announcing the girl's passage to adulthood. The preparations took months. A date was set for the spring. About a month beforehand, we all went to Cuernavaca for new clothes. Octavio and Miguel went off to buy new shirts and also a sombrero for Octavio. He had not had a new hat in several years, and he shopped in many stores to find just what he wanted.

We agreed to meet some hours later. Carmen and the girls suggested I go with them for the dresses. Mexican girls wear very beautiful clothes for the quinceañera. In some families it is a more elaborate occasion than a wedding. The family is presenting their daughter to the community as a young woman. It is a lot like a bar mitzvah, with the confirmation mass in the morning and then a festive, day-long party. We looked at many, many dresses, all long to the floor, in all sorts of fabrics, all pretty. The twins were going to dress alike for this occasion. After considerable agonizing, Carmen and both girls, with their somewhat different tastes, agreed on a pale blue cotton with tiny pleats and lace around the open necklines. The dresses were very simple compared to most of what was offered. Measurements were taken, a deposit given, dates discussed. The question of a hat or veil came up. Nothing was just right. Most of the headpieces were too citified and elaborate, or too expensive, or suited one girl and not the other. I offered to make coronas of flowers for their black hair and the bouquets they carried in the church. Everyone liked the idea, and we decided on red and pink roses. Carmen chose a simple outfit for herself, something she would use for a long time afterward.

We met Octavio and Miguel and suddenly things were not calm. Octavio had on his new hat, a natural white "panama" straw hat, the type seen all over Mexico. Carmen disapproved of this hat and expressed her objection immediately. Octavio was annoyed at her annoyance. I wondered what had gone wrong. At home late that afternoon Carmen told me the hat seemed to challenge fate. Its crown was at least an inch higher than his old hat, and the shape of the brim was much more oval. It was too proud. Octavio was stepping too far out of place. Better to wear the same style, with a low crown and traditional brim. A few days later, Octavio and I happened to cross paths in the garden. He told me that he was going to wear the hat — he was proud of his daughters, and he had come up in the world. He had come to a time that he could wear such a hat. Very quickly, they found themselves on good terms again, he wore the hat, and Carmen was even proud of him in it.

When the day was approaching I joined the family in cleaning the church. The stone floors were scrubbed and flowers set at the altar. The arched doorways were draped with garlands of homemade pale blue paper flowers. The night before, Carmen and her relatives and friends assembled mountains of food. Huge cazuelas were taken down from the shelves, and the men laid fires and set up tables. There was a steady sound of chopping and patting for hours. Chicken and pork were cut and added to the earthenware casseroles. Baskets of onions, garlic, peppers, and tomatoes were slowly browned. The moles (chocolate and pepper sauces) had to be stirred for hours, and everyone had to be fed while the next day's feast was prepared. The stirring and storytelling continued through the night. Young people rarely dated before fifteen, and this was an occasion for seventeen-year-old Miguel to smile at a pretty village girl, who smiled right back. The paseo, going out, was a prelude to engagement. More than one young couple considered each other under the starry sky. Near dawn the fires were banked and everyone went home for a few hours sleep before mass.

Carmen and Octavio had asked me to be the godmother and stand with Maura and Mauricia when they confirmed their faith at the morning mass. No one in the family was religious or went to church, but the confirmation mass was an essential part of the day. They walked down the aisle of the church in their long blue dresses. I had made their bouquets and crowns of pink and red roses for their hair. The priest preached his sermon on the theme of land, and spoke of the importance of not subdividing their precious heritage for city people's weekend houses. With brief vows and photos on the church steps, the ceremony was over. Doña Elvira, with huge relief, took off her huaraches. She had put sandals on her feet so that her going barefoot did not embarrass the children, and those few hours were enough for her.

The fiesta was a wonderful day of music, dancing, visiting, and neighborliness. The mariachi band played for hours. The parents and relatives ate and drank and reminisced. Everyone danced until the light faded. My compadres, Octavio and Carmen, were so proud of their children, so happy with them, and I was honored to have been included.

My dear friend Perla came to visit once in a while with her two little children, Sofia and Daniel. My Daniel was usually there on the weekends, and I have a lovely photo of him, about age fifteen, in the rocking chair in front of the fireplace with the baby Daniel on his lap. My Daniel is almost tall but still with a boy's face, with curly dark hair and a soft smile. He had turned from a shy child to an adolescent who was private and self-contained. He went his own way and faced his own doubts. What a gentle and generous person he was turning out to be. He had another specialty: he was great at finding titles for my work. He would cruise through the studio and come up with just the right words, sometimes even from my poems. There was a time that I thought titles were unnecessary, but I came to see that they serve as a kind of bridge and give the viewer a guideline, a starting point to meet the work. Daniel was good at that construction.

While I was still in Mexico City, my older son, Stephen, called from the College of William and Mary, where he was a student. He proposed that we take a car trip, just the two of us, when he next came to Mexico. He was about nineteen, probably in his sophomore year. This was an unexpected delight. Of course! I was so glad and thought, rightly, that this might be my last opportunity to have sustained time with him. We decided on the state of Michoacan and the city of Morelia, about an eight-hour drive away. It took us two days to get there. The trip was hilarious. Steve began remarking on the cows—brown cows, white cows, cows with curved horns. Every cow became the occasion for lunatic laughing. I had a collection of baskets from all the places that I had lived and visited, more than fifty examples by then. Along these country highways, open trucks passed us with towering loads of baskets swaying precariously. As each one passed, Steve advised, "Mom, more baskets. Hurry!" Steve was the navigator and kept the maps open on his lap. Whenever something appealed to him we turned off the main road to explore. We found apparently nameless ruins and hidden *miradores* overlooking the wide valley floor below the road. At one interesting hillside, we were speculating, inventing a story, when a man climbed up after us. I wondered if we were trespassing. Sort of, but he was eager to tell us the story of the rock wall he guarded, a fragment of a lost ruin with a lost story, and we stayed until his story was done. In Morelia, we went to the orchidarium, which houses the more than two hundred different orchids that grow in the highlands of Michoacan, at altitudes of eight thousand feet and higher. We cruised around the markets and bought some delicate white cloths from the weavers. Years later, I gave one as a keepsake to Steve's wife, Melissa. We took in the sights, went to the old colonial buildings, ate well and often. We talked about his courses and plans, about the sights along the way, about places to explore some day. The Michoacan pine forest at eight thousand feet smelled fresh and resinous as we drove back toward Mexico City.

Both Steve and Daniel had jobs each summer they were in Mexico. After I had moved to Tepoztlán, they came together many summer weekends. We went to the Sunday market or explored the region nearby. Of course, I did not discuss the proximate cause of the separation, and I don't know what Edwin chose to tell them. The two fellows spent long hours together and made good use of the swimming pool and ping-pong table.

Daniel was all right in Mexico City. He was busy with school and advanced rapidly. In the end, he graduated a year early because there were almost no courses left for him to take. In his last year we went to visit a few universities, as we had with Steve, and finally he chose William and Mary. He and Steve overlapped there for one year. When we first arrived in the city he could go anywhere safely. As conditions got worse, he had to promise to go directly from a movie to someone's home, by taxi. It became too dangerous for youngsters to be walking around downtown. The son of the Mexican neighbors next door—a big, burly soccer player at the university—was briefly kidnapped and very badly beaten. He nearly died of his injuries. An American acquaintance was kidnapped and fortunately released after just a day or two. The increasingly difficult economic conditions were making for some desperate people, and the first incursions of the narcotics gangs added to the mix. The most dangerous of all were the police, who were both underpaid and corrupt.

I drove to the city pretty regularly to visit friends, or go to art openings, the theater, or a concert. I couldn't stay long since the gray, traffic-polluted air brought back the asthma that first sent me to Tepoztlán. Usually I stopped at the house in Las Lomas to arrange with Juanita whatever housekeeping issues and shopping needed attention. She was very kind and competent, and cared a lot about Daniel.

LIVING EVERY DAY • *I always felt a sense of relief to return to Tepoztlán*, to the streets and sights that seemed like home. Walking through the village on some errand, I picked a few bright red, sweet coffee beans from a branch overhanging the street. Don Rubén delivered milk on horseback. I liked the fresh cheese that he made, and when I went to pick it up at his house, he told stories of his boyhood, when he had been with Zapata in the

Revolution. Tepoz had changed hands three times between the Federales and the Zapatistas, and Don Rubén had been a runner, a child carrying messages over the hills. In September, those same hills were covered with wild orange zinnias, which were picked to decorate all the fences and churches for the fiesta of San Miguel. Every parish had its own fiesta, with mock bullfights, amateur mariachis, and fireworks. The celebrations for the Day of the Dead were very animated, with huge masses of marigolds (the Aztec symbol of death), cemetery picnics, fireworks, and candy skeletons.

The house of Adelaide Foppa was a few blocks from the zócalo. She was a journalist and poet and had gone to Chile around 1982 to report on the *desaparecidos*, the people who disappeared during the rule of the junta. A few days after she arrived there she disappeared. She was never heard from since. The name Foppa was on the iron gate enclosing the front patio. Over the years since Adelaide had disappeared, people had tossed messages in envelopes through the locked gate, far enough inside that they were out of reach. I did so as well. Leaves had blown off the trees onto the paving and mixed with the envelopes. There was no damage and no graffiti on the house. If she ever came back, she would find everything as she left it.

The Carnival preceding Lent has been the subject of many books. The men who couldn't sew on a button spent months designing, sewing, and embroidering their long velvet gowns and improving their masks from year to year. One year Miguel gave me a gift of his childhood mask. It was too small for him, and he had made a man's mask for himself. As the *chinelos*, the men danced in the zócalo for three days, eating and drinking, more intoxicated by the dancing than drink, although it was a close call. Carnival was a special tradition, and they had kept it for centuries, with small gradual modifications. Around forty thousand tourists came every year to the village of about six thousand people. The income was important, but the carnival remained Tepoztlán's.

One spring day, I was walking back home along the road from Amatlán when a small pickup truck swerved onto the shoulder. I was thrown in the air and landed in a clump of bushes, briefly knocked out but, I thought, nothing worse. The young guys driving took me to the tiny clinic in the village. The medic on duty, there mostly to sew up Saturday-night machete wounds, did a light examination and said that, apart from some bruises, I was okay, just go home and put some ice on my shoulder. I didn't even need to see a doctor. Three days later I still had no use of my left arm and hand, except for the two outside fingers. I went to the city and saw a regular physician who said that I had damaged the nerve, and it was too early to say what might happen. I was to apply moist heat, rest, and it would heal itself if it were going to. I had had a small concussion but that was clearing up well, and the headache gradually went away.

I drove back to Tepoz and fell into bed. For the next couple of weeks, people dropped in to take care of me. Roger came right away and many times after, tenderly putting hot compresses on my sore shoulder and back, making chamomile tea, and bringing supper and conversation. He had been teaching me to play the recorder, which he played very well. We talked about the music he brought. I couldn't practice, of course, because I didn't have use of my left hand. It gradually improved, the long line of the nerve repairing itself slowly from the hand to the shoulder, but it was a couple of years before I had complete use of it again.

The days returned to normal. I believed that I could keep the sweet and comfortable life I had begun to make for myself. I started to look for a house to buy. Everyone I knew had a suggestion. I had a little money saved. I had sold a few pictures, although not enough to live on. I thought I could teach English and cobble together enough income to stay permanently in Tepoztlán. It was the aftermath of the second peso crisis and a tiny house could be had for about $15,000-$20,000 US. A friend was trying to sell his large and elegant house on several acres and hoped to get perhaps $40,000 with luck. Foreigners still could not own land directly. There was a device whereby a Mexican citizen could hold the property in trust. I thought if I found a house my cousin Jacobo might do that. I looked at one or two houses a week and after a while found a four-room house with an orchard and a mountain view from the veranda. Very gently I started to talk to an intermediary to begin the process of negotiation. The legalities of a purchase with a *fideo comiso*, a trustee, were complex. Legal affairs are complex everywhere, I suppose. Mexico's Spanish colonial heritage made the legal system ponderous and opaque.

Life had a nice rhythm in Tepoz, and I lived without hurry. But there were complexities. During the week I worked steadily in the studio, concentrating and experimenting. I was neighbor and friend, occasional resource, recipient of kindnesses small and large. I was Daniel's mother, talking to him by phone during the week, and spending the weekend with him. Edwin called every week about something or other having to do with Daniel. The artist-writer circle reappeared each weekend, and many Sundays I had dinner with them or at least dropped by in the evening. Perla, Jacobo, and other people came from the city. I did two exhibitions, in Mexico City and Guadalajara, and participated in some very nice collective exhibitions, including a traveling show sponsored by the Secretary of the Treasury. A few galleries were showing interest in my work. It turned out to be a busy life, not at all solitary.

I dropped by to have a coffee with an acquaintance one day and met her neighbor, Leonardo. He was a great huge man, with heavy black hair and big hands. He was a painter, and lived in Tepoz not far from me. We took many walks, and he dropped in at my house. He invited me to his, which was largely studio space. I saw his mature and abundant work and recognized the power of his art. We saw each other frequently and stood very near each other when we looked at work in progress, talking about painterly problems, among other things. He had interesting news about the art world, told me about a pyramid I should see, or a new place to walk to. He is the one who introduced me to the sweet delight of ripe, raw coffee beans. I didn't know how to respond to what I thought might be his interest. I had had no experience since my college days in interpreting or sending these signals.

DAVID • *One sunny afternoon, I met David. He was a very lovely man, interesting* and talented, a composer. He was building a house for himself on the outskirts of Tepoztlán. His wife had recently left and taken the two children back to her native England. He was not widely recognized yet but was very ambitious and had great expectations for his music. The first afternoon we spent together, we drove around and then walked over the hills, chatting and getting acquainted. The next time we met, he picked me up in the afternoon and brought me to see his unfinished house. We set out and walked for several hours over the hills, climbing over stone walls and across the dry beds of little erosion streams. He offered me his hand in the roughest terrain. We admired the landscape and walked until we could hardly see the ground in front of us. We returned to his house at dusk and he invited me in.

We sat on two chairs in the open French window with a glass of wine and watched the dark fall, still talking, looking — and not looking — at one another. At some point David said he could make some *quesadillas*, tortillas with melted cheese, how would that be? As he got up, he brushed my chair and bent over with a delicate kiss. A few more followed, and he went to make the quesadillas. We put some candles on the low windowsill and ate our little supper, looking intently at each other. A few more embraces and he took me home. With one more kiss, he said he would come and pick me up the next evening, if that was all right. It was and he did.

That Day

If you knock your elbow against the edge of the door
    the funny bone will send a thrill of shock
    right to your brain.

On that hot morning
our eyes knocked.

In that instant
    every bone was funny
    every muscle laughing
    every hair breathless.

In the aftershock I kept touching
that electric pain
leaning against the doorframe
until my heart could move again.

We enjoyed our new love affair with its subtleties and surprises. A good deal of our conversation was about making art, his and mine. He admired what I was doing and my new work engaged him. He was experimenting, too. It would be a few years before he found his own voice, in the creation of operas on Latin American literary themes. Meanwhile, he made a ballet, chamber music, and music commissioned for ceremonial occasions.

Perla came to visit around this time and asked me straightforwardly if I was seeing someone. I was a bit hesitant to reply. She put her arms around me and said that I should just enjoy it. It was time to have such a good thing in my life. Daniel usually came on Friday afternoon after school. Time with my son had precedence before anything else. These were difficult times for him, and I wanted to avoid adding any more stress or awkwardness to his life. When Daniel stayed for dinner on Sunday afternoon, I joined the writers later on for coffee or met David at his house in the evening.

We were more often at David's house than mine. His bedroom had a wide porch, but sometimes after we made love, we climbed through a window and sat on the tile roof and watched the red sky become night. He was a tall man and loaned me his striped polo shirts, long as a dress on me, in place of a robe. We sat on the clay tiles, listening, talking, smiling, one of his large hands covering both of mine.

He had an enormous, brass bathtub that sat on short legs on the terracotta tiles of the bathroom. The sun came in for a while in the morning, and the whole bathroom glowed. We luxuriated in the hot water, not washing until the water was tepid and the sun had moved around the corner. We took the towels out to dry on the porch railing. Sometimes they didn't quite make it to the railing, but instead became a nest for us there under the blue sky. Everything we did was for our pleasure: smiles while we waited for slow-steeped pots of tea, suppers interrupted by kisses, bodies charmed by our good fit.

We loaned each other books and read aloud and told each other about the places we had been or dreamed of going. He had left home in his teens, studied in England, lived a year in Florence. I had spent much of my adult life in East Asia. He asked me to tell him about Japan. He had me read his doctoral dissertation about *Don Giovanni*, and I told him my ideas about *The Marriage of Figaro*. He gave me a volume of Mozart's letters to read; I loaned him Japanese poetry translations. When I could stay over on Saturday night, we got up late on Sunday morning. His friends dropped in — unannounced since he had no phone — and we sat around with whatever breakfast was on hand and the newspapers they brought with them from the village. One time a neighbor came riding over the hill. Without dismounting from his horse, he chatted with David a bit and then turned to me and asked if I had moved in yet. I had no expectation of leaving my house in paradise, no desire to change anything.

Although he officially lived in the city, David spent a lot of time in Tepoz. He came to the village on Thursday or Friday and went back to the city on Tuesday morning. He asked me to come and have lunch with him in the pretty restaurant in Chapultepec Park or to go to a concert with him. His apartment was very small, a bachelor's place where he had many, many records, the black vinyl disks that were being replaced by tapes around then. One morning, before breakfast, he pulled out Borodin's quartet, and we stood an inch apart, wrapped in the nocturne. It was all very romantic, companionable, and enriching.

He took me to meet his mother, a really lovely person, and I visited there several times. He told me about his family, the grandfather who had emigrated from Turkey. David resembled him a bit, with his bushy moustache and wavy blond hair. I was startled the first time he said he loved me. I didn't believe it. I knew his music was his first, truest love. And it still is.

David was very serious about making music and also about becoming well known and having his music and his name recognized. He worked hard in the studio at the top of his house. He had to climb three flights of outdoor stairs to get there. It was a very simple room. If I was at the house, I read in the living room or wrote at his desk in the bedroom while he composed on his upright piano, which was always out of tune.

Edwin still called me often, and at one point he offered to buy a little farm for me in Vermont or New Hampshire as an inducement to leave Mexico. He was preparing to depart and tried very hard to find a way to have me leave also. I didn't expect to go, but when I told David about it, he said he wanted go with me if I went.

Looking back now at David and the time I spent with him, I can only smile. We said then that this could not last. It was not our time, but that we would always like each other. I have never had any regrets that we enjoyed being together for this brief and happy time. Twenty-five years later he told me that knowing me had changed his life, and I thought the same.

A MYSTERIOUS PUZZLE • *If this were a novel I could not write what happened next.* How did Edwin persuade me to leave the happiest place I had ever been? Why did I agree to leave? I had arrived a stranger and I was almost home. It was a kind of waking dream. And like a dream it had its subtexts and complications.

In Mozart's opera, *The Marriage of Figaro*, the Count behaves very badly. He is unfaithful and schemes to promote his own desires. Other people are objects in his life, and he cannot clearly see them or himself. Eventually, his wife, the Countess, shows him the truth and he is repentant. She sings her forgiveness. Toward the end of her astonishing aria, her voice and the music tell us that it is within our power to forgive and redeem ourselves. The Countess's aria lets us understand the almost divine quality of forgiveness, and we are redeemed on this earth.

Forgiveness is a transaction between willing partners. The injured party has to find it possible to allow the injury to heal. The offending party must recognize the injury, repent of doing harm, and offer contrition. I wanted to forgive Edwin. Although he said the words, he never recognized the hurt he inflicted. Still, he was the father of my children. We had a long history together. The unresolved issues were a heavy burden on both of us. For a long time, I believed he might choose to open his mind to our reality, to the longstanding difficulties we experienced, and we could be reconciled. But things didn't happen that way.

The week I packed up to leave Tepoz, I could hardly believe I was doing it. I said so many good-byes. At the last hour, Octavio came in to help carry things to the car. Tears ran down my face. He took my two hands in his and said that I would be back in just a while.

As I drove away, I thought that I would never recapture the happiness I had had there.

I have thought about those last days in Tepoztlán. It took me the next five years to untangle my life but eventually it was done.

I drove away from Tepoztlán into the heart of a puzzle.

TWO

New York: Our Pasts as Prologue

MEMORY • *In the sunlight, a stranger held me in his arms against the beautiful,* deep golden brown of his scratchy wool jacket. The light made every color intense, almost too brilliant. The stranger's big hands surrounded me. When I awoke again, it was the prickly, tan wicker seat I felt, the bench of a train rocking toward New York City. The train was full of soldiers. I don't know if they were off to the war in Europe or going home.

More than six decades later, this memory of being on the train, the earliest that I am sure is really mine, seems to foreshadow what became the principal elements in my life: a line of travel — full of colors and light and mysteries — in motion toward an unknown destination.

As a child and in adolescence, I was always eager to finish, to grow up, to leave the furor of my family and start my "real" life. A long line of events — starting out from New York and bending through Baltimore, twisting around Korea and Japan, passing the cities and suburbs, lingering through a Mexican dream state — has finally drawn me here and now, to tell you this story. As I write, I am surprised that this is not the solitary undertaking I expected. The people I knew are right here with me. They keep me company as we travel along and remind me how it was between us. I can hear their voices, and see them where I knew them last.

THEIR PASTS AS PROLOGUE • *My parents carried me home from Doctors* Hospital in a wicker laundry basket on Saturday, the day before Pearl Harbor was attacked. I am named for my paternal grandmother, Sophia. My mother, Edythe, insisted on a name that was as plain as possible, and agreed only to use a name with the initial letter "S". No middle name at all. My father yielded to my mother's adamant insistence, the standard pattern of innumerable family upheavals throughout my youth. Life with my parents was dangerous and uncertain. Their clashing personalities and aspirations erupted endlessly. There was war in the Pacific and in Europe, and in our apartment. I stood on the line between them and yearned for a peace treaty. They could negotiate a temporary truce — a concert in the park, a summer stock play at Sea Cliff, maybe dinner at Lum's Chinese restaurant, possibly a drive up the Taconic Parkway — but soon things were back to normal.

My father, Sam, was not qualified for military service in the war because of his age (thirty-two) and having had thyroid surgery. He was a social worker in his day job, and in the evenings a counselor at the Boys Club. He cared deeply about both roles. With the opening of the war, he added a third, home-front job as a civil defense warden. Mother, meanwhile, was learning that her premonitions had been accurate. She really did not like keeping house or taking care of a baby. Besides that, she found it very difficult to cook. Her ideal was to live in a hotel, with room service.

My mother didn't like being a mother. All her life she said, rather proudly, that she really never had any maternal feelings. She told me so for the last time a few weeks before she died.

In 1942 we moved to Flushing, to a beautiful apartment house built in 1908, with marble floors, red velvet drapes, and sofas in the lobby. The lovely apartment and close proximity to her two sisters did not make Mother any happier with domestic life. Before long, my parents separated and my grandmother Dora accompanied my mother and me to Florida. The pretext for the move was that we would be safe from a possible — if unlikely — German submarine invasion of Flushing. I don't know why Mother considered St. Petersburg safer than Flushing. She was not a person to analyze things dispassionately. Maybe its appeal was that it was far from my father.

Even with my grandmother there to help, Mother did not find herself at peace in Florida. Wherever she lived, she restlessly threw away and bought dishes, furniture, clothing, and especially little objects — flowered teacups, great quantities of stationary, disparate items too varied to be called knick-knacks. Less than a year after arriving in St. Petersburg, we packed up and returned to New York on the train. We rejoined my father in apartment 1A of the Terrace Gardens, on 165th Street in Flushing. In our absence, he had made me a little oak table and two chairs. They served me for years, then my brother, then cousins. Mother told me that my first real sentence, at two years old, was, "Don't worry. I'll manage." I said this often to my dolls as a young child, and to my mother for the next sixty-six years.

When I was about three, I learned to write at that table. My dolls shared the chairs, and I made pictures, "wrote" letters, and "read" them stories. We had tea in tiny, pretty, china cups. My library books were piled up on a corner. A pencil or crayon was always in my hand. Later, my parents laughed remembering that I sat there working for hours, saying I was too busy to go play.

As a small girl, I had many dolls: fancy store dolls with eyes that closed, rag dolls my grandmother made, a Mexican doll with a baby of her own, a baby doll in a yellow dress and a bonnet that I won as a prize from the *Long Island Star* newspaper for the best essay in a contest for children. I had old-fashioned dolls with china heads and beautiful clothes, and traditional baby dolls. They all lived on the floor of the hall closet.

The closet was about seven feet long, with double doors opening onto a short hall that connected the living room to the bathroom and bedroom. The dolls were arranged there with their clothes and other necessities in a white cardboard box. I often played in the hall, or moved everything en masse to my little table. It was dangerous to set up in certain spots — my mother was liable to shove me and everything else out of her way, or deliver a straight-armed whack as she shrieked, "You're going to kill me!" She and my father fought nearly every day, set off by almost anything — a bottle of milk left out, a newspaper thrown away, a radio program. Minor disagreements quickly escalated. Maybe they both needed the rush of adrenaline. Their shouting frightened me, and I was embarrassed — our neighbors in the building could hear. Sometimes, I went to the doll closet (as I thought of it), climbed in with my dolls around me and the clothes hanging overhead, and closed the door with a little strip of wood I found to pull on. The dark, the dolls, and the safety of invisibility contained my fright.

Once the shouting died down, I could rearrange all the dolls, letting them sit next to each other in the white box, tucked in amidst the blankets and bonnets, and quietly open the closet door again.

After St. Petersburg, my grandmother went back to Connecticut to live with her friend, Mrs. Spanner, in Bridgeport. Around 1945, Grandma had a heart attack. Her daughters—Diana, Ruthie, and my mother, Edythe—insisted that she move to New York. She was about seventy, and they all thought she probably was going to die soon. She lived almost twenty years more, but never had her own home again. At first she lived over Ruthie's garage, in the former maid's room. When she recovered from the heart attack, she moved out, going from one Flushing rooming house to another. She spent much of her time working as a volunteer, especially for the American Cancer Society. And she spent many days with her three daughters, who lived within six blocks of one another.

When my mother was frantic and overcome with rage, Grandma said, "Calm down, Edythe. Sit with me. We'll have tea." Sometimes, briefly, the tea and time helped. But, just as often, Mother responded, saying that no one could understand how she felt. Being in the apartment, with that child, was her waking nightmare. Grandma took me out — even in winter, all bundled up—and we'd go somewhere: to one of the little neighborhood shops, or for tea, or, in summer, for ice cream at Cook's. Many afternoons she took me on her capacious lap, brushed my hair, sang a song, and soothed the wounds of the day. She loved to use her big, graceful hands. She might rummage through her sewing box and come up with some little scrap that we could sew into something for one of my dolls.

A FATAL ROMANCE • *My parents first met in 1932, when my mother,* Edythe, had been in New York City for about a year, living with her sister Ruthie. Edythe was eighteen, with good looks and an eagerness to say anything daring and outrageous. It was summer, and in the evenings there was free dancing in Central Park. Sam came along, asked her to dance, and that was the end of the fellow Edythe had come with. Sam was tall and slim. His Baltic ancestry had given him blue eyes, a gently ruddy complexion, and wavy, reddish hair. He was twenty-three, with a vibrant smile and a great liking for women's company, qualities he retained throughout his life.

It was the Depression then, but Edythe had a job. Ruthie's husband, also named Sam, owned a store on 125th Street, in Harlem. Clocks, watches, and jewelry were sold on the street floor. Downstairs, Edythe was the office staff. She lived in an elegant apartment with Ruthie and Sam, their children, and their maid. Responsible only for enjoying herself and having fun, she had beaux lined up. Sam hadn't had a regular job for months and lived hand to mouth, working at whatever he could find. He hadn't had a permanent home since he was eight years old. On the night they met in Central Park, Sam had one nickel in his pocket — the subway fare home. They danced until the music was done and then walked through the park, along the river, through the sultry night streets. They arrived at her apartment around five in the morning. For a while, they saw each other often.

Sam joined the CCC (Civilian Conservation Corps) and was sent to Montana. He fell in love with the forests and the mountains and the camaraderie of the men on the line. Assigned to the Ninth District in Montana, he worked on a Forest Protection crew, cutting firebreaks and doing conservation work. The men in this crew were paid $36 to $45 per month, part of which was sent directly to their families. Later, my father remembered this time in Montana as the best of his life, and that he wanted to stay. He didn't though. Instead, he returned to New York when his mother, Sophia, became ill with leukemia. He began his long career as a social worker and counselor then. After Sophia was released from Montefiore Hospital, Sam and his sisters, May and Sally, nursed their mother at home. They moved her bed into the living room of the small apartment and took turns staying with her. All their lives they talked about Sophia's sweetness, her patience, and her "angelic" quality.

Somehow, during this troubled time, Sam and Edythe met again and took up where they had left off more than two years earlier. Sam took Edythe home to meet his mother and sisters. Edythe remembered Sophia's gentleness and beautiful blue eyes. Their only meeting was short. Sophia was very frail, and died soon afterward.

My parents shared only a love of books and a lack of pragmatism. They married in July 1936 on their lunch hour, she expecting a carefree young life, he craving a home, a wife, and children. At her insistence, they kept their marriage a secret for a while. They finally moved into a bohemian apartment on Hudson Street, in Greenwich Village. There was a refrigerator they named Oscar and two names over the doorbell. Edythe didn't use a married name for five years, until she became pregnant with me. She agreed to it only if she and Sam both changed their separate surnames — to Gardner.

At the start of their marriage, Sam was already ill with worsening but undiagnosed Graves' disease, which at that time was fatal. He lost weight. In a few months, his 5'11" frame weighed less than a hundred pounds. He worked less and less, and was nervous, anxious, exhausted, and sleepless — the classic symptoms of an overactive thyroid. Edythe was furious. She had expected to be taken care of, and here her new husband was lazy and no fun at all. They searched for medical help, and finally found Dr. William Hitzig. Willy was about Sam's age, a young, gifted doctor with innovative ideas. He offered an untried, radical solution: they would remove part of the swollen thyroid gland. The surgery had not been done before, and was thought to be very dangerous. It soon became the standard treatment, and remained so for decades. Sam recovered immediately. He and Willy were friends for the next fifty years.

Sam was soon able to go back to work. They moved a few times to better apartments, and eventually found themselves in the Sunnyside community, in an apartment they later remembered with pleasure. Sam very much wanted to have children. After five years of married life, and under considerable pressure from him and her own family, Edythe finally agreed.

DAD: ALL CHARM AND BUSINESS • *Dad had friends everywhere in the* city. If he didn't find a friend, he made one, even if only for that day. He knew a little of many languages and loved using them. He flirted relentlessly and women smiled at him, flirting right back. His friend, Virginia, had a restaurant downtown in Chinatown. When Dad walked in the door she already knew what he wanted, even what I wanted. The same happened at diners along Queens Boulevard, where it seemed that the owner or a waitress always knew how much he was going to like the lemon meringue pie. After the war was over, he bought a black Pontiac. Even in chilly weather, he liked to drive out to Cold Spring Harbor, on the Long Island north shore, where the fishing boats, filled with just-caught clams and oysters, sold their catch right off the boat. He had lived in Harlem as a boy and was at ease in the black community there. He learned Spanish as he met people resettling themselves from Puerto Rico. He could walk comfortably into Merrill Lynch, then a very stuffy, old-line office, and be met with the same level of courtesy as in those downtown diners and Chinese restaurants, which he enjoyed so much more. Besides his regular counselor job during these years of my growing up, he was building a side business in the stock market.

Saturday mornings he sometimes took me with him to a broker's office. He worked for years with white-haired Maxie, developing a business of advising clients on stock market investments and eventually advising businesses on going public. He and Maxie studied the markets and gave me an office while they did it. I packed my briefcase with pencils, paper, crayons, and a book, and we set off in the subway. Dad set me up in an office, with a typewriter, a phone, and a chair that twirled around. I "did business," checked Moody's (the investment publication's thin, translucent paper had a gorgeous, rustling sound), and generally was very busy until it was time to go to lunch. Maxie took my cheek between the knuckles of his second and third fingers—in the approved pinch style—and said that since I was going to grow up and take away all his customers, I should plan to come and work for him.

Dad wasn't home much, but he had an imagining of the life he wanted and made time for pieces of it with me. He loved to go to Topsy's restaurant on Sunday afternoon. Mother wouldn't eat there. I loved the chicken in a basket. You were supposed to eat it with your fingers. They must have had silverware for the salad, but I only remember the delicious and illicit pleasure of greasy fried chicken and the afternoons with Dad.

Dad was a great storyteller. He made up characters and spun them out for months of stories. Right to the last morning of his life, he told and retold me the stories of his childhood. My father, Sam, had begun childhood in an ordinary way until his father died in the influenza epidemic of 1918. There was no life insurance. Within days, the family went from slowly rising working class to abject poverty. The children, Sam and the two girls, May and Sally, were farmed out to their half-brothers and cousins. Their mother, Sophia, began to take in laundry. She boiled linens in large pots, strung them to dry in the alley, and then ironed them with flatirons heated on the stove. Sam, the man of the family at age nine, soon went to work as a newsy, selling newspapers on the streets and learning to smoke. Tobacco was cheaper than food, and it took his mind off eating. He quit his three-pack-a-day addiction in his sixties. He longed intensely for a home of his own. On many of our Sunday outings, he tried to give me pieces of the childhood he had missed.

Every spring he took me to the Ringling Brothers, Barnum and Bailey circus, a three-ring extravaganza. As soon as the newspapers ran pictures of the circus train arriving in New York from Sarasota, we started dreaming of the big event. Without fail, Mother told Dad not to waste too much money on the seats and, invariably, he bought very good ones for the two of us. I admired the beautiful, sparkly costumes, gasped at the acrobats, and worried mildly about the clowns. We threw away the brown-bag lunches Mother had packed and ate all sorts of forbidden junk; we never got sick on it, and were careful never to tell.

One of Dad's great pleasures was the horse races. New York had several tracks and he took me to all of them. The best was Belmont in the summer. We always visited the paddocks and watched the horses in the walking ring, checking out their splendid form and estimating their chances. I still love to see the horses run for their own joy, and I still don't care who wins.

MOTHER: CLOSING TRAP • *Mother, meanwhile, was restless. She tried* typing envelopes at home, piecework that was very tedious. I learned to count the packets of addressed envelopes, stacking them in crossed piles of ten, then in place-marked hundreds in the boxes. This typing money went for the things that made domestic life bearable for her, especially going to "the city." She didn't want to stay at home. She already had a terrific aversion to being alone and so, as I was handy, she took me with her. These were the best times we ever had together. The tens of thousands of envelopes bought hours of freedom, hours when all the commotion, anxiety, fear, and rage were put aside in the calm, shining, marble halls of the city. Favorites were the Frick Collection and the Metropolitan

Museum of Art, the Museum of Modern Art, and, at the very top of the list, the New York City Ballet.

By the time I was three, we were going to the Wednesday matinees at the ballet. Top balcony seats were $2.60. It was high, dark, and completely magic. I started ballet lessons at four, at the YMCA. Mrs. Whitecoff's classes were filled with twenty girls, mostly outfitted in leotards and pale ballet slippers. (Mother sent me to these lessons in my leftover summer shorts and black slippers, which didn't show the dirt.) The class started with classical barre exercises and then moved to the center space, little girls to the back, following the older girls in front through a series of floor exercises. All the steps were called out in their French ballet names, the time kept by Mrs. Whitecoff tapping a stick on the floor, accompanied by the patient pianist. Then came dances, some original and some versions of traditional ballet pieces — the *Mexican Hat Dance*, the fan dance from *Don Quixote*, pieces from *Coppelia*, and so on. Of course, in the fall we prepared for an abbreviated *Nutcracker* performance, and in the spring, for a June recital. Mother did not allow me to perform, but, nevertheless, I continued classes, with a few short pauses, until I was sixteen. By then I was using my baby-sitting money for the tuition of one dollar per lesson. I loved to dance and still do.

I saw the film *The Red Shoes* when it came out in 1948 and several times since. The ethereal Moira Shearer lives to dance, to make art, to do her work in the world, and dies for love. Coincidentally, for my eighth birthday, Dad gave me Arthur Szyk's exquisite *Tales of Hans Christian Anderson*. Of course, it includes the story of the red shoes; the story of a woman who cannot help but dance, cannot stop, and at last dies because she accepted the shoemaker's invitation, the temptation to dance.

The first ballet I can remember, when I was about seven or eight, was with Maria Tallchief. I had already been to many dance performances, mostly the classical story dances. This was entirely different. From where we sat in the dark balcony the stage glowed blue. It was bare, with only a blue scrim illuminated with lighting from the floor. As a line of ballerinas in simple, floating, knee-length dresses entered from the left, Tallchief moved onto center stage. The line of her white arm was vivid against the blue. She moved through the music with the clean grace that made her such a delight to watch. For the first time I experienced the way a gifted performer can invite the audience into the act of art. It was the most beautiful thing I had seen. I was in love.

Balanchine, through Tallchief, created the possibility of this experience. His belief in the human capacity for beauty, his expression of that belief on the blue stage, invited me to share that possibility. I accepted.

ABORTED DREAMS • *Although my parents had reunited after a lengthy* separation, their goals and aspirations remained far from harmonious. Dad wanted conventional family life, in a single-family house, and the steady presence of his wide circle of friends and acquaintances. My mother wanted none of these things, especially the house and children.

I was timid and inward-looking, but wanted to be intrepid at the same time. I dreamed of being an explorer. With my friend Regina I played at being a Flash Gordon-type space traveler, sailing up the Amazon, or exploring farthest Africa in the vacant lots and alleys around Broadway Flushing. I heard of Stanley and Livingstone and always wanted to be Stanley, bravely to the rescue in the nick of time. In these games I was always brave.

But I did not feel brave. I was always doing something that was contrary to my mother's wishes, and therefore, was punished often. Mother would grab my arm, pull me up short, and tell me to go get her hairbrush. She told me how many strokes to expect in my spanking. I had to bring the brush to her in the living room. She turned me over her lap and counted out the sentence with each straight-armed stroke while pushing my face into the burgundy brocade of the couch. Afterward, I was not allowed to talk to anyone while I thought about what an awful child I was and what I needed to do to improve. Then I stood in front of her and made a report on how I would change, always with a tearful apology, always meaning to reform enough so that she could love me. I didn't know that I never could.

I was what was called a "picky eater," afraid of many foods, and with a small appetite. At my mother's table, a plate loaded with too much food was to be finished no matter what. I had to stay at the table looking at congealing grease and gray string beans, "if it took all night." I was to think about how to deserve the food I had, think about starving children in Europe. (I would have been happy to send them the liver.) Dad often tried to cajole me to eat a certain number of bites so that he could give me a little sweet. He put us in league together against Mother, saying otherwise there would be hell to pay. By the time I was three or four, I had a pretty good idea what this "hell" was: dramatic confrontation, complete with mutual screaming, accusations, and threats, with one or the other storming out the door. This all transpired because I didn't finish my lunch.

As long as I can remember, Mother had said that she needn't do what people expected of her because she was going to be dead soon. She hospitalized herself, with back problems and strep throats, every winter, more than fifty times over her adult life. She didn't want to cook, and by the time I was four I could wash potatoes and put them in a special pot to bake on top of the stove. Without crossing a street, I was sent two blocks around the corner to Tony the greengrocer, to Sam the butcher, to Mr. Kuhn at the delicatessen, and to John the pharmacist at the corner. All these merchants extended credit to most of their customers. Sometimes I took money to be paid on the account. Sometimes the bill was too high, and one shopkeeper or another sent me home with the message that at least part had to be paid. Dad ranted and reasoned but nothing could keep Mother on a budget.

The late forties were a time of explosive prosperity and social conservatism as people recovered from the war and the economy shifted to consumer-driven movement. The emerging social milieu insisted that the single family belonged in a single-family house, preferably with three or four children and perhaps a dog. Psychiatry, pop psychology, and advertising all presented this as the much-desired norm.

Mother was depressed, anxious, and volatile. When they sought professional help for her, amazingly, the advice was the same as it was from her family: have another baby! The theory was that all this distress was due to hormone imbalance and an under-stimulated uterus. A baby would take her mind off her problems and peace would prevail. By early 1949, under great pressure again, Mother agreed, and they embarked on another pregnancy.

The prognostications and diagnoses did not turn out to be correct.

With three jobs and a good economy, Dad earned enough for them to afford to buy a house. They had a little stock and some savings for the down payment. In the summer of 1949, they put a deposit on a house in Flushing. Dad was overjoyed. He would have his own home at last, permanent and secure.

But within days of giving the deposit, Mother was so overwrought at the thought of owning a home that the builder was persuaded to refund the deposit. For many years, they retold the story — she feeling it was a triumph of will, he desolate at the loss of a home.

Instead, my parents rearranged the apartment, putting the baby's crib and me in the bedroom. In the living room, they had new twin beds for themselves at one end of the room, and moved the sofa and chairs to the other end. The entrance to the little hall was between them. They were on a waiting list for a larger apartment in the building, but because of the general housing shortage, nothing better was immediately available.

Dad had bought Boeing stock some time earlier, believing that air travel was the way of the future. (He bought Boeing about half a dozen times in the succeeding decades.) But in the midst of the expanding economy, there was a temporary recession in 1949 as postwar demand settled down. Stock prices were fickle. Mother was frazzled by this. She seemed constantly on the edge of an explosion. She grew less and less able or willing to control her words and actions. In the face of Mother's extreme upset, Dad felt forced to sell the Boeing stock. Within months, it was obvious that he had sold at the worst possible moment, and that his original insight would have given them considerable financial security. This tale of the Boeing stock, often retold, became emblematic of all their lost opportunities. The futile pattern was repeated: hysterical scenes, followed by appeasing actions that could not appease, followed by recriminations on all sides, some lasting for decades. All fall, while we waited for the new baby, chaos threatened to overcome us.

BOBBY • *My brother arrived with much travail on December 19, 1949.* Mother stayed in the hospital for ten days. Many of those mornings, Dad made his specialty, funny eggs. He said his mother made eggs this way when she was a girl in Russia. He let the eggs set in the buttery skillet, folding back the delicately browning edges, to make a light, airy, beautifully patterned circle, flipped it over for a moment, and slid it onto a plate with toast cut into triangles, all the time telling a story about his childhood. He took me to the Rendezvous dinette around the corner for many of our meals. The waitresses wore little aprons and big smiles, always asking after Mother and the baby.

Finally, it was time for them to come home. They arrived with bags and boxes. An English baby nurse in a starched white uniform, with an equally starched manner, carried in the baby. At last! Mother wore a black silk crepe dress, draped elegantly at the hip, with a pin on the folds. Her sisters came over to greet her. I ran to her, but she pushed me away. My aunts said that I had to be careful because she still hurt a lot. Mother recounted the story of Bobby's difficult birth all her life. She did not want to take care of the baby at all. Dad was there but talking to one of my uncles, not involved with the baby either. He was unwilling to have much to do with Bobby until he was six months old.

I just *had* to hold this baby, touch him, see what his fingers and feet looked like. In the bedroom, Nurse had me sit on a chair with a pillow across my lap, and, hovering close by, she let me hold my brother. I had expected something like a big doll, but here was this beautiful miniature person. I was astounded and ecstatic. I told Bobby, within the nurse's hearing, that I would always take care of him. And to the best of my young ability, I tried to do it. Over the next few weeks, Nurse showed me how to give Bobby a bottle, pick him up, change his clothes and diaper. She even let me help with his bath. My grandmother was there often as well. As Nurse's time ended, Mother found a woman named Lily to take care of our household.

Wonderful, sweet Lily lived near us in Flushing. She was a heavy-set, very black woman, with the gentlest voice that can be imagined. She came a couple of times a week. Although my parents always fought about money and neither felt there was ever enough, they managed to have Lily stay with us for about two years, until she was dying of cancer. Grandma filled in on the days Lily didn't come by, letting me be part of everything. Mother was still focused on how difficult the birth had been. Pretty soon she began working for temporary agencies like Kelly and Manpower, wanting to be out of the house and back at work. Dad was absent pretty much, too.

FIRST STEPS • *So that's what it was like at home when I was eight years old.* I was beginning to have a life outside our apartment and inside my head. I was in the third grade and my teacher was Mrs. Florence Neunzig, to her students the most beautiful woman in the New York City Public School system, possibly in the world. Her classroom was famous in our school as the most desirable. To this day, I can remember and name each of my elementary school teachers, and Mrs. Neunzig is still at the top of the list for her empathy, her calmness, and the pleasure of learning in her room. My new baby brother was the subject of a show-and-tell presentation. Monitor jobs and endless reading offset the trials of penmanship and spelling. Although I am somewhat dyslexic, no one had a name for it, and I had already invented some strategies that let me move through the school day nearly without incident. At that point, I read the *Herald Tribune* or the *Times* when my father brought them home in the evening, was working my way through our *Book of Knowledge* encyclopedia, went to the library a few times a week, and had a stack of books at hand at all times. Old habits die hard — or not at all. On a recent trip to Spain, I took a suitcase with twenty books as well as the usual clothing.

The Flushing branch of the New York Public Library had been moved from a storefront to a nicely remodeled space at the triangle where Crocheron Avenue and Depot Road meet Northern Boulevard, about five blocks from our apartment. The children's section, with a separate entrance, was five steps above the main floor, with the librarian's desk near the door. There were maple tables and chairs, smaller versions of the adult furniture, and open shelves for the various ages of the young patrons. Children could look past the stairs to the main library but enter only with an adult. Reading with the soft, hushed rustle of pages turning, bindings sliding across the tables, and the quiet clicks of dates being stamped on the paper slips inside the back covers of books being borrowed. With necessary whispering only. Perfect. I was a regular. I'd had my own library card at age three, as soon as I could write my name. I knew the librarians very well. I longed to see what was on the main shelves but for a long time never broached the barrier of the five steps.

Mother thought I needed to "be on a program," and not just fritter away my time. Sometime in third grade I started art lessons, which went on for a year or so. The teacher used a store for her studio and classroom, and the after-school class included some older students as well as the beginners. We had minimal instruction, with help from the teacher and her assistant as needed, everyone working on the same project. After a few months, I was moved to another class with students in their teens. Many projects were on various kinds of plates: pine, glass, heavy paper. In that class, I tried oils for the first time, painting a cherry tree for George Washington's birthday and signing it with my full name and age: "8 years old." For Mother's birthday in May, I made another painting on a wooden plate, lavender spring flowers with her initials. The teacher improved the painted initials, EG, but the painting was mine. In June, some of my pieces were selected for a display at the Flushing library, my first exhibition. My next art lessons were not to start until two decades later in Korea.

In the meantime, I kept notebooks and sketchbooks and hurried through my homework so that I could "do art." In 1951, an apartment finally opened up on the fourth floor of our building, and we moved from 1A to 4B. Bobby and I shared a bedroom — eventually partitioned down the middle with furniture — until 1959. Bobby was sent to nursery school at the Flushing Progressive School, as I had been, and the school car dropped him off in front of our building around 4:45. It was my responsibility to meet him, give him a snack, and look after him.

My grandmother stopped by once or twice a week, and sometimes stayed to eat with us before she returned to whatever rooming house she lived in at the moment. Often she got out her old black Singer sewing machine, which was kept in the front hall closet of our apartment. She sewed for a charity while she talked the afternoon away. With a needle in her hand, she told me about the actresses she had known. We folded the edge for a hem and bent back the fabric to take tiny stitches, catching two or three threads so that the hem would be strong and invisible. All around the edge of the skirt, the story would circle around. Grandma had started her career at Maisie's, a nineteenth century millinery for New York society ladies. After a while, she was designing and making dresses for actresses who performed in the 14th Street theaters. She had loved to go to the plays and could relay the details of many performances of fifty years before. I am surprised to notice that I can do the same.

BITTER TIME • *In 1951 my mother didn't have a job anymore. I don't know if she quit or was fired, but it was over.* At about the same time she accidentally became pregnant again. It was a catastrophe. She was distraught beyond reason. She said she would kill herself rather than have another baby. My father was horrified at the thought of abortion. Mother insisted. My father resisted. He was repulsed by the idea and the reality of it. She grew more wild and hysterical. In the end, he helped to arrange for a legal abortion based on the fact that she was increasingly and persuasively suicidal. (Abortion was legal in New York State under very limited circumstances.)

They told no one. When Mother went to the hospital, and ever after, she said it was for an appendectomy. Subsequently, their differences became even more bitter. Years later, when my father told me about this episode, I understood that, for him, that abortion was the end of hope for their life together. Their conflict became a war of attrition, without pity or mercy. Decades later, he was still very angry and bitter about his role in obtaining the abortion. Yet, under the pressure of the situation, he had done what he always did: give in and then protest that he had no choice.

Though my birth had been planned, however grudgingly, the fact of my existence ruined any chance of my mother having the life she wanted. Bobby was conceived only after medical advisors prescribed that female hysteria would be cured by pregnancy and domesticity. That concept was definitively discredited with Bobby's arrival.

For as long as I can remember, Mother talked of dying, of my being the cause of her death, not in the figurative sense but as a prediction. I believe she felt that parenthood was a kind of death for her. Once, in my presence, she said to my great-uncle, Grandma's brother Charles, that parenthood was "nothing but a kick in the ass" that would soon kick her into her grave. When he tried to calm her, she began to cry and scream and ran out of the apartment. I can still see her, frantic and despairing, as melodramatic then as it seems now.

I was timid and ambitious, bookish and constantly alarmed, always feeling guilty for all the grief I caused. I was also fairly intrepid. By six or seven, I traveled alone to visit aunts in Philadelphia and Syracuse. I walked alone to my aunts' and grandmother's homes in Flushing. By the mid-1950s I was taking Bobby with me on the subway to Manhattan, to the zoo, the botanical gardens, the movies. I wanted more than I knew. I was superficially obedient and quiet for the most part, but profoundly rebellious within.

Mother recovered. She took other jobs, which lasted days or weeks or months, and between them went back to temping. She didn't like this, that, or another aspect of a job, but liked being home with us even less. Everyone in her family was very heavy, and now she began to gain weight. Food had been important before, but at this point it became her central satisfaction.

Most days, Bobby and I were on our own together after school. We got our first television in 1952. Bobby loved to watch the little puppet Howdy Doody while eating straight from a jar of peanut butter. Many times he asked me to stay with him, and we wound up sitting together in the blue velvet chair. Usually I started dinner, putting the potatoes in the stovetop baking pot, gradually learning to make simple meals. Mother was trying to reestablish a working life, and she eventually landed a secretarial-administrative job she loved in Rockefeller Center. She left early, wore nice suits, had her hair done, and didn't seem to mind the commute very much. But if dinner were not started when she walked in the door around six-thirty, she just exploded.

NINETEEN FIFTY-FOUR • *The spring of 1954 was an amazing time. Television* was still somewhat novel. I was allowed to stay up late for *Your Show of Shows* with Sid Caesar. Another show, *I Remember Mama*, was on Friday nights. I was the same age as the youngest daughter, Dagmar, and was devoted to the whole Norwegian immigrant family. My favorite show was Edward R. Murrow's interview program, *Person to Person*. The McCarthy hearings were televised live in the afternoons.

Lucy was my very good friend. She lived across the street in another building and we played together nearly every day. Lucy's father was openly political. Perhaps in the 1930s, he had been a Communist. Now he worked at a low-paying job and the family was always tight for money. Lucy's parents and mine were friendly, especially the men. Lucy's mother and father were sweet and gentle with the children and I was always welcome there. One day, my father sat down with me and said that I couldn't go to Lucy's house. I was bewildered. The following day he told me that Lucy and her family had moved away the night before. I couldn't believe it. I ran across the street, up the six flights of stairs. The door was locked (it never had been before). Lucy, her brother, her parents, and her dog were never seen again in our neighborhood. Dad said, in his most serious voice, that I was not to talk about Lucy and her family to any strangers, or anyone else.

They just disappeared from our lives. In the political atmosphere of the times, my twelve-year-old mind connected Lucy's departure to Joseph McCarthy. The McCarthy hearings, and Roy Cohn, Robert Kennedy, and other people of similar mind, had become a national obsession. The Army-McCarthy hearings were telecast live. After school I raced home to watch it. Finally, I saw Joseph Welch, lead counsel for the U.S. Army, stand up to McCarthy and the committee. He was furious and brave.

Senator Joseph McCarthy had been building his career by finding Communists everywhere and the cruelly labeled "fellow travelers" (those culpable by a figment of McCarthy's imagination). Everyone was suspect. Even if you had no sympathy for leftist ideology, you were a dupe if you did not report them as un-American. After the Army hearings, he began to sputter out.

In school that spring, we practiced "duck and cover." We made an envelope of oilcloth. Girls sewed their own, boys' mothers made theirs. Then we neatly folded a white sheet, put it in the envelope, and kept it in our lift-top desks. When a certain bell signaled "air raid," you grabbed the envelope, marched silently into the corridor, sat against the wall, and put the sheet over your head. When the "all clear" was sounded, you refolded the sheet—neatly—and returned to the classroom. If there was not enough warning time, a different bell sounded, and you ducked under your own desk, covering your head, especially your eyes so that you might, perhaps, avoid being blinded in the nuclear blast. We started geometry and learned to calculate the blast zones from New York landmarks. Concentric circles rippled out from the Statue of Liberty, the United Nations, and the Empire State Building. Within those circles we calculated damage: total destruction zone, damage estimates (burns, radiation sickness, destroyed buildings, etc.), and survivability within each concentric circle. What percentage of people in Flushing would be killed? Injured? We were supposed to understand how near the threat of nuclear war was, and how dangerous was our enemy. These exercises contributed to making a lot of young people pacifists ten years later, in the sixties.

About this time school became more political in other ways. Nineteen fifty-four was the year that "under God" was added to the Pledge of Allegiance. My parents had no religious faith at all. Each of them, to varying degrees, believed in the idea of free will, and democracy was the closest they came to fervent belief. I came home with the new Pledge (always spelled with the capital P) and wondered if I could still go to school. Reciting and believing the Pledge of Allegiance was a required part of being a New York school child then. Mandatory profession of a religious creed was not new to the educational experience. Throughout my school years, we had learned and recited the Lord's Prayer, sung religious hymns, and studied the basic tenets of Christian belief as part of holiday celebrations. Nevertheless, this was the federal government telling us children that a publicly professed belief in God was part of being a patriotic American, at a time when it was necessary to prove you were loyal and patriotic. Mother said, "Just say it," and make no fuss, go along. Dad advised that if I couldn't say it, then move my lips past the words and let it be. McCarthy might have been in the next room.

GIRL IN SCHOOL • *At the end of the sixth grade, likely children were evaluated* for Rapid Advance (RA) or Special Progress (SP). These programs were intended for bright students who were ready to move forward more rapidly than the standard curriculum. An RA or SP student attended a different school and completed seventh, eighth, and ninth grades in two years. Everyone else stayed in elementary school through eighth grade and proceeded to high school as a ninth grader. Students had been tracked since kindergarten, via reading and math groups. I had been reading since I was three, was a regular library patron, and in fifth and sixth grades had read on an independent program. Rather unwillingly, my parents had gone to Manhattan to buy the necessary readers and workbooks, which I finished quickly so that I could get on with my own books. When I was recommended for the SP, my mother was adamantly opposed. I was not special, she maintained, and had no need to attend a special school. PS 32 was good enough.

So, in 1954, with McCarthy, the bomb, Communists, Dien Bien Phu in Vietnam, *Rock Around the Clock*, the discovery of DNA, and Brown vs. Board of Education, I spent a good part of the year learning to make lumpy white sauce and a skirt that didn't fit. I had always liked or loved my teachers, but seventh grade became one of the worst trials of my school life. I had to stay in step with the other students and write spelling words one hundred times (torture for a somewhat dyslexic person). The boys left the room to go to shop class, use tools, and make some awkward object their mothers would love for Christmas or Mother's Day. As long as they finished it, they were home free. Girls had home economics, in which they theoretically learned to cook, clean, wash dishes, and sew. Sewing was done in class, so that it would be evident that no one had helped you. Getting or giving help was one of the many illicit impulses that were to be curbed at any cost. We were being prepared to manage our future suburban homes, to be the wives and mothers pictured in the magazines.

The art of housecleaning: Girls were divided into groups of four (Gangs of Four?), with every effort made to separate friends. Then we swept, dusted, put down and took up shelf paper, made beds with hospital corners. The Marines could have used these lessons. The teacher bounced a coin to see if the blankets were tight enough. Did anyone ever actually sleep this way? We washed windows, washed glasses that were already pristine, set tables with six-piece place settings and put it all away again in drawers that were aligned with military precision. And we made white sauce.

I hadn't heard of white sauce. My mother never liked to cook. She was very happy when Swanson's TV dinners came along. Over the years, my brother and I ate hundreds of them. I had no knowledge of white sauce. It was from a different world.

Here's the recipe: each girl, in teams of four, puts on the white apron she made in sewing class, and a kerchief over her hair. (I hadn't seen someone actually wearing an apron except in ads. My mother didn't wear an apron when she cooked. In fact, she often didn't wear any clothes at all for cooking and housework.) Girl 1 stirs together white flour and unsalted butter until they hold together (more or less), then s-l-o-w-l-y adds milk, helpfully measured out by Girl 2. Keep stirring over the flame until it is perfectly smooth, like cream, but with no taste. Meanwhile, Girl 3 washes and peels white potatoes, and Girl 4 puts them in a pot to boil. She is responsible for putting them onto the four little white plates exactly when the white sauce is ready. She is the assistant stirrer, and also sets the table with white napkins for the occasion. Girl 4 pours a glass of white milk for each of her teammates, gives a helpful assist as needed and does the actual pouring of the white sauce over the white potatoes.

The undesirability of this presentation as food cannot be exaggerated. It preceded conceptual art by only a few years.

NEW HAMPSHIRE • *The term finally ended. Mother again felt that I needed* "a program." I had been to sleep-away and day camps, usually for about three or four weeks. The best of these was a farm in New Hampshire, north of Mount Washington, almost at the Canadian border, on a tributary of the Connecticut River. The owners were teachers during the school year and farmers in the summer. They had no children of their own and each summer took a dozen girls and boys from ten to sixteen years old. We participated in all aspects of the farm as if we were a family. The girls slept on cots in two tiny screened-in "cabins"— something like wooden tents — without electricity or running water. The boys slept in two big camping tents. In each sleeping shelter there was an adult: a woman with the girls and an older teenager with the boys. We cared for a vegetable garden, my first sustained exposure to anything other than a decorative city flower garden. The girls baked bread and cooked farm dinners of beautiful colors and amazing smells. The boys helped in the fields. Everyone cared for the animals. I rode a little donkey, bareback, and graduated to a sweet bay horse. If you rode on the farm, you were also responsible for currying your animal and mucking out the stalls, saving everything in the compost. Those patient animals let me climb on, and I was soon allowed to ride to the road to collect the mail from the rural box. A handsome gray helped me learn how to sail over a wall. Afternoons, the children walked together to a nearby lake to swim. Sooner or later, each of us emerged with a leech clinging to a leg or arm. The hired man, assistant farmer really, taught me to fish. I used a little pole, string, a hook, and worms dug from the woods. I could walk by myself across the stepping-stones and over the small dam to a spot where the sun came sparkling through the trees. There were salamanders to admire, and sunfish. He said let them live, take only what we need. My one or two trout wound up on the dinner table.

Sundays we made ice cream, the smallest children cranking first and the biggest boys pushing the almost ready ice cream through the dasher. Then there was an interminable wait while the ice cream set. Finally, we had sweet, cold gorgeousness. This treat was followed by singing, stories, and at the last, as the chill evening darkened, a fire in the fireplace on the porch. The farmers, husband and wife, loved their life on the farm as much as they loved their life as teachers. Every task, however humble, had a place, a value, in their scheme of things. They let us city children have a glimpse of the integrity of their stewardship and the pleasures of the land. They have stayed in my mind ever since my two brief visits with them.

WORKING ON GROWING UP • *I still didn't know how to swim, and I was* the handicap everyone dreaded when it came time to form up teams at school. I took dance lessons and was fairly coordinated, but I never connected with chasing balls. The summer of 1954, when I was twelve, I had my first job, minding the children of a neighbor couple. They belonged to a cabana club, which was a club for swimming, consuming summery food and drink, and gossiping. Someone had to watch the children so they didn't get sunburned or drown. This was supposed to be a vacation for me, too, since I was to be at the pool every day. I was expected to bring my own lunch, and most days I took a brown paper bag with a peanut butter and grape jelly sandwich, an apple, and Oreo cookies if possible. If there were any potato chips in the kitchen I put those in, too. The kids were little, their mother was occupied, and it was hot on the concrete apron of the pool. I earned five dollars a week and gave my mother one dollar of it toward my board. She said everyone who worked should contribute to his or her own expenses. Bobby went to day camp.

All that summer I worked through my "program." The librarians agreed to allow me in the adult stacks. I started to read American novelists in alphabetical order: Alcott, Cather, Crane, Hawthorne, Lewis, London, Steinbeck. I began a lifelong friendship with some of the books I found.

Eventually, the summer of 1954 was over. The eighth grade curriculum included choral speaking, similar to singing, except that the voices spoke poetry. Long poems were no longer learned by rote, although we still had to recite some short pieces from memory: Kipling, Teasdale, Whitman, Longfellow, Lowell, and their cohorts. Choral speaking was all joy once the class got into it. Our teacher, Mrs. Ober, obviously loved it. It was taught as the reward for getting through spelling or completing some other drudgery. By the spring, we had a small repertoire. Mrs. Ober spread her arms in a wide circle and said that now it was time. We moved to the perimeter of the room, spoke the poems, our teacher's open arms directing us much as an orchestral conductor would. Poetry as reward!

In the winter of 1954, my Great Uncle Harry and his wife, Great Aunt Rhoda, came to New York from California. Harry had rapidly advancing cancer, and had come to New York to say good-bye to his remaining sisters and brother, and to try some last resort treatment at Sloan Kettering Institute.

Harry and Rhoda were artists. They were very loving with one another, and very open and free with their affection. One afternoon, Harry found me drawing at Grandma's old desk in our apartment and said that I was an artist, too. I should keep on and try everything I could. I think that, during my childhood, Uncle Harry was the only person who said anything to me about being an artist. I am almost the same age now as he was then and I see his advice was right. Making art, being an artist, seems in large part to be a matter of paying attention and keeping at it.

THE DRESS • *There was a ritual torture to be endured by the girls of PS 32:* THE DRESS! The eighth grade teachers decided on the pattern and fabric, and the girls had to make and WEAR it to graduation at the end of June. But first, we had to make the jumper.

During the fall term, every girl made a jumper, a sleeveless, waistless, princess-seamed dress to be worn over a blouse or sweater. The girls could choose dark green, navy blue, or very dark maroon, of a fabric chosen by the teachers. It could not have been dowdier, but once it was finished, you wore it for a day and then it could go to a rummage sale. The graduation dress was next.

In January, the teachers announced the pattern: puffed sleeves and a round neck, both edged in ruffled lace threaded with baby-blue velvet ribbons; a very full skirt, attached at the waist with more lace, threaded with more blue ribbons tied in a bow and falling over the skirt. It was a dress for the dolls we had outgrown just a while before. The fabric, to be purchased at a particular store, was sheer organdy with roses embossed, all white. The shoes would be white, flat, or with a Cuban heel, no more than one and one-half inches high and no less than one inch at the base. Girls were to wear a full slip, white, strapless if possible, no bras showing through the sheer fabric, and white stockings. Bare legs not permitted. Short white gloves required. We would each carry a nosegay, obtained from the designated florist, edged in white lace. The boys were to ask their mothers to be sure they had a blue blazer, white shirt, and red tie.

The dress pattern was purchased in the size that the mothers guessed their daughters would be by June. The fabric was laid out, pinned, and cut without anyone actually measuring any girl. Various sections were loosely basted together, ruffles gathered, eased, fine basted by hand. The inner seams were machine sewn, and then the rolled French seams were hand finished for the whole dress. It took months of afternoons of school time. Most girls would sneak pieces out to do at home. In school, by late May, the skirt was attached to the bodice and the zipper put in. The horrible lace was painstakingly threaded with the ribbons and attached to the waist. The whole thing was a nightmare fantasy. In my case, the teacher had pinned the skirt backwards, the left of the bodice to the right of the skirt. It was also too small. My mother was livid, furious at the waste of money and the fuss. Fortunately, my grandmother came to the rescue. She and I ripped open all the French seams that had been so painstakingly rolled. She took apart the whole dress, found little margins everywhere, and rebuilt the mess on my body, all the while vigorously expressing her opinion of the whole project. It was a marathon weekend of tears, pins, thread, and strong words. The dress was gruesome, but it was done. The graduation dress was even more grotesque on me than it was on the typical girl, as I was already over 5'5" tall. I had never been one to choose ruffles and flounces, and this dress cured me for life from any misapprehensions in that direction.

In 1955, the year I was to graduate from eighth grade, politics prevailed. The students were given a form to sign. It was a loyalty oath in which each child declared that he or she had never been a member of the Communist Party, and did not advocate the overthrow of the government by violent means. Some children were uneasy or reluctant to sign, hardly because they were Communists. I think we had never before considered that we might be politically powerful enough to matter at all, much less overthrow the government of the United States. Again, very quiet discussion took place in my family and the families of some of my friends. Eventually, everyone signed. Without it you couldn't graduate, and therefore, wouldn't be going to high school.

So, at the end of June, we marched with the hesitation step down the aisle of PS 32, girls singing "Look for the Silver Lining" and boys, "Stout Hearted Men." We received our diplomas. After a short break, we entered the gym for the dance, the girls still a mass of billowing, mandatory, white organdy. The school had given everyone lessons in social dance and "social deportment." The girls had practiced sitting demurely with ankles crossed, and the boys had practiced a bow from the waist and "May I have this dance?" I was the third tallest girl, taller than every boy, with no sign of the Marilyn Monroe figure that was the exemplar of femininity. My still very short friend, David, asked me to dance. David was brilliant at science and planned to become a doctor. Through seventh and eighth grades, he had shared his chemistry set with me, letting me help to set off small explosions, mixing powders into colored liquids, and doing other magic. After a few turns around the floor, we went for the Kool-Aid punch. Finally the dance was over. Summer was allowed to begin.

MAY AND MIKE • *My girlhood was much taken up with traveling to visit my* aunts. My first solo trip was to Philadelphia when I was about seven. My father took me to Penn Station, put me on the train, and stowed my little suitcase. He kissed me good-bye, with instructions to get off at North Philadelphia where his sister, Aunt May, and her husband, Uncle Mike, would be waiting. I had packed my books and pencils and paper for the trip. As I would for all the future, I loved looking out the train windows. Eventually, the conductor came along, took me and my bag to the door and, as the train pulled in, there was Uncle Mike on the platform waiting right at the door of the car.

Aunt May was my father's twin sister. She loved to say how much I resembled her. I used to visit her a couple of times a year at school holidays, and she came to New York for holidays or just a quick visit. It is only an hour on the train from New York's Penn Station to Philly's 30th Street.

In Aunt May's young life, things were hard, as for all the family. She went to school only through junior high, graduating when she was fifteen and going to work immediately afterward. Like my father and their older sister, Sally, she had a great craving for education. Perhaps it is hard to understand now, when almost half of all the high school students voluntarily, eagerly, drop out without graduating. But for May, as for her siblings, the hunger for learning was as great as the hunger for food. They were all avid readers, lovers of words. She was a demon Scrabble player and knew several versions of the game, including one, "dirty Scrabble," that required an off-color association for each word laid down on the board. It took all night to play a round. Children were not allowed to be present, nor were they given explanations for the great gales of laughter.

May never gave up. After her son, Stephen, grew up she took courses, became qualified as a teacher's aide, and worked alongside the same teacher in a local school for about fifteen years. After she reached mandatory retirement age, she found a job with the Better Business Bureau as a combination ombudsman, information service, and complaint resolver.

I have never met anyone kinder, with a funnier sense of humor, or more openhearted.

Aunt May's husband, Mike, was just the loveliest man alive. He was always ready with a smile that spread over his face from his dark brown eyes. He had a stocky, muscled, very fit body, just right for swinging little girls in the air. He was a builder who was very proud of his Carpenters Union membership, which he kept all his life.

In World War II, there was a rule that if an airman flew fifty missions, he got a furlough all the way home. Mike flew the fifty, went home for a few weeks to his new wife, May, and on his return to Europe, flew another fifty. He was the man in the Plexiglas gun turret of the B-17. One day the Flying Fortress was hit by German anti-aircraft fire. The pilot and several crewmembers were killed and most of the rest wounded. Mike, with no piloting experience, and only emergency instructions from the ground, managed to fly them all back from Europe, across the English Channel, and land them safely in England. General Pershing decorated him in a ceremony in Europe. He resolutely never spoke about it, except once to say that it wasn't heroism. He had expected to come back home from the war, and this was a necessary thing to do. He had wanted to throw away his medals and the certificates, but Aunt May wrapped them in a linen cloth and put them in the back of a closet. That summer, when I was thirteen, she showed them to me and told me the story. She said I was never to mention it to Mike. At that time, more than ten years later, he still had terrible headaches and intense nightmares about flying in the war and didn't want to bring it back.

Another decade later, he told the only war story I ever heard from him directly, about the bombing of Dresden. Virtuoso formations all the way over, the planes packed so tightly in the sky over the city that they blocked the sun. The fliers could see each other from every window, and endless fire below. Some people thought it was revenge for the destruction of Coventry (England) by the Germans. Mike said the war had to be won. He had his job to do.

Mike died a hero, too. Years later, after a long career as a builder, with their son grown, he retired, and he and May enjoyed life together. They often drove from Philadelphia to a nearby resort in the Poconos. One cold afternoon, a man was floundering in the pool. Mike jumped in wearing all his clothes, pulled the guy out, and gave him CPR. The man revived. Mike was tired. He went to the hotel room, lay down, and died of a heart attack a few minutes later. At his funeral, on a cold, rainy day in Philadelphia, my father held his twin sister in his arms and they cried together.

ALL READY • *Dad was still at the Department of Welfare in the 1950s, but had* given up the Boys' Club except for special occasions. His best energy was given to the stock market.

My father was a future-oriented person. He had traditional ambitions and values in some ways, but always thought the future was going to be better, more interesting. He was almost entirely self-educated, a very avid reader. After he died, I received some boxes of his books and found that, over the years, we had bought and read many of the same biographies, volumes of history and philosophy. His boxes, though, had very little fiction or poetry. His Schopenhauer was literally falling apart at the seams, pages falling out of the blue linen cover. A brown, leather-bound volume by Macaulay was very worn but in better shape than mine. He made a lifelong study of the Civil War and the American Revolution. Two whole boxes were books about the Civil War, many of them biographies. There were at least three biographies of George Washington. A life-size head of Lincoln hung in his bedroom. Most of all, he read about economics and the relationship between the worlds of money and politics. I sorted the book boxes, kept his copies, and gave my duplicates to the public library.

As a young man, like many of his generation, Dad thought that unrestrained capitalism was in urgent need of reform. For all the faults he saw, though, he believed that enterprise, and its embodiment in the stock markets, was the key to prosperity and empowerment. He studied it voraciously. He subscribed to *Moody's* and *Barron's*, both financial magazines, and read several newspapers every day. He began to invest. He made a little money, lost some. Mother liked the former but was terrified of the latter. From my perspective now, I believe she was also projecting her unhappiness and anger with Dad's philandering onto his preoccupation with the stock market.

Dad liked the company of women. He was charming and witty, made women laugh and feel desired. He flirted in front of my mother, and me—that was safe enough—but he also had many brief and not so brief affairs.

Mother constantly became infuriated over large things and small. One day she was in the kitchen and I did not respond as required. I don't remember the issue. She had a long carving knife in her hand. It was very old with a black wooden handle and a curved, smooth, steel blade held in place with brass rivets. She raised this knife, face livid, eyes opened wide. She screamed that she was going to kill me. She rushed toward me across the kitchen. I bolted for the bathroom, the only room that had a lock. She pounded on the door, yelling and swearing. I stood in the bathroom, shaking, my heart racing as I refused to open the door. Then, all was quiet. I stayed there for what seemed like hours. However long it was, the standoff lasted until my father came home. By then, Mother's fury had worn away, I was persuaded to unlock the door, and it was as if it were an ordinary evening.

On this day, as many others, Bobby ran into the bedroom we shared and hid under my bed, scrunching himself into the farthest corner. As usual, I had to wiggle in there and take his hands so that he could come out again. He remembers this day exactly as I do.

My parents were always repeating the same pattern, dramatic scenes followed by capitulation. They seemed to want to hurt each other to compensate for, or maybe balance, their individual pain. As the mid-1950s wore on, they were stranded in the fever of their mutual discontent and disappointment.

CAMMY • *In 1955, Dad met Cammy. That spring I was thirteen years old and* Bobby was five. It was still my job to look after him. I often took him to the park after school when we had late daylight. We were walking through the wide brick gate entryway and there, right in front of me, my father and a beautiful woman were holding hands, walking around the path. They were talking with their heads tipped toward each other, smiling, at ease, strolling through that neighborhood meeting place. I grabbed Bobby, spun him around, and we left at a run. There could be no other explanation: my father had a girlfriend.

Cammy was just about everything Mother was not. Cammy worked at what today is called Child Protective Services. Dad was a senior caseworker at the Department of Welfare. They met at court while addressing the same case. She was lovely. She had a very pretty face with a big, ready smile, long brown hair that she wore loose over her shoulders, and she had a very handsome figure. She was professional in her career and was a delightful, sociable person. She lived six blocks from us, in an attached row house, with her husband, a lawyer, and her two children—about the same ages as Bobby and me—and her Italian-born parents in the downstairs apartment. I grew to like Cammy enormously and felt conflicted every minute.

Cammy and Dad were in love. They were not discreet. They did not leave their spouses. Instead, our two families became friends. My parents went to their house for New Year's and Christmas parties and other social occasions. I can remember my mother, tense, dressed up, making some sort of hors d'oeuvres, wrapping the plate, and setting off with my father to the party at his lover's home. There was music and dancing. Mother didn't dance, probably hadn't in years, but Dad danced in the living room with Cammy, while her husband and their friends and neighbors looked on. Oddly enough, each of my parents chose to tell me about this party afterward.

Our families were friendly enough that I could go to Cammy's house anytime. Like many people, they did not lock the back door, and Cammy made it clear that I was welcome to stop by anytime. Sometimes I went over for the comfort of a quiet house. Cammy invited me to take something from the cake box — there was always some Italian treat there. Incredible but true, my mother didn't object. Through my high school years, I came to know Cammy very well. I felt very guilty to like her for the sweet and kind person she was. One afternoon when I was about fifteen, I walked over there and came in the back door as usual. The house was quiet, and I called to Cammy as I walked from the kitchen into the living room. She and my father were making love in a big armchair. I turned and dashed out.

I avoided Dad for a couple of days, but finally he asked me to sit with him in the kitchen. He and I had a habit of having a glass of milk and cookies together around eleven o'clock in the evening. We usually talked about politics, the news, his work, books. That night he said that he and Cammy loved each other and wanted to be together as much as they could. I asked him if he was going to get a divorce and marry Cammy. He said, no, he couldn't do that because he couldn't leave Bobby and me with our mother. If it weren't for us, he would spend the rest of his life with Cammy, his true love. Many times in the coming years, he reminded me that we, Bobby and I, were the cause of his decision to abandon happiness. I thought I was supposed to feel guilty. Through my school years, Cammy was a fixture in my life.

MISS BROWN'S • *In the summer of 1955, I went to Buffalo, New York,* ostensibly to visit my cousin Bennett but really to be with his wife, Roslyn. She was about twenty-five, sweet and hospitable. One day we were baking a cake from a mix in a box. While we waited for it to be ready, the conversation turned to clothes. Roz, kind Roz, gave me the lowdown. I needed a bra for high school, for the locker room. How could I have imagined that I might need to take my clothes off in school? I still was required by my mother's strict rules to wear an undershirt!

After a few false starts, I told my mother that I needed a bra. She laughed and said if I wanted a brassiere, I should go to Miss Brown and get one. Miss Brown's shop, opposite the Long Island Railroad Station, was an institution. My mother had all her corsets and brassieres made there. Even readymade underwear was custom fitted and altered. Miss Brown had an assortment of necessities, embroidered handkerchiefs, stockings, filmy negligees, and a small array of makeup. I was used to going there but making this purchase was very intimidating to me. Miss Brown got the gist of it right away, found a dainty little white eyelet bra and told me to try it on. I was so ignorant that I didn't exactly know how it went. Mother was proud of her advanced views on women's concerns, but she had neglected to tell me much about the details. She wore corsets and brassieres like full-body armor, with stays, steel, and laces. Finally Miss Brown came into the dressing room and made the necessary adjustments of straps and hooks, while I cringed in embarrassment. At about this point, Mother and Grandma came into the store and gave their approval to my purchase.

Miss Brown said that maybe I could use a little color on my cheeks. I had a regulation pale pink lipstick from the graduation dance. Mother said that Dad would never permit rouge. Miss Brown answered that she had a solution for that problem. She took out a delicate pink lipstick and put a couple of dots on my cheeks, and then smoothed them with her fingertips. Grandma approved. Miss Brown said, "Sam will never know. And she's not wearing rouge…. It's lipstick!" And so I walked out of the store, wearing my bra and "makeup," feeling like I was masquerading as a high school girl.

HIGH SCHOOL DAYS • *Within five blocks of our apartment, I had five first* cousins. They were older, as my aunts were older than my mother. (My father's older sister, Sally, also lived within walking distance, but she had no children.) Aunt Diana, the oldest sister, had two sons. Gerry had finished college and was getting into television and theater. Dick was a student who played the cello and basketball. Aunt Ruthie's oldest son, Bobby, had just gotten his doctorate in physics and married a girl from Belgium. Betty was an aspiring actress, studying at NYU, living at home and hating it. Closest to me in age was Judy, Aunt Ruthie's youngest offspring, about to start her junior year in high school. I was in and out of my aunts' homes and Judy was a regular companion. Ruthie and Sam were very well off, as the saying went, and liked to be sure that everyone knew it. It was arranged that I walk with Judy to my first day of high school.

I was ready early, dressed in a new, dark, straight skirt and new short-sleeved sweater. I packed my new, still aromatic, Italian leather bag. With my notebook in the bend of my arm, I set off for Judy's house. Oh, my! Judy opened the door dressed in a flowery summer skirt with crinolines and ballet flats. We walked toward the school, about a mile away, stopping en route to pick up Judy's friends, all in pretty skirts. You were supposed to use this day to show off your most feminine self, with several of the multilayered, ruffled, stiff petticoats, then all the rage. Apparently, the first day was only to get schedules and books, the opportunity to establish your image. I walked along in my sensible brown shoes, a few paces behind the three friends, whom I had known all my life, definitely the younger bumpkin. At the school door, Judy said I was to meet her there to walk back to her house for lunch.

I went into Bayside High School, along with the other four thousand students, trying to find my homeroom. I wandered around the building, through the abbreviated day's schedule, eight periods, to fill in forms, collect books. I was as naive as a tall, awkward, nerd of a girl could be. It was a day for students to reconnect after the long summer. My longtime playmate, Regina, had moved with her family to a house in Stony Brook. Several of my friends went off to other schools. I floundered through the few hours that constituted this first day, an innocent abroad in the foreign land of high school.

Ninth grade was a very crucial year for New York students. Right then, decisions were made that would affect your entire life. The courses in math, science, and English were on tracks: academic, vocational, and general. Within the academic track, if you, or your teachers, thought you were "college material," you took the hardest course within each subject area, on a four-year program that met the requirements of the New York State Board of Regents. If you started out in vocational, there was little chance to have the courses to qualify for college four years down the road. My mother was proud to work as a secretary and had signed me up for typing, with the plan that I would follow this traditional female career. I found out that students could volunteer for service, which meant being helpers to various departments and teachers. My guidance counselor, Mr. Deutsch, arranged for me to exchange typing for service in his office. I worked for him for the next three years, doing clerical work, fetching students from their classes for conferences, and organizing the deluge of materials that arrived every spring from colleges. I took the hardest courses every term, planned for the future, and began to see college as my way out of my family's chaotic life.

As it had been in grade school, classes were huge. Many classes had forty students or more, sometimes more than the number of seats and desks. In geometry I had to share both a seat and a book with another girl. I could only take the book home every other night. One evening my tenth grade geometry teacher telephoned and said to my father that I was a bright student but often came to class unprepared, with homework not done. My parents were incensed. How could I behave like that? I explained about the book. A day or two later, we again went to the school bookstore in Manhattan and purchased a geometry book, my parents grumbling at the expense and the classroom conditions.

Tenth grade English was a revelation. The major project of the year was reading Homer's *The Iliad* and *The Odyssey*. The class was divided and the various groups made skits, hallway exhibitions, dioramas, and reports. We read aloud, in English, of course, and I had a first taste of Herodotus. We went to the Metropolitan Museum of Art to look at Greek sculpture, models of ancient temples, mosaics from Crete. I had been going to the museum since toddler days and was familiar with the Egyptian and Greco-Roman halls, but now everything old was new to me. I loved the mathematical order of architecture, the calmness and sense of proportion. I thought about the people who had lived in those buildings.

I was drawing every day and my pictures became building plans. Dad had gone to advise a company, and as a souvenir brought me an anodized gold scale marked Apex Smelting Company. It is heavy, with clear numbers and two measuring scales on each face, still shiny and useful fifty-five years later. It took me a little while to get into it. I use it to this day. I began to see that my work in the world might be architecture.

In school we had to explore one profession or vocation, and the students were supposed to research the field a bit and interview someone. I wanted to choose architecture, but there were apparently no women architects. My parents said that being a teacher, secretary, or social worker was appropriate. Aunt Jessie, married to Mother's oldest brother, Mervin, was a sort of social worker. She was one of the earliest practitioners of the art therapy movement and worked with a psychiatrist in a hospital in Syracuse. I had visited Aunt Jessie and Uncle Mervin many times. Jessie's mother and my grandmother had been friends and made weeks-long visits to one another in the early part of the century. On those family visits, Jessie came to know and eventually marry Mervin. During the school holiday, I went to visit in Syracuse, interviewed Jessie, wrote my report about the job of therapist/social worker, and never for one minute considered it to be my future, no matter how much I loved Aunt Jessie.

For my fifteenth birthday, I had been given a Jaguar bicycle, black with chrome trim, with a fender ornament of a jaguar in motion, similar to the one on the automobile hood. My bike had skinny tires, gears, a leather bag with a tool kit, a light, and a basket. It was beautiful. I rode it everywhere I could. I was still supposed to be home for Bobby after school, but sometimes he went to play with his friends, or else Grandma, now over eighty, would come to babysit so that I could go out. In mild weather, I went to one park or another and did my homework there. Cunningham Park had bike paths through the woods and picnic areas, and around a pond. One of my favorite destinations was the base of the Whitestone Bridge, officially called Francis Lewis Park. The bridge is a soaring, simple sweep through the air, elegantly defining the place where the East River becomes Long Island Sound. It is one of the most beautiful bridges anywhere. The boulders piled around the base were perfect for climbing, sitting, and picnics. The park wasn't very developed then. You just pedaled through the pretty streets of Malba and Whitestone and arrived at the river. I did my homework and dreamt away many afternoons with the sounds of the water, the boats, and the airplanes taking off from La Guardia Airport nearby. I was still pretty faithful about being home in time to put up the potatoes, start dinner, and help Bobby with his homework.

Mother's Day was supposed to be a big occasion. Flowers and a gift were absolutely required. I usually bought something that would be from Bobby and me. In 1958, Mother's Day was a disaster. I had arranged with a florist to bring lilacs, Mother's favorite, as a surprise. It took a lot of baby-sitting money to do it. There were many deliveries and somebody had to be first, but it wasn't us. There were no flowers there that morning. Mother screamed out her anger at her ungrateful children and, in full fury, she stormed out. Dad went for a paper, which on a Sunday usually meant visiting with the men at the candy store for a couple of hours. I had meant to do something good but knew I had failed. I went out, too, with Bobby. I don't know where we went, but by the time we came back, the florist had left the flowers at the door. They were pretty wilted when Mother got back to the apartment. She dismissed it all as a misunderstanding; I was being oversensitive, and, anyway, Mother's Day wasn't important.

BOB AND THE BOYS • *Tenth grade was a social revolution for me. As an* adolescent, I viewed myself as a dorky girl, earnest, smart, and plain, too gawky to be attractive. I hadn't gone on any dates yet. No one had asked me. The winter I turned fifteen, I went to my first New Year's Eve party. Bob lived on the next block, played the tuba, had graduated, and gone to college in Vermont. When he came back for winter vacation that year, he invited me to the party. We danced to Johnny Ray, Pat Boone, and Bobby Darin. In the style of the times, various boys — older men of 18 and 19 — danced with me, too. In the rec room in the basement of someone's house, candles were lit; party food was set on the bar. I drank Coca Cola (a novelty for me) and ate unidentifiable, salty things. At midnight, Bob swung me in a low dip and kissed me. Over the next year or two, we wrote each other letters. When he came home on college breaks, Bob took me out for my first pizza and my first bowling date. He invited me for my first weekend away, to the University of Vermont homecoming, where he arranged for me to stay with his landlady. We walked around Burlington and the campus. He took me to a party, to the dance, and after two perfect, innocent days, I took the train back to New York. We knew each other as children, dated, were friends, dated some more, and are friends again. Around 1961 he was drafted into the army. We wrote more letters and saw each other on his leaves. He was focused on becoming a photographer. I was spreading my wings in other directions.

I was getting pretty busy by this time. In the Debate Club I was elected secretary. I joined the junior arm of the NAACP (National Association for the Advancement of Colored People) and NCCJ (National Council of Christians and Jews). I volunteered for UNICEF (United Nations International Children's Emergency Fund). I learned to sing "We Shall Overcome." I went to parties of girls who sat around singing folk songs and being high-minded, that era's equivalent of bluestockings. I still took dance lessons. And I was drawing houses.

Not everyone in school planned to go to college, but everyone I knew was thinking about it, getting catalogues, writing to admissions offices on blue stationery with blue-black ink, trying to make a good impression. Judy and her friends, two years ahead of me, were in the throes of the application process, but almost all of them wound up nearby at Queens College, part of the New York City system. They lived at home and continued their lives as before. I was sure I didn't want to do that.

NOT GOING TO MIT • *I still worked for the guidance counselor, Mr. Deutsch.* I started to write away to universities, and he encouraged me to aim high. I was dedicated to becoming an architect. At that time, MIT had an early admission process that matched a prospective student with an alumnus in the proposed field of study. His recommendation was required. I met this architect alumnus a few times, he saw my drawings and plans, talked to me a bit about the nature of being an architect, and when the time came, recommended me for early admission, which I received. My parents' reaction was immediate. Dad was sure that this was a field entirely unsuitable for a girl. I would be around construction, have to wear a hard hat. I should be a teacher, a good field to fall back on if, after I married, I ever needed something. Besides, I had no talent either for art or for engineering, and would definitely fail. MIT was no place for a nice girl. In that era, students needed their parents' signature to accept college admission. It was not going to happen. Mother had a different take. I didn't need to go to college at all. I could get a job, perhaps go to the Katherine Gibbs secretarial school first, and take night classes if I were determined. She hadn't gone to college, why did I think I needed to? We fought many a battle royal. Meanwhile, I applied to a couple more schools and was accepted with scholarships. At a parent conference, my counselor told my father that he had attended the University of Michigan and was sure I could get a scholarship there. Dad said it wasn't worth the money to apply. I was going to Queens College. All fall we raged at each other.

UNCIVIL WAR • *The warfare at home had escalated to a very loud intensity.* In the partitioned bedroom Bobby and I shared, Bobby had the side with the window. I had the side with the closet. He was about six when we moved into that room, and in no time he learned to climb over the dividing bookcase and tease me from his perch near the ceiling, looming over me. Mystery missiles sailed over the top. He knew, as brothers usually do, just what to say to get my attention. He was a frightened and yet very mischievous child. No matter how irritated I might get, I also wanted to take care of him. There was no one else in those years. I was always conflicted, needing to leave, not wanting to leave my brother, needing to grow and at the same time be a grown-up.

I knew I was going to leave home. I began to plan my escape. I accelerated my high school courses and graduated after the fall term. I received letters for service, (less prestigious but comparable to athletic letters), was elected to the National Honor Society, and knew I had very good grades. Nevertheless, I was surprised to be called up to receive the gold medals for both English and History, one from the Flushing Women's Club and the other from Kiwanis. My aunts and uncles came to the apartment afterward for a little celebration, and the day was over.

Finally yielding to my parent's resistance, I had applied to Queens College as a last resort, and started there a week later. It was a short bus ride or bike ride away, almost in the same neighborhood. People I had known in high school were there. People who knew my family were there. The domestic turbulence at home was at its usual high pitch. Dad's affair with Cammy rolled on. Mother was eating more and more, putting on weight, although she was not yet obese. You could still see a hint of the woman she had been. She started college classes when I did, was working toward an Associate Arts degree, and had a job she liked.

After a particularly stormy session between my parents while Mother was ironing his shirts, Dad said some last word and Mother, crying and swearing, threw the hot iron at him. It narrowly missed his head and smashed a hole in the wooden door behind him. Dad stopped calling Mother by her name and addressed her, at home and in public, as Woman. That year, for her birthday, he gave her a check for a hundred dollars, a lot of money in 1958. The check was made out to Woman Gardner, and he told her that to cash it she had to sign it that way. That wasn't true, but she didn't know. She begged him to change it. He said that she could tear it up or sign it, but he was not going to change it. She cried, called him names; he was adamant. His "gift" was the occasion of one of their most bitter confrontations. At times, she was beside herself, beyond sanity. She packed a small bag in haste and went to one of her sister's nearby. After a little coffee, they sent her back home, to her husband and children, "where she belonged." She didn't belong there, of course, but she was more afraid of being alone. Even the ignominy of her present life was less fearsome than the unknown of a solitary new life.

And so, I struggled against the entangling threads of their discontent and started at Queens College.

QUEENS • *I registered for a heavy program and wallowed into college life.* I was so distracted by my family that I hardly knew what was going on. It was like high school but more so. There was more homework, of course, bigger classes, more distance to cover between buildings.

An acquaintance from Bayside High, Jimmy, asked me to play bridge. I had no knowledge of bridge whatsoever. He offered to teach me. He was a lovely young fellow, tall, slender, with long flat hands, and beautiful, caramel colored skin. I wasn't very good at cards but played often between classes. Jimmy kept saying I would get better if I practiced.

There was a social network in New York called house plans. Fifteen or twenty fellows or girls would form a group for the purpose of meeting the opposite sex at parties held on Friday evenings in someone's house. The members of each house plan would come from just one or two neighborhoods and always attended the same university. I was barely seventeen and especially inexperienced. Most of the girls seemed very worldly by comparison. For a party, I had a gray wool dress with a Peter Pan collar and long sleeves. Single pearl earrings and pumps with two-inch heels completed the outfit. Despite my somewhat square style, fellows asked me to dance occasionally and asked for my phone number.

In February, I met Joel at a house plan party. He was an art major, planning to be a sculptor, intense, sensitive, and twenty-one. He took me home from the party where we met, and soon after, I had a boyfriend. He had to endure the classic treatment of picking me up, submitting to my parents' inspection and interrogation, promising to have me back at a specified time. Sometimes one of them was awake, awaiting my return at the witching hour. Joel and I went out once or twice a week, to arty movies, and parties, and just out to drive around, talk, and have ice cream. Joel had an old car with a bench seat and drove with one arm around my shoulders. We parked under the trees in front of my apartment house until the windows fogged up. It was a major physical escalation when one button came undone. One rainy spring evening, we went to an arty movie house in Queens. The picture was *Specter of the Rose*, a 1946 classic, an atmospheric ballet/murder mystery. Afterward, we went to a diner. Joel took my hand and pulled out a traditional sparkly ring to put on my finger. I wanted him for my boyfriend, not to marry! I knew I was too young. My secret plan was to leave home soon.

I always said I could manage, but I couldn't manage Queens College and my home life at the same time. I was saving my babysitting and summer job money as diligently as possible. Inspired by my two youthful visits to the farm in New Hampshire, I set that town near Mount Monadnock as my goal. I wanted to be there, in that quiet place in sight of the mountains. I planned to get a job and go to college there. Just be there. I made lists on yellow, lined legal pads. I planned a route, by Greyhound bus. I planned the clothes to take — only the nicest and most grown up to go with me. I estimated how much money I thought it would require. I wrote and revised. Turbulence at home was the order of each day. I was going.

For a few years, I had sporadically attended the Flushing Friends Meeting House. It was an austere brick building built in 1645, when Flushing was a Dutch town called Vlissengen. The Quakers had met there continuously, as they do to this day. It is the site of the 1657 Flushing Remonstrance, in which citizens risked their lives and fortunes to protest wrong-minded government actions. My understanding was very imperfect, but I was profoundly attracted to the creed of a quietist life, peace, and the concept that each person manifests her ideals and beliefs by the actions she chooses. For all their history, Quakers have valued the lives and work of women, even children, each one for her own sake. I didn't understand or profess the Christian part of the dogma, but I was welcome there anyway. I often went to the historic Bowne House and sat in the garden or under the giant beech tree. Those people had chosen the life they wanted for themselves. The same idea was emerging in my mind. I continued to plan on my yellow pads, growing more desperate and daring.

ON THE BUS • *One spring day, I packed my little cardboard suitcase. I left a note in the foyer of our apartment.* I took the subway to the Port Authority in Manhattan and bought a bus ticket to Boston. I had wanted to go all the way to New Hampshire but didn't have enough money. My amended plan was to get a job in Boston, save as fast as I could, and go to New Hampshire as soon as possible. I wore my good tweed suit for the trip. It was evening when I arrived in Boston, and I asked the way to the YWCA, some blocks away. Wanting to save money, I trudged with my suitcase through the dark streets behind the bus station. A taxi slowed next to me and the driver asked if I needed a ride. I said I couldn't. The cabbie said, "Come on, Miss. You don't want to walk here. I'll take you. No charge." I checked into the Y, put away my few things, and ate the last peanut butter sandwich that I had packed at home. The next day I started to hunt for a job. I stopped in every store, art gallery, and restaurant I passed. I searched the paper. By the following day, I had a job on probation at Lord and Taylor department store. I was to go the next morning to a suburban branch along the trolley line for orientation. On the ride out, I met a woman who lived along that line. After we had chatted for most of the way, she invited me to her house for dinner the next night and wrote down the address and phone number. She told me to call my parents. I intended to call as soon as I had a job and a way to go on my own.

The orientation went fine, and I was told to report to the store the next day. I returned to the Y and minutes later there was a knock at the door. There stood my father and another man, identified as a police officer. The officer cautioned me to go home like a good girl and then left. My father said we were flying back that night on the shuttle. I packed and we went to the airport. Dad said that since I liked to write, I should write my version of events and he would do the same, and we would compare notes. But that didn't happen. All the rest of his life from time to time he referred to my running away, laughing ruefully at such a silly act. Mother was solicitous at first and then dismissed my attempted escape as a stunt, done for attention.

Despair was the order of the day. I went back to Queens College and was persuaded to see a counselor. He had me take a personality test. It seemed that I was smart, determined, and a "sex kitten," a "clinging vine." What could this mean to a virginal seventeen-year-old? The description was a mystery to me, then as now. I didn't think it was supposed to be a good sign. I had no idea what I should or could do about it. The counselor was ready with some analysis. With his hand on my arm, he suggested I return to his office for further evaluation. I never did.

Joel was there. We saw each other a few times, but he was involved with graduation and a new girl, whom he married soon after. I didn't miss having a boyfriend. I finished the term, dropping some courses, completing a few. The situation in the family did not change.

My parents decided that the problem was that Bobby and I still shared a bedroom. That summer they moved to a large, three-bedroom apartment on Kissena Boulevard with two bathrooms and a dining area off the living room. My room was toward the front, with a six-foot wide window half a storey up from the street. The space was a vast improvement, but once we had settled in the new apartment we all fell back into our old habits.

A NEW JOB • *When the term was finished in June, I got a full time job at Premier* Knitting in the Manhattan garment district, around 38th Street. Premier made clothes for teen-age girls: angora and cashmere sweaters, and pleated, plaid skirts in Scottish tartans. They advertised in *Seventeen* Magazine and sold to stores like Bloomingdales and Marshall Field. My job was to do clerical work in the one-man advertising department, enter the hours of the mill workers in the New Jersey plant for the woman who did payroll, relieve the receptionist who answered calls on a PBX telephone board and greeted customers, and wear the clothes, which I could buy wholesale. During Fashion Week, especially, I tried on various garments for the buyers, constantly refolded the sweaters, and tidied up the displays. I was paid ninety cents an hour. When the minimum wage was increased, the boss told me I was getting a raise to a dollar twenty-five. The hours were 8:30 to 5, with an unpaid forty-five minutes for lunch and one coffee break. I walked or took the bus to the subway in Flushing, and walked a few blocks at the city's end. You were docked if you came in late. I left the apartment a little after seven in the morning and returned home around 6:30. After social security and taxes were deducted, I made about thirty dollars a week. I gave my mother five dollars toward my room and board. I opened a bank account and saved something every week.

The company's founder, called Senior, was an old man of about sixty-five. He came in almost daily but on an unpredictable schedule. His son, called Mr. Arnold, was there more often. The showroom had a wall of windows, and the two Mr. S's had windows in their adjacent offices. The rest of the office staff, about twenty-five people, were together in a large, grim, florescent-lit room furnished when Senior expanded the company more than two decades before. Maybe he had even inherited the furnishings when he took the space. When buyers came from out of town, the salesmen were protective. They told the buyers, "Not her. She's a college girl." They asked out the receptionist, who had to include entertaining the customers in her job description. Except for the showroom, it was pretty dingy. I learned from everyone. I was a working girl. I loved having that job.

HUNTER COLLEGE • *In September I began classes in the open night program* at Hunter College at 68th Street and Park Avenue. I was seventeen when I started classes. I took philosophy, art history, and European history. I finished work, ate in the terrible Hunter cafeteria or at the automat, went to class, and took the subway back to Flushing around ten-thirty. I had matriculated and intended to study philosophy. The term was momentous for me. I ended with three As and met the woman who proved to be a demanding, life-altering mentor, Beatrice Hyslop.

The classes were filled with a wide range of students. I sometimes ate with two women who were runway models. We took philosophy together. One was about to marry and wanted to improve herself for her husband, while her friend wanted to read more. Behind me was a fellow studying chemistry, needing a humanities course to complete his degree. (They allowed men in the evening courses.) Stan was tall, nice looking, in his mid-twenties, and I dated him, more than others, for the next couple of years. Most of the students were working part or full time, most were studying for a degree, most were in their twenties and thirties. Professor Hyslop's history class was the hardest I had ever taken. Evening class or not, she expected, demanded, required scholarship. Her commitment and expectations were something I had not experienced before.

BRUBECK • *In this pivotal term, I celebrated my eighteenth birthday. From a fellow I dated, I received a record album,* Dave Brubeck's *Jazz Impressions of Eurasia*. I had heard jazz, of course, but nothing like this. I fell in love on the first cut and have remained so ever since. Brubeck's elegant cool is as vibrant as ever. Not long ago, in Barcelona, he gave a concert. He had not been there for decades, and it was my luck that he was playing just around my birthday. Somewhat bent, he walked slowly across the stage and told the audience that to celebrate his eightieth birthday he was about to play a concert with his sons in London. The commissioned work was "London Flat, London Sharp." At the piano, the years dropped away. He played with his trio for two hours. The music was interesting, original, and satisfying. As an artist I still feel a deep kinship with this music after fifty years.

At Premier, I was more confident. Around December I told Larry, the office manager, that I was going to start Hunter full time and wanted to keep my job. He and I made an arrangement whereby I could come into the office about ten hours a week and take some work home, so that my hours were reduced only a little, but I could attend Hunter as a day student. I registered for five classes. I stayed with Premier, with some short breaks, for the next three years.

THREE

Incidents of Change

THE COLLEGE • *Hunter College was a historic women's college founded by* Thomas Hunter in 1870 to train teachers. Hunter was an idealistic, progressive educator, even radical. He required all women to study mathematics and science as well as history and literature. He required physical education and exercise and prohibited women from wearing tight corsets to class. He believed that the constriction of breathing limited brain function and was unhealthy for intellectual development. In my time, on Founder's Day, alumni joined the students. We heard about their "firsts" in law, medicine, theater, and scholarship. In attendance were some who had graduated in the previous century. Founder's Day was a celebration of possibility and excellence. New students were told at orientation that it was far harder to get out than to get in, to graduate than to be admitted. We paid twenty-four dollars tuition per semester and could rent the textbooks for one dollar apiece if we couldn't or didn't want to buy them. It seems to me that Hunter was the epitome of the democratic ideal. It was elitist in the belief that talent was valuable and found at all levels of society, and that excellence and achievement were worthy, attainable goals for individuals and society as a whole. Most of the four thousand women did graduate and many went on to do significant work in the world.

I signed up for another history class with Professor Hyslop as well as philosophy, English, French, political science, and art history. Throughout my career there, I always took a load like this. Whatever else I was lacking, I had endurance. Larry, my boss at Premier, allowed me to work lighter hours and come to the office less during exam periods as long as I got my basic work done. I took home the advertising billing cards and other clerical work, often doing most of the tasks on the subway if I could get a seat. My daily life was better because I was hardly ever home. Dad still waited up for me often, wanting to talk about the day. These conversations grew shorter as my schedule required homework and papers. Many Friday nights were for parties and Saturday nights for dates. I stayed out late, stayed up late, and began to make my way.

REAL POLITICS, REAL LIFE • *My political education continued. I was* active in and eventually president of the Collegiate Council for the United Nations and the International Relations Club. In 1960 the Greensboro boys conducted their daring sit-in, and soon after, northern students, including me, began to boycott and picket Woolworth. I doubt that anyone I knew believed that formal southern segregation would collapse within a few years, but we said to each other, a bit sanctimoniously and very sincerely, "It has to begin, and if not now, when, and if not with me, then who?" Medgar Evers was heroically leading the NAACP in an effort to desegregate the University of Mississippi and end separate facilities everywhere. In 1957, after the Montgomery bus boycott, Martin Luther King, Jr. formed the Southern Christian Leadership Council. He was thirty-one then, speaking out in his southern voice, acting on his beliefs, and inviting us to join in. There were many other leaders, but King's gift of oratory stirred young students as no other.

Hunter was as polyglot and polychrome as a place could be. Daughters of United Nations diplomats, daughters of the New York ghetto, and middle class girls from every background, sat in class, ate together, shared the locker room. My brother's favorite chess partner was a black boy who lived in our neighborhood. It wasn't all sweetness and light but neither was it Mississippi. We were lucky to grow up then and to come to believe that each one of us can do something.

Gandhi and the creed of nonviolence inspired most of my friends. When Nehru visited New York around 1961, I was invited to some of the receptions. Adoring students mobbed him. After espousing nonviolence, and forming the third world moment, he shocked us all by sending a military invasion to Goa to remove the Portuguese. We were going to become less shockable, but not yet.

Movements against nuclear war ranged all over the political map. Reinforcing the awareness of how close war could come to us, in 1961 and 1962 we had the two Cuban crises.

President Eisenhower's administration had planned the Bay of Pigs invasion to remove the Cuban leader, Fidel Castro, depending mostly on émigrés in Florida and an expected popular uprising within Cuba. In 1961 President Kennedy had to approve or cancel it. He let it go forward. It was an ignominious disaster. Cuban-American relations have not yet recovered. The aftermath changed the western hemisphere, including South Florida. The Republican senator from New York, Kenneth Keating, went on television in the summer of 1962 to warn of a missile build up in Cuba and urge President Kennedy to be proactive. After the McCarthy excesses, Keating was ridiculed and accused of scare tactics. Of course, this time he was right.

The missile build up was too impressive and too obvious to ignore. In October 1962, after an agitated and dangerous run up, Kennedy went on the air to tell us that the threat was intolerable. The United States had quarantined and blockaded Cuba to force the Union of Soviet Socialist Republics to retract its shipment of missiles, then on the high seas approaching Havana. It was a classic ultimatum, such as the ones that had begun the world wars and many others. If the Soviets didn't turn back, we would stop them, even if it meant firing on them. It was clear that war could happen, might happen the next day. Many professors cancelled classes or abandoned the scheduled lesson. In my political science class, the professor, Peter Juviler, told us to leave or stay and talk. It was within the realm of imagination that this could be our last time together. He led an informal discussion, what was soon to be called a teach-in. He sent us on our way, wondering if Kennedy's threat to the Soviet ships might lead to the incineration of New York. My friend Bob, then stationed at Fort Hood in Texas, was one of the legions of soldiers moved to South Florida and poised for invasion. Eventually, all parties appeared to stand down and the crisis became a historical incident instead of annihilation.

Hunter's building at Park Avenue and 68th Street had sixteen storeys and three basements. The physical organization was by floors instead of by separate buildings as on traditional campuses. History was seven, political science nine, music fifteen, and so on. I spent a lot of my college life on those middle floors.

I took another history course with Professor Hyslop, and she enticed me from the philosophy department to be her student in an interdisciplinary program of international studies. The program was history, political science, and economics. At Hunter, almost half of the total bachelor's degree consisted of required courses in math, science, languages, literature, history, humanities, and physical education. The program honored the original concepts of Thomas Hunter. I took as many philosophy courses as I could fit into my packed schedule and spent the rest of my time on the sixteenth floor in art history classes. One of my science courses was geology, which was such a great course I nearly changed my major. The fieldwork was done in Central Park, a few blocks from the building, and one of the most geologically interesting sites anywhere.

GOLFING • *Everyone had to take the basic gym class, which was essentially* exercise and fitness training (although it wasn't called that then). Then you could choose at least one sport and at least one dance class, for a total of two years. The fourth floor was Physical Education. I didn't know anyone who played sports seriously. Weekend tennis or tent camping was about it. The PE department included people preparing for careers in physical therapy and the like. Sports were so minor a factor that I cannot remember if we had teams that competed with other women's colleges or only played intramurals. Many students regarded PE as just so much inconvenience cluttering up their schedules.

I had stayed with dance lessons for over ten years and enjoyed the courses in modern dance and folk dance. For my sport, I signed up for golf because it fit into my schedule. We undertook to consider the history and social significance of golf while getting used to the clubs. The gym was two storeys high with square grating over the windows. The horizontal window frames marked the target areas for the ball—if and when you hit it. We were assigned to watch golf matches on Sunday television and write up the games. At that time, no women players were seen on television. For optional extra credit, you could go to a city golf course and hit a couple of buckets of balls. I was TERRIBLE at hitting the ball but good at writing reports and so did well enough in the class, if not on the course. A few years later, my husband, a golf enthusiast, gave me a gift of clubs, a green-and-white bag with matching club socks, and green and white golf shoes. All this gear was accompanied by a series of lessons with the pro at the golf club in Seoul. It was worse for the pro even than for me. I have never seen the point of chasing little white balls. I couldn't ever get the hang of it. Finally the pro said that maybe on the course itself I might be more comfortable or at least do a little better. He could escape my lessons. I went with two athletic friends, regular golfers, and hit just over one hundred—for nine holes, not counting mulligans. My golfing days were almost over. A few years later, I gave the whole set to a friend in Osaka, who made much better use of it.

Aside from my athletic career, I was doing well despite the tight schedule I always had. I took the maximum course load of seventeen or eighteen credits. Student organizations were all over the political map and we all assumed we should take part in the public dialogue. Student conferences were a big item, and we went to each other's campuses to enact mock UN sessions. I volunteered in John Kennedy's campaign. I was one of those cute girls in white gloves. We were too young to vote but were political and sincere. We hadn't lived long enough to be blasé.

NEW YORK EDUCATION • *New York was a great place to be a young* person. The restaurants, the jazz clubs, and the Village were filled with groups and couples on the weekends. I went out just about every weekend. Nice young guys invited me to the opera, the ballet, downtown jazz clubs. We went to Broadway and off-Broadway shows. Stage actors were as famous as movie stars. We made dates for the Museum of Modern Art, or a hip gallery to see the experimental art of John Cage, Robert Rauschenberg, or Helen Frankenthaler. We took it for granted that there were dozens of theater performances all the time, and much discussion concerned what to see, what would signal the next great thing.

We went to see the Knicks play basketball in the winter, the Yankees, and, after 1962, the Mets in the summer. I had been a Brooklyn Dodgers fan, devoted, constant, faithful. Then they moved to California. Nothing in sports has been the same for me since. When he was home from college, I went with Bob to baseball games, dance performances, bowling dates. It was the custom to end a date with a ferry ride to Staten Island, just like the Edna St. Vincent Millay poem, "Recuerdo." Outbound, across the harbor, the stars were vivid. On the return trip, we sailed to the lights of the Manhattan skyline. Most of the fellows came and went, brushing the surface of my life. Although I still tried to be around for Bobby, New York was too rich an environment to resist.

I often went to the museums on my own, running over during a break in classes or traveling to Manhattan on the weekend from home. I looked at everything. Even now, many decades later, I can rummage through the files of my mind and find, from MoMA (the Museum of Modern Art), the glowing and sometimes very melancholy Rothkos, the high energy Pollacks rushing across the huge canvases, the grandeur of Motherwell's elegy, and most of all, the beauty and color and lyrical quality of Matisse. I loved the Egyptian and Greek collections at the Metropolitan Museum of Art and also the Met's magnificent rotunda filled with sculpture. I often went to sit for a few minutes in the second-floor replica of the Chinese garden. Very often, I saved a cruise past Cezanne for last. The collection is huge and you can see how Cezanne's imagining evolved. I think I learned more about seeing the world — about color and perspective and form — from those stolen hours than from anything else I have studied. I believe this intense acquaintance with Cezanne is the strongest visual influence on my photography today.

Libraries have had a special significance to me since my early childhood, when I sat in the quiet security of the children's room at the Flushing library. The New York Public Library at 42nd Street was a beacon of purpose and possibility for me. The front steps and lions are famous symbols of New York. The century-old Beaux Arts building allows you to enter with a sense of occasion and importance of purpose. Even though there are street-level doors, I usually walked up those hallowed front flights and entered through the main rotunda. The reading rooms were open long hours then, and I did most of my studying there, often staying until the midnight closing hour. The room had very long tables, each with chairs for about thirty readers, each four lit by a glass-shaded library lamp. In the card catalogue room, you went to the small oak drawers and found the materials you wanted. Then you took the request on a thin, yellow paper slip into the immense general reading room. The library clerk rolled the slip into a heavy brass cylinder, and it whooshed away through pneumatic tubes. A few minutes later your stack of books was delivered, yours for as long as you wanted to stay. The sounds of the room, filled with hundreds of people, were hushed: soft talking at the desk, pages turning, pens scribbling, shoes crossing the marble floors. The table lamps shined gold on all those heads bent over their books.

In all my travels I usually like to check out the libraries. Whether it is the great new ones like Vancouver or Seattle, or little rural one-room facilities like El Bruc in Spain, the same spirit seems to be present. A free public library is the most democratic institution I know of. Two decades after I sat through my studies in the general reading room, the library gave me a grant to assist in my research, and I spent most of a year there in Room 112, the Allen Room.

Hunter was located very near the concentration of midtown museums. I often went to one or another — Modern Art, the Metropolitan, the Frick — between classes. I took classes in renaissance art and modern art with Leo Steinberg. He was intellectual, handsome, a heartthrob to the students. He was also a terrific teacher. He sent us to the Met to spend the term with one — any one — painting, making it the basis of a term paper. Meanwhile, he showed slides. His classes were about looking for what is there, seeing with more perception, asking more than answering. I read Bernard Berenson and Nikolaus Pevsner. Leo Steinberg pointed our eyes toward modernism, which filled the halls of MoMA on 53rd Street, and galleries all over the city. Leo Steinberg later became renowned for the work he was doing right then, in the early sixties. His classes overflowed, with thirty, even thirty-five students. I reorganized my program, created nightmare schedules in order to study with him. Leo Steinberg held up a glass and pointed your sight toward what he could see. I brought everything I knew to that usually dark, image-filled classroom and left with confusion, questions, and the beginnings of insights that would develop in the coming years. I was used to museums and paintings, but I hadn't known there was more to art than beauty and color. Leo Steinberg's teaching changed my life.

In the first class with Leo Steinberg, I sat next to Dianne. She was slender, with copper-colored hair, beautiful eyes, and an engaging smile. She was an art major and spent most of her student life on the sixteenth floor. Having been told so often that I had no aptitude for art, I did not consider taking a studio class but nevertheless hung out with art and music people. Dianne and I hit it off, and we saw each other almost daily for several years. I often visited her family home, and sometimes slept there. We went to dances and parties together, sang folk song duets. Premier's quietest season was the summer, with few work hours for me, and I took jobs as a summer camp counselor. Dianne and I went together. We sang, flirted with the same fellows, and walked with our arms around each other. Oddly, we married men with the same name but, as happens, our lives took separate turns.

Hunter had the philosophy that no one would be denied an education because of lack of money. The fees were extremely low, but even so in many cases the students, of necessity, worked at outside jobs, as I did. There was a fund, administered by the Dean of Students, and students could borrow emergency funds on their signature alone. I was acquainted with Betty, a girl from the uptown ghetto. She worked part-time but it was a sacrifice for her that she didn't take a full time job to help support her family. She was a good student and had dreams of leaving that difficult neighborhood on the magic carpet of her education. She borrowed two hundred dollars for subway carfare and book rental for one semester. Her crisis abated, and she became a teacher when she graduated.

Another close friend I remember from that time is Tin Tin. Her father was Burma's representative to the United Nations. In 1962 there was a coup in Burma, the origin of today's regime. Many people were shot or disappeared, including Tin Tin's fiancé. She had been engaged to this man for several years. Although it was an arranged betrothal, she liked and respected him and felt great loyalty to him and to her country. Within days the Burmese delegation was packing up, some to seek asylum in the U.S. and some to return to Burma. Tin Tin was to graduate that spring. Couldn't she stay just the few months until then? No, her family was returning to fight and evict the usurpers. The military could not be allowed to take the country. Students were protesting, being arrested, being killed every day. Tin Tin needed and wanted to be part of the effort to save the country. Women had played an active role in politics and public affairs in Burma. Tin Tin was part of that tradition. She went with her brave family to the futile battle. She was twenty-two years old. She disappeared from my life that day. When I see a story about Aung San Suu Kyi, the Burmese leader who is of the same generation, I often wonder if Tin Tin has survived the trials of her country and made her life there.

Each one of these people, each experience we shared, became part of my education. They are part of the person I have become.

BEATRICE HYSLOP • *My mentor at Hunter, Beatrice Hyslop, was a remarkable* person. As a teacher she took her students seriously. She pushed, coaxed, and browbeat us to aspire to and achieve excellence. The facts of history were important to her but were not as valued as judgment, intellectual honesty, and integrity. You had to be as earnest as she was to survive her classes. During the time I was her student, she received her second major recognition from France, the Palm of the Legion of Honor. Officially it was for her work on the history of the French Revolution. Those who knew her well speculated about it. She had been in all the hot spots before World War II, sometimes in the company of her sister. She was in Algeria from time to time during the struggle for independence from France. Once during the term she simply dropped all her classes and left on a day's notice to go there. She was a tiny woman, hardly more than five feet tall. As a student at Mount Holyoke College in 1919, she was the captain of her basketball team. She had a wry sense of humor, and she taught me to make a wonderful Dutch colonial stew.

Around this time, I met Edwin. Bea Hyslop introduced us at a reception for Nehru. Edwin was a heavyset man, with deep blue eyes. He was older and well traveled, had been to Europe several times and was about to go to the Soviet Union. He was there during the missile crisis of 1962.

Because of his work at an NGO and his other affiliations, he had access to the Delegates' Lounge at the UN, one of the most glamorous places in New York. He took me out from time to time, to plays and concerts and nice restaurants.

I continued to see Jimmy in bursts. We'd go out in a flurry of dates and then back off for a while. We didn't play bridge anymore, partly because I wasn't very good at cards, and partly because we had a lot to talk about, a lot to do. Even in New York it was not always easy, in the early sixties, for an interracial couple to find a comfortable place to go on a date, have dinner, listen to music. We went to Pablo's near Hunter, and to Greenwich Village. Jimmy was a slender, handsome man, and he did a lot of martial arts. I don't remember the color of his belt. What I do remember are his grace and charm and how much fun we had. One evening we were walking along, surely holding hands, when some guy spit at me. He missed, but the intention was obvious. Jimmy assumed a karate posture, ready to defend my honor and his. The situation was defused, and the incident became yet another reminder of the need to change ourselves, and our city.

ON THE HOME FRONT • *Those years at Hunter were very conflicted. My family's situation was worse than ever.* Dad continued on with Cammy. He even took her on a couple of business trips where he presented her as his wife. He told me that it made him happy to pretend for a few days that they were married, that he had a wife he could be proud of, that they could have a taste of the forbidden life they denied themselves. I squirmed mentally, maybe physically, profoundly embarrassed. Why didn't he get a divorce? Mother was an emotional wreck, growing more mean-spirited as she grew fatter. Her cruelties were, I think, an echo of the pain in her life, the circumstances she labored under. Why didn't she get a divorce?

Bobby was still in elementary school, very good at sports and very enterprising. He made pocket money by returning the supermarket carts that people borrowed to take home their groceries. (They walked home and then left the carts in the hallway of the building.) He had other projects, too: collecting deposit bottles and helping people with errands.

I was used to taking care of Bobby. When it came time to tell him about sex and money, I was the one he asked and who answered. I wanted to protect him and be sure that he was safe. To do that, I had to be there. I felt I had to choose what I understood to be right and to fulfill the obligations I had. From very early childhood I learned that because I was able to, I must do whatever was required of me.

I wanted the life I was just beginning to imagine for myself. Achievement could be the route out of my present circumstances. I could be a professor, or join the new Peace Corps, or be in the UN. I was very earnest — preposterously earnest. It was a good thing that I had friends and boyfriends who showed me how to have fun. I could pack up my sense of responsibility for a Saturday-night date, but once the long Flushing Line subway took me back to the Main Street station, my conscience was reactivated. I managed to have a lot of good times in my student days, but I continuously renewed my commitment to myself to work harder and do better. I was going to find my way.

My grandmother died late in 1962. About a year and a half earlier she had had a fall and been forced to move into a nursing home. She still tried to go out every day, to keep up with the news and the rest of the world outside. She developed cataracts that, in addition to her fading hearing, made life steadily more difficult. The ophthalmologist she consulted refused to operate on her cataracts, saying it wasn't worthwhile for someone in her eighties to have this operation. He seemed to feel that it would be a waste of medical resources. Later that autumn my grandmother developed bronchitis and was hospitalized. She told everyone that she had decided to stop taking the digitalis that had made her heart beat for twenty years. She did not want to become isolated and dependent, cut off from what was important to her. She recounted that she had lived from the era of candlelight through whale oil lamps, gaslight, electricity, and space travel. More years had no meaning for her if she couldn't be part of the world. The doctor said he could force her to take her digitalis. She answered that of course he could hold down a weak old woman and force the pills down her throat, but did he dare face her afterward? She said good-bye, washed her stockings, and hung them on the towel bar. She put on her best nightgown and waited. It wasn't long before she was only semiconscious from lack of oxygen. A day or two later she died. My mother grieved for a long time. My grandmother had been her best support, her safety valve. She kept a small snapshot of Grandma on her dresser. I heard her cry. I heard her say, "Mama, what can I do? Tell me, what can I do?"

That year, 1962, I went to a lot of weddings. Several of my cousins and friends married, more were engaged in 1963. Most of the brides wore ballerina length dresses of white organdy or lace, and looked just like the romantic ideal they aspired to. However, I had no intention of getting married. I dreamed of a future that was more solitary, quieter. Marriage seemed to be exactly what I did not want.

Approaching graduation, I had several graduate school offers, the best from the University of Chicago and from Johns Hopkins University. Bea Hyslop offered to help secure a research position in Strasburg so that I could continue the work I had done on my honors thesis with her. I was tapped for Phi Beta Kappa, and also for Phi Alpha Theta, the history honor society, and Pi Sigma Alpha, the political science honor society. I was to graduate in May.

PHI BETA KAPPA • *The Phi Beta Kappa installation was on a mild evening.* I planned to go out afterward with my parents and Bobby for a celebration. My distracted parents were very proud of my election to PBK and knew this was an event they couldn't miss. I had been seeing Edwin more and he asked for a ticket to attend, which I gave him. He showed up with a beautiful, huge orchid for me, and my mother told him it was entirely unsuitable. He ran back to the florist and exchanged it for the wrist corsage she preferred. The ceremony was just as such occasions must be, complete with the practiced secret handshake (descended from the Revolutionary War period), the gold key, and exhortations to high aspirations and great deeds. As we milled around afterward, students hugging and professors beaming, Edwin announced that he had reservations for just the two of us at a fancy restaurant nearby and handed me my coat. We left. We didn't stay for the cookies and punch or more mutual congratulations or celebrations. I'm not sure who was more surprised, my family or me. His possessiveness that evening began a line of bitterness that neither he nor my father or brother ever were able to cross.

Edwin was a man of great determination, for better and worse. He knew that I dated other people, and that I did not expect to "settle down," just the contrary. The satisfaction and pleasure of that ceremony are mixed forever with my chagrin at being so far from the center of decision-making, however small and unimportant those decisions may have seemed. I had no ability to evaluate what this might suggest for my future.

DANGEROUS ENGAGEMENTS • *I was in a hurry. Because of the light* summer hours at Premier, I temped and took camp jobs and went to summer school. Altogether I attended Hunter for three years and two summers, with time out in my last, graduation term for viral encephalitis. It's an illness contracted through a mosquito bite. I was in Mount Sinai Hospital in Manhattan for about six weeks, but I remember only a little of that time. Contracting encephalitis is something like having a stroke. You may not survive the trauma, and, if you do, with what damage? The reflexes on the left side of my body were affected, and I experienced short-term memory loss.

While I was in the hospital, many people came to see me, especially as I started to recover after a month. My three aunts helped to speed my recovery. Aunt Diana, Mother's oldest sister, was an ardent Zionist. Knowing my thesis was about peacemaking in the 1920s, she talked about the Balfour Declaration. Aunt May came from Philadelphia several times. Dad's older sister, Sally, came and said that she made a promise to God: If I recovered she would cut her hair. This was a gigantic sacrifice. Aunt Sally's hair was her crowning glory, very long, still the soft red color of her girlhood. When I left the hospital she did cut it off.

When it was clear I would recover the doctors allowed my parents to give me the acceptance letters from Johns Hopkins University in Baltimore and the University of Chicago. Each had offered me support for graduate study in their Ph.D. programs. I sent my return acceptance to Johns Hopkins. The ferocious headaches were to persist for many months. I couldn't stand yet, but I started to read. I had to finish my courses and my thesis in time to graduate. I had to get to Hopkins and start my real life. I had one of those yellow pads and began a list of what I needed to do.

Friends came. Sometimes I could see them and sometimes not. Several of the fellows I dated were at the hospital from time to time. Edwin visited steadily and walked with my mother up and down the halls. When I went home he was there, visiting as if it were a date, as if he were already part of the family. They were terribly offended.

I sent my acceptance to Johns Hopkins University in Baltimore. Edwin proposed over the phone. He came the next day with an armful of presents, a record album, and flowers. He presented me with the traditional little velvet box. It contained a diamond solitaire. Edwin showed the ring to my mother to announce our engagement. I was still in bed almost all the time. Noise set off terrific headaches. I weighed less than a hundred pounds and slept long hours. Edwin started commuting out to Flushing after work and then going home to his apartment in Manhattan. He sat with me in my bedroom for long hours. Eventually, most evenings, he closed the door and climbed into bed with me. I was too frail to have much inclination or capacity for sex, but he wanted as much intimacy as he could get. He just wanted what he wanted.

I was so fragile and exhausted. Where were my parents? Who was taking care of me? Why did everyone leave that door closed? Perhaps they were so used to my being able to manage that they didn't realize I couldn't take care of myself then.

I started writing again. Several professors let the work already done stand for the grade with just a pro forma final. The biology professor parted only with a B because I had not done all the lab work. (What silliness we remember to rankle ourselves with!) I was taking a graduate course with Bea in the evening — coming full circle to the first course I had at Hunter — and I worked maniacally with her to complete a respectable honors thesis. I had done much of the research before I became ill but nearly all the writing remained. The thesis was titled "The Peace That Failed." It investigated the relationship between France and Germany between the world wars. The heads of government, Gustave Stresemann and Aristide Briand, came so close to finding a way to live in peace or at least avoid war in the aftermath of the destruction of World War I, but failed in the end. Ultimately the thesis became a reflection on the nature of politics and peace as well as historical research.

Mother was going to type it. She used a blue ribbon on erasable bond and swore steadily about the footnotes. The typing was full of errors, a disaster. It was June and time was growing short. Full of trepidation, I took the essay to Bea's apartment in Jackson Heights. She told me to come back in three days. She had marked up the paper using the title page, the contents, and every white space on those hundred pages. We sat down and she proceeded to attack every weakness, every mistake. What a labor of love! She gave me the name and number of an academic typist and asked if I could afford it. She knew that I had had a job throughout my academic years, and she offered to help with the typing cost if necessary. The afternoon passed. As I left, Bea smiled her wry smile and said it wasn't at all bad for a draft. Still recovering, I was resolved to do my best and also not disappoint Bea's faith in me. I went back to work. I thought about Hopkins.

Edwin was about to join the Foreign Service and was moving to Washington. He wanted me to cancel Hopkins so that we could be together in D.C. I left my enrollment in place. Meanwhile he was eager to plan a wedding for August, just six or seven weeks away.

His was a traditional family. The first time I met them, his Grandmother Rose took my hands in hers and smiled right into my face. She brought out the honey cake she had made, a sweet gift that the bride may live a sweet life. Rose was a delightful and original person. She had emigrated alone from Austria as a young girl. Her son, Dave, Edwin's father, had the same blue eyes and the same sunny disposition as his mother. At family weddings and parties, he and I always danced together. He taught me the Peabody and the two-step and danced a mad Lindy with arms flying through double and triple turns. He was good with the slow numbers, too, and did a deep dip at the end of each dance. He was so kind to me, so gentle, all the years I knew him. He was just a good person. I was very much influenced by knowing him. I thought he was the model Edwin would follow as a husband. After I was divorced, Dave hand copied a poem by John Masefield and sent it to me with a letter telling me to follow my heart. Edwin's mother, Blanche, was very nervous that first day we met. I doubt that she ever had a comfortable time with me. I was not the bride or the wife she wanted for her son. Her criticisms were intended to make her son's life better, to make me a better wife. Edwin's sister had been married for several years. Although I knew her for twenty-five years, I don't think we ever understood one another very well. The gap in our experience and aspirations was very wide. Her husband, Bill, was a charming guy. They had married as teenagers and had two little girls by then.

If we were going to be married in August, it seemed I needed a bridal shower. I was recuperating and very involved with my studies; I am not sure how it happened, but Cammy was to host it. Mother seemed to feel that it was the right choice. Very startling. But the invitations went out to my girlfriends, to Edwin's large coterie of cousins, sister, and aunts, and to my female relatives. On the appointed day in June, we dressed up in nice dresses and went to Cammy's living room for the shower. She made a lovely party of it. I suppose most people thought that she was Mother's friend. I was deluged with domestic supplies and equipment, almost ready for my wife life. Dianne gave me a little Wedgwood box and said I should keep it apart and think of her when I used it. I keep barrettes and pins in it, and I do think of her. For most of my friends, this was the last occasion we were together.

After the shower, I headed back to work, back to what I thought of as real life. The thesis was revised, Bea looked at it again, there was a little more revision, and then the whole thing was ready to be typed. Another struggle! Mother was upset that I was going to waste money paying a stranger for what she thought she could do better. Still, I got the draft to the typist and safely delivered to Bea. With just a few more comments she accepted it. There was paperwork to do for Hopkins. There was a wedding to plan. There were medical appointments to see if I was still breathing. Willy Hitzig, in charge of my care, said to let me rest and fatten up a little. I finished everything Hunter required of me, and they mailed my diploma. Was I going to Baltimore or Washington? Or anywhere?

By July when I completed my academic obligations at Hunter I had little physical strength. I could not drive yet and was unable to walk any distance alone. The short-term memory loss and weakness on the left side of my body both were dissipating. I am very fortunate that the residual effects are minimal, but the recuperation took many months. Even now, decades later, I still have some small remainders.

I think the fright and commotion of the spring had made Bobby very agitated. He was angry with me for leaving and angry with Edwin for taking me away. It seemed like he was being abandoned. Edwin tried to take on a big brother, older man role. They went to ball games and such, but it didn't touch Bobby's anguish.

One summer night in the front hall of my parents' apartment, I told Edwin I couldn't go through with the wedding. I didn't want to be married. Not to him, or anyone. He didn't agree to call it off. He banged his head on the wall. He punched the door. He said we had already told everyone and couldn't break it off. Eventually, he left with his ring, with the understanding that we would not be seeing each other, at least for a while.

I closed the door with relief and went to bed.

BALTIMORE • *In August 1963, Dianne went with me on the train to Baltimore* to find an apartment. I had a very small budget: a C. L. Pack Fellowship and a University fellowship. They provided my tuition and a stipend of four hundred and fifty dollars a term. I didn't know exactly what it cost to live there, but I imagined something like fifty-five dollars a month for rent. With some small savings, and a student loan for fifteen hundred dollars at three percent interest, I could just barely get by. In the August heat, Dianne and I trekked all around the University neighborhood searching for my new apartment. On St. Paul Street, two blocks from Hopkins, I found a building that seemed to be all right. The superintendent showed us a few available apartments. My name was all right with him, but he probed Dianne, trying to determine if she was Polish (okay) or Jewish (not okay). I was going to take the smallest studio, but we also saw a somewhat larger apartment. The departing occupants assured me that it was fine. It was a little more than I had budgeted. I apprehensively signed the lease for sixty-two dollars a month, and we went back to New York. Dianne gave me a color photograph of herself, signed, "for sharing childhood's end." She went back to her job teaching art and soon met the man she would marry the following year.

Finally, it was moving day. I took the train again, with as much as I could carry, and arrived in Baltimore in the sweltering remains of the summer of 1963. The apartment wasn't going to be ready for another day or two, so I checked into the Y. The next morning I went to the Hopkins

Homewood campus. It has a very stately quality, and its buildings and proportions are elegant and welcoming. I had been to other universities, weekends at Yale and Vermont, conferences elsewhere, but I had never been part of this kind of academic landscape. I was more than a bit nervous but also elated as I set out for my first appointment with Dr. Robert Tucker.

Dr. Tucker was well known for his work on international relations and was to be my advisor. The program was meant to grant a Ph.D. in three or four years, with a master's degree after the first year. I arrived at Tucker's office and introduced myself. He was leaning back in his swivel chair and sat forward when I walked into the room. He greeted me, "Well, good morning, Miss Gardner. It's too bad you're here, but the university has decided to admit women to this program. You were the best qualified. I hope you aren't wasting a space that could be better used by someone else." I had had no idea I was to be the only woman in this international relations doctorate program. Hopkins had many female master's students and had had women in the medical school for decades. I was accustomed to the company and guidance of many women of achievement at Hunter, and their male colleagues who were perfectly comfortable teaching hard subjects to capable women. I wasn't blind to the obstacles a woman might encounter, but I had not had the practical experience of it since the time my father refused to allow me to go to MIT.

Tucker outlined the course work. While there were optional letter grades for all courses at the doctoral level, he, as my advisor, decided when I advanced through the stages of the program. Over the next couple of days, he took me to meet Professor Gottfried Dietze in the history department. Dietze took a copy of my honors thesis to read and decided that the work, equivalent to a master's thesis, could stand for the Ph.D. history component. I met with Dr. Tucker regularly and sometimes we chatted briefly in French. One day he said that he had arranged for me to take the French language qualifying exam, scheduled for the next day. I needed to get it out of the way right off in order to begin to study German. It was one step completed toward my degree.

Shortly afterward, he said that I needn't waste time on the master's and from now on I was to come to the doctoral seminar, meeting at his office on Tuesday afternoons. I had been at Hopkins only about a month. I was still tense but a little more confident. I should have been on guard. The doctoral seminar met in his office at two o'clock on Tuesdays. The other four or five students were already working on their dissertations. I had a general idea of where I wanted to go with my research but was more ready to listen than present. We sat around the desk, each reading from his work and making a short informal presentation. Each participant was expected to respond, critique the evolving theses, and support each other's progress. This seminar was the heart of the program. Everything else was optional. Without successfully negotiating this seminar, you didn't have a degree.

IN FRONT OF THE BAR • *Each week, after the first presenter, about forty-five minutes into the seminar,* we gathered up our voluminous stuff and set off across the campus, then down St. Paul Street. The first of these Tuesdays, Tucker asked if I didn't live nearby. Then we stopped on the street in front of a bar about a block from my apartment. They were accustomed to finishing the remaining two hours of the session there, with a beer. In those days, in Baltimore and other places, most bars were off-limits to women. They usually had a ladies' night and sometimes a ladies' room that was accessed by a side entrance, and not generally in use during the day. Tucker and the guys did not change their habit just because I was tagging along. They all said, "Good-bye, see you next week," and went in for their beer. This custom was honored — if that is the word — all the time I was at Hopkins. Gender discrimination was not a crime, yet. But pretty soon there were remedies.

I was also in Irma Adelman's seminar in development economics. Irma Glicman Adelman is a brilliant person. She has the ability to conceptualize and synthesize ideas. In a thin, dense, yellow book she devised a system of mathematically modeling economic development in emerging economies. It is the hardest book I ever read. Her contributions to development strategy and design are among the most influential in the field. In 1963–64 she was in her early thirties, in her second year at Hopkins, and in a rich, productive phase of her career.

Professor Adelman, later Irma, was born in Romania, educated in the United States. She spoke with a gentle accent. In the seminar room, she stood at the blackboard, speaking in her very soft voice. Seven or eight men sat around a heavy table. Some were professionals on leave from their government jobs abroad. Their papers mostly reflected their pragmatic interests. The rest were doctoral students in economics. Before registering, I had gone to see Irma and described the project I wanted to work on for the year. I had done some graduate work in history at Hunter but not in economics. This was an advanced seminar but, despite my deficiencies — I did not have the prerequisite graduate economics courses — she allowed me to enroll. For that year she welcomed me to visit her office, especially on Tuesdays. We had many conversations, on many topics, and her generous support was deeply appreciated and is gratefully remembered. Our paths were going to cross lightly in the coming years, and we ran into each other from time to time in Washington.

I became friendly with one of the development seminar students, Basil, who recently had been the deputy development minister in his Caribbean country. He had a wife and children at home and had never been through a cold winter before. Basil and I fell into a routine about once a week. He brought some groceries and I cooked. Basil helped me to buy a short little Christmas tree, the only one I have ever had, and carried it to my apartment where we decorated it very modestly and put it on a card table. We talked a little about the course, a lot about his family and home. It was very companionable.

NEIGHBORS • *Carol was my next-door neighbor. She was a Baltimore native,* had just graduated from Goucher College, and was teaching kindergarten in a public school nearby. This was her first apartment and she was having a lot of fun. Our doors were at right angles together in a corner of the fourth-floor landing. We could tap at each other through the wall. Carol took me around Baltimore, introducing me to the city. There were some lovely residential neighborhoods. A small area of downtown had department stores and shops, but the harbor was a dangerous, mob-infested slum. Many areas of town were heavily infested with rats. Everyone who lived in the basement apartments that were cheap and popular with students was afflicted with rats. I saw Norwegian wharf rats bigger than a house cat. I was glad to live on the fourth floor, even if it was a walk up.

Soon after I moved to Baltimore, my father came to visit. He was by himself. The apartment horrified him, especially the kitchen. I had tried to clean, but it was almost beyond the beyond. The stove was so dirty with generations of student use that most of it didn't work anymore. The fridge was on its last feeble legs, more of a rickety cabinet than refrigerator. Dad complained to the super, threatened him with the health department, and in a day I had old but clean and functional replacements. When they carried out the old stuff, there were rodent body remains, hundreds of roaches, decades of dirt, grunge, unmentionables. We cleaned up the mess and passed the rest of his weekend sojourn with a campus tour and chitchat. He returned to New York on the train on Sunday. We would see each other only three more times before I left for Korea.

Carol and I often tapped on the wall to say we were coming next door to see each other. Many times we shared whatever odd combinations of food were around and gabbed the evening away. Lovely Carol had a lot of her friends over and came over to my place — my place! — ahead of time to make sure I was ready. My hair was very long, very dark, and curly, spreading out over my shoulders halfway down my back. I wore it piled tightly on my head or sometimes in a single braid. Carol helped me spiff up for her parties, pulling my hair loose, and even lending me her dresses a few times. Girlfriends shared a lot of clothes then. We made food together, southern wonders I had known about only from books. We consumed astounding amounts of junk food and, among the boys especially, astounding amounts of cigarettes. At those parties, there was no agenda, no ferocious ambition, just nice young Baltimoreans having a good time, looking each other over. Carol was as exotic to me then as anyone I met in the coming years. She was carefree and represented a new way of life — new to me, anyway. She was a lovely girl without many complications, just very nice. She was too busy having fun to be earnest. She shared with me an attitude I had never seen outside the movies.

Our apartments were at the top of the stairway. There was no place to go up from there. And yet there were noises above. By late fall Carol told me she thought there was a ghost in the attic of the building. I heard footsteps, too, but I didn't credit ghosts. It was pretty creepy, though, and a few times we spent the night together in one apartment or the other. Finally, we went to the super. After a while, and a few more reports from his two wide-eyed tenants, he went up to the roof and sure enough someone had taken up residence next to the chimney. Apparently this person had observed that we were not home in the daytime and used our working hours to come and go. That was the end of ghosts in the attic.

Despite all the writing necessary for my courses, I was an avid correspondent. It took a day for a letter to be delivered in Baltimore from New York or even Texas. Dianne and I were in touch steadily. She was teaching in New York and enjoying a new romance. Some other college friends wrote for a while.

I still corresponded regularly with my old friend and sometimes boyfriend, Bob. The winter I was at Hopkins, he finished his military service. We arranged by letter for him to visit on his way home to New York.

My life in Baltimore was underway. My work at Hopkins was moving along. Despite the doctoral seminars on Tuesdays, I was starting to develop an idea for a thesis and Bob Tucker began to encourage me. All the rest was coming together. Those professors who chose to give letter grades all gave me As. My fellowships would be renewed. I had a carrel in the library, the beginning of friendships, and could even manage to balance my new checking account most of the time. My little apartment was pretty Spartan. For all its shortcomings, it did have sunny windows and a huge claw-foot bathtub. And, of course, it was mine.

THE NEXT TURN • *Edwin called and I answered the phone. We had met* in New York in August, and I had given him my address in Baltimore. He just wanted to keep in touch. He did. That fall he called. And called. He was so sincere, so contrite over his behavior the night I had broken off with him. He said he loved me and just wanted to make sure I was okay, he wanted to help, wanted the best for me. He wanted a lot. In November he took me out to dinner before I went back to New York for Thanksgiving. All December he came often to Baltimore, hopping the commuter train after work. I needed to be focused on my research and class work. He focused on me. He called and said he was about to catch the train, he'd see me in an hour. I had work to do, and he countered that I had to eat anyway. He would just come for dinner. He would just ....

ASSASSINATION • *My research took me to Washington, the Library of* Congress, and the Hopkins School for International Studies. I was in D.C.

on Friday, November 22, 1963, the day President Kennedy was murdered. The news came over the radio with a sickening sound.

I had worked in the campaign a little, was one of the girls in white gloves with wholesome smiles, full of hope. When JFK came to speak at Hunter College, he was fantastically late. Everyone waited for him. His presence had an effect on young people very much like President Obama's. Kennedy had great speechwriters. He told us that we must reach higher, do more, be more. He made a point of assuring us that religion played no part in his political decision-making. He used television in new ways and campaigned everywhere, using the energy of tens of thousands of people still too young to vote.

Since the election of 1960 a lot had happened. We had passed through the Cuban crises almost intact. We weren't too clear about the war in Vietnam, although coups happened and masses of American troops were already there and in preparation. Race was a very big issue. Improvements were happening in civil rights but so were violence and resistance. The Peace Corps was a reality. The Pill was easily available. The Beatles were an institution. Jacqueline Kennedy redecorated the White House and set the standard for American fashion.

That November day, I met Edwin and we wandered around through the evening, like the crowds of people we saw on the streets of Washington, dazed, confused, and worried. Lyndon Johnson spoke to us but it was hard to hear while looking at Jackie's bloody clothes. The next few days were entirely occupied by the astounding events—the drama of the funeral, the news bulletins, the capture of the assassin, Lee Harvey Oswald, and his murder by Jack Ruby. You could hardly keep your head on straight. You couldn't sleep, didn't dare sleep, for wondering what new astonishment was going to befall you.

LIFE RESUMED • *The following week I went to New York for Thanksgiving.* Nothing and everything was different with my family. The same old dissensions and issues still raged, but now I was the odd girl out. We ate turkey, celebrated Dad's and my birthdays, and skittishly tried to avoid the sore points. I happily returned to Maryland after three days.

Back in Baltimore, I pushed on toward the end of term deadlines. Edwin put himself on that commuter train more often. On some snowy winter nights it got too late or was too hard for him to go back, and he stayed over and took the early commuter run in the morning. He was pressing me to renew our engagement, with daily calls and near daily visits. He was not happy with the prospect of Bob coming to visit me and wanted me to cancel the visit. It was not "fair" to Bob. I saw less of my neighbor, Carol, and her friends, less of my Hopkins circle.

Midwinter I was looking forward to the long-planned visit from Bob. I bought a semi-comfortable cot for him. I didn't know what his feelings were, nor my own. We had a long, friendly history full of companionship and shared experiences. We had dated rather enthusiastically but that had been a while before. I was not willing to be distracted from getting my degree, and I wanted to see the world. I was sure I didn't want to settle down or "settle for" getting married. I wondered if I wanted a long-distance love affair with my sweet, safe friend.

Bob arrived. I was so happy to see him. He was just finishing his military service, very fit, out of danger. He had large, very blue eyes, further magnified by the glasses that he had worn since childhood. He was a graceful man from all the dance and athletics he had done. It was comfortable and reassuring to be with him. He amused himself with his camera while I went to class. We had a good time together. He slept on the cot. Perhaps he was too shy to reignite our past romance, especially in the presence of the phone calls. Edwin called once or twice each evening. It was difficult to abbreviate these calls.

When Bob left we embraced as always, and although our paths did cross geographically, we didn't talk again for more than forty years. We loved each other for a long time but were never in love. Right then, it would have been good for me to have a love affair with him, a man who cared about me gently, with the comfort and security that comes with years of knowing each other, and through the intimacy of growing up.

WEDDING WITHOUT BELLS • *In February, around Valentine's Day, I* agreed to marry Edwin and changed the trajectory of my life. With that same diamond on my finger, we went to New York for a long weekend to get a license and arrange for a wedding. Edwin's family had traditional values and would have been distressed with anything other than a Jewish wedding in a synagogue. We settled on a simple ceremony in a rabbi's study, for mid-March. Edwin himself had no traditional religious faith and neither did I, but we honored his family with this gesture. The vows were the conventional kind, without any personal modification. We went over the ceremony and promises with the rabbi, and he counseled us as best he could in the short time available. We should have listened more carefully, for he had things to offer that echoed in my mind in the years to come.

I had had the bridal shower first time around. Planning the wedding itself was very strenuous. I suppose all couples have issues that arise during this process. It is a time when the basic parameters of the future relationship are being established. I had originally thought to wait until the end of the academic year. By then Edwin would have finished his language study, and we would be able to prepare for our first assignment abroad. He was determined to have his bride with him in Washington and wouldn't wait the extra two months. He was insistent and, after considerable discussion, we went ahead with his plan for a March wedding. He had no idea who I was or what I needed, and evidently I was unable to express those needs in the face of his persistence. The pattern of our relationship was established. Given our personalities, there could have been no other way.

Even a simple wedding has a lot of elements. I was back to planning on the yellow pads again, and pages were rewritten often. Apparently lawyers know what they are doing. Those legal pads come in bundles. Decisions had to be made, very quickly: the number of guests and the degree of consanguinity (up to first cousins but we didn't expect most of them to come from out of town), friends — I had just Dianne as maid of honor, his brother-in-law, Bill, was best man — reception, flowers, invitations, rings, dress. Paying for it all.

Edwin and I were going to pay for the wedding ourselves. It was to be simple, with just immediate family at the ceremony and then, at Mother's strong urging, a cold supper at my parents' apartment rather than a restaurant meal. My father had a friend who was a florist. He arranged for me to go there for the flowers. Mother went with me to conclude all the arrangements. Even though it was March, I wanted white roses for myself, and pink for Dianne. Mother told the florist to keep it simple. He asked about flowers for the table. Nothing fancy was required, she said, just a little something low, that would not interfere with the food, which was going to be set out as a buffet. Flowers checked off.

For the wedding cake, we went to a very nice neighborhood bakery. They had many pretty designs. I asked about a round white cake with a tiny top tier. Mother ordered a rectangular sheet cake, easier to cut, with thin icing, because "no one" liked the traditional kind. The compromise was to have a spray of sugar roses to one side. Rolls and breads were added. In another store, trays of cold cuts and cold fish were ordered. Food checked off.

My budget was getting perilously tight. I still hadn't bought a dress. Mother and I headed for Fifth Avenue in Manhattan. One afternoon in Baltimore, I had tried on wedding dresses — long, white swathes of prettiness. I was slender, about a hundred and five pounds on my 5'6" frame. It was easy to find sample dresses to experiment with. I wanted something elegant, silky, and memorable, no flounces or ruffles. I had not been clothes shopping with my mother in some time. We went into the stores, to each bridal department, and rummaged through the racks. Mother told the saleswomen that we needed something simple, not extravagant, and ready in a few weeks. We looked at the sale racks and samples and kept going from store to store. The day wore on. In Henri Bendel a salesperson, after several false starts, brought from the back an elegant, short, white wool dress that was beautifully made. It required only a few alterations. It fit into my budget. The woman gave me a little swatch from an inner seam and promised the dress would be ready on time.

Off we went for the accessories. We went to the garment district where each block has its own specialty, each notions and findings store specializing in one category of the small items essential to sewing and the garment trade. I sorely missed my grandmother that day. She had died eighteen months before. She would have enjoyed the tiny stores and would have enjoyed even more making me a veil. I bought a little pillbox hat frame, white silk to cover it, and a square of the sheerest white silk net to make a shoulder length veil.

Back in Baltimore, I tried to catch up on my studies, which were beginning to be in arrears. Long phone calls every night from Edwin unless he came to have dinner and stay overnight. He brought a lot of homework for me: paperwork to do for the Foreign Service, information forms for a security clearance, medical matters and immunizations to start, preparatory to the departure for Korea the coming summer. I went to Planned Parenthood

for contraceptives. We talked about children, of course. He was older —
twenty-nine — and wanted a family right away.

The weeks flew by. It was time to return to New York for the wedding.
As my granddaughter, Fiona, has taught me to say, OMG! Everybody
had a different agenda. Plans started to come together. The dress was
delivered, the refreshments and the florist reconfirmed. I slept in my old
room. My schoolgirl clothes were still in the closet. Some of my childhood
books were in the bookcase along with the college texts that I had not
needed in Baltimore. Edwin stayed with his parents.

In Flushing all was not sweetness and light. Since the spring and our
first engagement, Dad and Edwin had had a visceral dislike for each other.
Bobby was bopping around, without a good place to light. Not only was
I going to get married, I was going ten thousand miles away. Not good.
Mother was more agitated with every passing hour. Was she thinking of
her own marriage? Wanting me to not marry at all? She didn't share her
thoughts. All I saw was increasing anger, distress, and disturbance.

Late in the afternoon of the wedding day, I was almost ready when the
florist came with exquisite bouquets for Dianne and me, corsages for
Mother and Blanche, lapel flowers for all the men. On a second trip, he
brought into the apartment a low arrangement to run down the length
of the table and, as a gift to me, a fan of flowers in a vertical container
to use in a corner or hallway. He brought it to wish me well. Mother
exploded, told him his horrible flowers were going in the incinerator. He
was crazy to think she wanted such a monstrosity in her house! The poor
man fled as quickly as possible. She went on with her tirade, after all she
had done, etc. Dad cleared a space on a round table in the corner. We put
the vase there, even took my picture next to it. Mother was beside herself.
She wasn't going to stand for this, she was leaving, and in her winter
coat, on a snowy spring evening, she started for the door. Bobby took her
by her arms and literally pushed her back through the apartment into the
bedroom. He stood over her and shouted that she was going to go to the
wedding. She was going to be good. We all got in the car and made it
to the synagogue without death or dismemberment, but you couldn't say
it was a tender leave-taking.

We arrived at the synagogue in one piece. I was hustled off to the bride's
room. Dianne arrived shortly afterward. She fulfilled her maid of honor

role and had instructed me in the tradition of "something old, something new, something borrowed, something blue." She came prepared with handkerchiefs, hairpins, and hopefulness. Her bouquet of winter roses was waiting with mine.

The ceremony went almost as scheduled. Edwin's two adorable little nieces — blonde, blue-eyed, dressed up for their first wedding — were there. We fell for each other at once. I loved being their Aunt Susan. In a few minutes the ceremony was done. Everyone hugged and smiled at the end. Then, back to the apartment and the reception. It was snowing more heavily, but everyone got there eventually. The earlier drama was tucked away, just part of the furniture. My new mother-in-law said she was surprised that I looked like a bride, and she was happy that I did. No one in Edwin's family had ever had such a simple wedding. There was kissing and stories, and most of the relatives gave checks to Edwin as their gifts. The party was finally getting started. Edwin said, "Let's cut the cake and go." A bottle of champagne was opened. No taxi was likely to come out in the snowstorm. Bill and two uncles organized to drive us to the airport hotel. We were to be back at work on Monday. Edwin went to his language course. I began living at the Chastleton on 16th Street in Washington and tried to salvage what I could of the term at Hopkins.

WASHINGTON, D.C., 1964 • *We spent the first months of our married life* studying and intensely preparing for our respective new careers. Edwin offered me his worldly experience and sophistication as a guide for my education as his wife. I studied hard and tried to incorporate his direction into my understanding. I hadn't had a clear picture of wife-dom, except that I did not want to make the same choices and mistakes as my mother. She was a reverse model for me. I tried to accede to my husband's needs and desires as much as possible. In any case, he would not have accepted less. We both started out with this unrealizable premise. In the first weeks and months of married life I was confused and conflicted. I believed I had made promises that had to be kept. I wanted to keep them. But I also wanted to be myself and grow into whoever it was that I was going to be. There in Washington, I no longer saw friends or went out by myself. My whole life began to take on a new shape.

THE CHASTLETON • *Our apartment was in the Chastleton at 16th and R,* in the Dupont Circle area. The building was a physically amazing environment. In 1964 it was a bit rundown and past its prime, like the rest of that neighborhood, echoing its former glories and pretensions. And what a past it had! Wallis Simpson had lived there before she married the King of England. Douglas MacArthur had been a resident, and, gossip said, kept his mistress there.

The Chastleton had been built in the 1920s. It reeked flamboyantly of romantic movie theater excess. The stone façade was a menagerie of gargoyles and grotesqueries surrounded by and supporting botanical creations in profusion. It was decorated with an abundance of geometric stone moldings, ogees, ornamental window trims, and pretty much anything that the effusive architect could have thought of. The glorious, tall, center-parting windows had French-style latches and were mullioned with tiny panes that glinted onto the street at thousands of slightly differing angles.

The lobby was a two-story extravaganza, sympathetic with the exterior, and with a reception desk. To the rear, the telephone switchboard operator still plugged in sets of rubber tubes to connect and announce all the calls to the apartments. The wiring from the twenties did not provide for separate lines. Certainly the level of gossip was magnified by the fact that the operators could listen in undetected. They weren't supposed to do it, but it happened. I had subbed on the telephone board at Premier and had done the same thing a few times. Much later, in Tepoztlán, the hotel clerk considered it a regular function of his job. Maybe in the ancient days of switchboards, listening in was a normal occupational perk. It added a lot of amusement to the workday. The Chastleton operators provided many useful services. For example, if you had a guest, they rang upstairs if your spouse arrived home unexpectedly. It was from the front receptionist and the operator that I garnered my tidbits of rumor and history.

Our apartment was on the top floor. We looked down from a little balcony onto the mimosa trees of the Masonic temple next door. The balcony proved to be a most wonderful amenity. We ate out there almost every evening, overlooking the yellow-blossom-covered trees and the Masons' garden. There was very little air conditioning in the mid-sixties. When the humidity rose to ninety percent, many embassies, theaters, and even restaurants closed and the city population seemed reduced to half.

Our two rooms were huge and beautifully proportioned. Everything was finished with elegant details: moldings with beautiful profiles at the high ceilings, inlaid wood floors, solid, trimmed doors on the wall of closets in the bedroom. On the other hand, the closets were a bit shallow. We had to put clothes in crosswise for the hangers to be hung. The bathroom and kitchen were as minuscule as the rooms were grand. Neither could accommodate an iota more than the minimum essentials. That was all right because we didn't have much more than essentials and the shower presents, mostly still in their boxes. On the first morning of my married life there, bending down to get something from under the sink for breakfast, through the ample holes around the plumbing in the wall, I saw two bare legs, knees to hips, Edwin innocently shaving on the other side of the pipes.

That spring I bought a true indispensable: Craig Claiborne's *New York Times Cookbook* in its first edition. I was becoming more of a cook and loved the whole process, except perhaps for the cleaning up afterwards. Claiborne's style was clear, simple, and straightforward as he taught the most sophisticated techniques and elegant recipes. There were sequences of photographs that showed how to make *vol-au-vent*, carve a turkey, produce Neapolitan ice cream molds, and many other useful procedures. Colored photographs displayed categories of foods I hadn't even known existed. Over time, I made almost every recipe in his book. The recipes were in a clear font, easy to find, and came with suggestions. None of this sounds very novel now, but cookbooks were much more utilitarian then. Claiborne was my teacher.

I took a class in knitting with two elderly French sisters from Alsace who had a tiny yarn store downtown. In French they taught me to knit in European style and extended my academic vocabulary into domestic areas. My first effort was a Shetland wool sweater that Edwin wore for years. Women came into the store to knit and visit, something like you might have imagined a sewing circle once would have been. There was some gentle teasing and lots of helpful information for a bride without many models of happy domesticity.

I became a commuter, taking the train to Baltimore to finish my course work and organize as much as I could for my future degree. Edwin wanted me to be with him. He would not agree to my staying in my apartment. I didn't sleep another night in Baltimore but always returned to Washington, taking up my wife life en route. Hopkins said they retained credits for five years. Surely I wouldn't be gone so long. I would come back, finish the degree, and probably be a university academic.

FOREIGN SERVICE LIFE • *The State Department required officers' wives to* take a course called the Foreign Service Wives' Training Course. There were no officers' husbands because if a female officer married she had to resign. So in addition to Hopkins, knitting, and Claiborne's cookbook lessons, I enrolled in this two-week class. The dozen or so women were of varied backgrounds and the few experienced in Foreign Service life were there to mentor the new and ignorant so that they could meet the department's rules.

And how ignorant I was. Much of the course was spent on seating charts, packing and shipping, children's education (with a subsection on boarding schools), health hazards, record keeping, the pros and cons of storing your silver for security or taking it to have the comfort of home at post. A fair amount of time was devoted to the subtleties of professional entertaining. It was necessary to understand the requirements of creating and facilitating the environment in which diplomatic business can be informally conducted. Calling cards. Despite my education to date, I had a hard time mastering which corner of my cards to turn down. Each corner, turned down and marked with lower case letters (abbreviations of French phrases), with a tiny gold or silver pencil, signified a different message to the recipient when you called.

In Washington, a particular stationer specialized in diplomatic needs. It cost more to engrave than emboss the necessary calling cards, note cards, letter paper, envelopes, invitations, etc., but with engraving you received the tiny copper plates and could use them for the rest of your life. Besides, engraved text felt so much better under your thumb than the raised embossed text. You needed social cards of your own, Mrs. John Smith, social cards for the husband, Mr. John Smith, Second Secretary, and joint ones, Mr. and Mrs. John Smith, in one of two or three script fonts, placed on bright white or cream paper. The rules on how and when to use these cards, and in which combinations, were complicated and extensive.

Etiquette sounds stuffy and seems to be useless rules from another era.

In my Foreign Service life however, I came to appreciate that etiquette, once it is stripped of its unwieldy superstructure, gives a commonly accepted frame of reference, a common language of behavior, so that people can be as comfortable as possible if they live in a world of strangers. In 1964, wars and pot and flower power were beginning to influence a new etiquette for young people. The Foreign Service was not young. A great many officers were people of independent means. Many officers had a father or uncle in the service. Our generation was the first to begin to "look like America," to represent the diversity of the country. Before the late fifties there were very few Jewish officers and, until the sixties, almost no black or Hispanic members of the service. The wives' course was a fairly recent innovation, serving the role previously filled by a relative or older friend in acclimating new wives to the intricacies and requirements of the service.

The course had a small component about personal security and keeping yourself from being kidnapped or shot, but it was a small item. Two and three years down the road, I could have used more information in that area.

I fit in the voluminous paperwork for my security clearance. Wives were not compensated for the official work that was required, but we had some of the characteristics of employees. A wife could be a potential security risk, inadvertent or deliberate. She could be a conduit into informal cultural and social areas of life. On occasion, she might convey subtle messages. Wives created the quasi-social atmosphere and social network for building confidence and for conducting business. They also got the officer and his family from pillar to post, moving from one city, country, language, and culture to another every two years or so. All was expected to be done invisibly, gracefully, efficiently, and without the expression of personal opinion.

Edwin had passed his intensive, ten-month-long, Korean-language course. The language institute had a system for jamming a tremendous amount of new language skills into the brain in a fairly short time. It was hard work. When a "hard" language course was finished, the student had a good basic working knowledge. Wives were not qualified for the courses. Sometimes simple language study for wives was offered once they arrived at their post. Edwin got off to a good start. He was looking forward to his new career and imagined a dynamic and interesting life ahead.

We had been immunized against about a dozen health hazards — small pox, cholera, tetanus, typhoid, etc. We sorted our separate and mutual possessions into storage and shipping. At many posts, the Embassy provided housing, furnished with basic essentials. Some posts didn't have adequate housing or the economy was not developed enough to support foreign families. Korea was only ten years out of its shooting war, still very poor. There was no housing "on the economy," so we planned to store what little furniture we had and take only those personal things that fit into our weight allowance, determined by rank, family size, and destination.

In July 1964, we said good-bye to families. They didn't say much about our upcoming adventures. It was a new relationship for all of us. We packed our bags, sent our minimal crates, and were ready to begin our great adventure. We left the Freedom Summer in Mississippi, the conventions that nominated Lyndon Johnson and Barry Goldwater, shorter skirts and longer hair, Joan Baez, the Beatles, and safe drinking water.

ON OUR WAY • *We planned a leisurely trip, a deferred honeymoon. It was the* first time I saw San Francisco. There was a popular song, "I Left My Heart In San Francisco," and it was played often in honor of the thousands of troops sailing from there to Vietnam. I have visited there more than a dozen times. It has always seemed to me to be one of the most interesting and enjoyable cities in the world. We climbed the hills, walked along the bay, ate wonderful food in glamorous restaurants and little dives, heard jazz in dark clubs, did the tourist sights for five or six days and then traveled on to Japan.

We arrived in Tokyo in early August. Edwin was to have consultations at the Embassy there. I did sightseeing during the day when he was busy. Japan was getting ready for its first Olympics in October. They were adding English lettering to street signs, the subway system, and everywhere foreigners might go. Streets were being repaved. Hotels were being built or refurbished. The Olympics was seen in Japan as the opportunity to reenter the world stage as a fully respected player. They went all out to present themselves as a modern, peaceful country. In August, the process had reached a frenzy of activity.

We stayed at the old Imperial Hotel, exquisite inside and out. The approach to the main entrance was a long drive along a rectangular lily pond. The scale and materials were perfect. As part of the project, Frank Lloyd Wright designed all the chairs, beds, and tables. I think he was more interested in conceptual integrity than the guests' comfort. There was not any place to sit at ease. I think that is as much a hallmark of Wright's designs as is the beauty of the buildings.

The design had originally been intended for Mexico City. The client there backed out when he saw Wright's novel concept. Wright looked for a long time to find a client who agreed to try his idea for an earthquake-resistant structure. The whole tall building sits on a platform under the foundation. The theory was that when the quakes hit, the building would move on the platform and remain undamaged. The Imperial Hotel was completed in the early 1920s and withstood the massive quake of 1926 with almost no damage. Afterward, this construction system was widely used, and it is effective in the most common type of earthquakes.

Tokyo was sweltering in the August humidity at the end of the rainy season. Still we got around the city and saw some of the palaces and gardens. The World War II bombing had intentionally left the Imperial Palace and gardens untouched. Huge sections of the city had been destroyed, especially in the firebombing, and were now being rebuilt as fast as possible. Miles of gray concrete were going up, the apartment houses the Japanese referred to as "rabbit warrens." The department stores were full of goods. They offered art exhibitions, formal tea ceremonies, and flower arranging classes. Young girls in white gloves and French designer uniforms bowed at the door and at the foot of every escalator. The Japanese economy had been given a heavy lift by their huge efforts and the profits of the Korean War, and they were spending the money to rebuild the whole country. It was all an education.

FOUR

Korea

SEOUL • *Seoul is surrounded by an ancient city wall. Almost anywhere you* were in the city, you could see the surrounding mountains. They are obscured now by the growth of the city, with its forests of high rises. Several palaces are in the downtown area. The buildings became museums and their grounds were turned into parks. The scale was intimate and human. The palaces had very intricate, colorful painted designs and were set in gardens with old trees, ponds, and lakes, with few flowers and almost no statuary. Most palaces had not been renovated and still had the patina of age and history. Economic activity was primarily in two or three large outdoor markets, especially East Gate Market. In the evening the vendors had candles in lanterns or pedaled a stationary bicycle to power a tiny bulb so the customers could see what they were buying.

When we arrived in Seoul in 1964, the city was growing at a tremendous rate as people moved in from the countryside. It was eleven years after the end of the Korean War. The city had suffered three waves of battles. Bullet holes were visible on many buildings in the center city. There was still a midnight-to-four o'clock curfew when no one was allowed out on the streets. Korea was a very poor country then. Electricity was uncertain, and there was no clean water anywhere. North Korean guerilla soldiers were caught regularly, and from time to time a bus was blown up or some similar attack occurred.

We were required to live in embassy-assigned housing for security reasons, and because there was no housing available locally. Although the date of our arrival was set many months in advance, no housing had been designated for us. In the sixteen months we were in Seoul, we lived in five different places.

We were taken to The Guest House for an indefinite period, with just the suitcases we had carried en route. It was the private business of a middle-aged American woman, Mrs. Wissberg. She intended it for dependent wives not authorized by the military authorities. For their monthly rent, the wives each had a small room and could prepare their meals in a shared kitchen. There were very simple shared bathrooms and a bathing room with a shower and tub. Most of the eight or ten American wives were young. Some had found jobs teaching English. One woman played solitaire for hours at a time.

The day after our arrival, we set off to do the administrative chores associated with a new post: identity cards, money, security briefings, and orientation for spouses, called "spice." Then Edwin went to his office and sent me back to The Guest House with instructions to prepare to call on the wife of his superior.

From the start, Edwin told me that he was hoping for a child right away. I stopped using contraceptives in August and became pregnant the very first month, while we were traveling. After a stop for a couple of weeks in Tokyo, we had arrived in Seoul in the midst of the heavy, murky August humidity. I was indisposed in the ordinary way, with morning sickness that persisted much of the day. I didn't know anyone yet and had very little idea of what to do.

It had been emphasized to me that wives were required to formally call on one another. At least the more junior wives called on the wives of officers of higher rank. I had a very minimal wardrobe with me. One of the young wives at The Guest House loaned me a pale yellow silk dress and her church hat for this first occasion. In the ninety-percent humidity, ninety-degree temperatures, I put on the required stockings, white gloves, and a hat, and took my brand-new cards to the homes of other women who were obliged to serve tea and cake and make small talk for fifteen minutes. One surefire way to be excused from at least some of this activity was to be pregnant or nursing a new baby. Some women had a new baby at every post, at least for a while.

The pecking order for the wives mirrored that of the officers, and in time the senior officer's wife indicated to her husband the strengths and weaknesses of the junior wife. That information was incorporated in a file on the wife and also in the officer's evaluation each year. The wife being evaluated had no right to see or answer any negative comments. It was an almost Confucian hierarchy, rigid and coercive. The required calling, coffees, teas, luncheons, receptions, and service activities within an approved range of choices, all took time and involved the consumption of a tremendous amount of coffee and baked goods. Many wives played bridge in the afternoon, waiting eagerly for five o'clock and the arrival of sherry. I was not the only junior wife instructed to bring hors d'oeuvres or dessert for a party that I was not invited to attend. Like other young wives, I was expected to do as I was told and to keep my opinions to myself.

I had an image of myself as a person who would do useful things in the world. When I married, it was at least partly for the adventures I imagined, living in a new culture, seeing the wonders of the world. I was innocent and romantic about this, but not wrong.

KFEA: TEACHER AND LEARNER • *Gradually, I made my way around* some of the obstacles. When I had been in Seoul only a few weeks, through one of the cultural officers I met the staff of the KFEA (Korean Federation of Education Associations). They were beginning to plan for the first international conference to be held in Korea and needed to learn English. Bernie thought I was just the one to teach them. He was right. I met with the staff members two or three times a week for most of a year. They were diligent in their efforts. More difficult than some of the language lessons were the cultural necessities for the international event.

I suggested to them that handshakes were expected. We practiced at the beginning and end of every class. The idea of shaking hands was strange, its practice all but unknown, except in a very small circle of Koreans who had foreign contacts. Bowing, with its many subtleties, was the norm. People didn't touch one another in public; least of all would a man and woman have physical contact. Together the staff and I persevered for almost a year. We needed every day. I helped with the preparation of conference materials and brochures, corrected speeches, and invented dialogues that applied directly to the conference. I learned almost as much Korean as they learned English. I took some time off to have the baby. On my return, the director asked me to deliver the welcoming speech to the several thousand delegates. I was honored to do it. Besides the pleasure of having a job I liked, and knowing that I was useful and respected, we liked each other and they gave me a chance to know something of Korea when I was new there.

This was far from the usual charity work that wives were expected to perform. My education had prepared me to question, to form and express opinions, to enjoy energetic discussion. I expected to keep right on doing it. Surely I was unreasonably optimistic. I had little interest in the traditional activities that were standard for officers' wives. I did all that was required but not more.

PACKING AND PACKING • *After those first few weeks at The Guest House,* we were assigned a house at Yongsan, a military base about fifteen minutes from downtown. The area was divided in two sections. The larger was the U.S. military base, with housing for married and single officers, enlisted barracks, a school, the 121st Evacuation Hospital, a Post Exchange (like a poorly stocked Wal-Mart), and a small library. There were chapels, mess halls, and an outdoor amphitheater where the comedian Bob Hope gave Christmas shows with pretty actresses entertaining in the frigid air.

During this first year, we had plenty of practice packing and moving. We were first assigned to a house on a steep hillside in the smaller, civilian area of the Yongsan base. All the houses were furnished with the same government furniture, in one of two or three neutral color schemes. The rest of our baggage arrived a month after we moved in. I unpacked dishes and linens and the few other things we had shipped. I expected to live in that bungalow for our entire tour, the next three years. I imagined the new baby in the bright bedroom to the front and looked at catalogue pictures of cribs and bassinettes to furnish it. I learned the drill for wife-life and did it better than before, but never perfected the techniques. The nausea of early pregnancy cleared up. I taught at KFEA, and went often to the palace parks. As autumn grew cooler, the ponds lost their foliage and the dried lotus pods and stems made twisting sculptures in the shallow water. Only the palaces had old trees, and the foliage was especially intense against the backdrop of the gray, treeless cityscape.

Just before the winter holidays, we were ordered to move to another house a few blocks away. It was the identical model. Edwin's boss, Harry, expected his wife to arrive at post in time for the holidays, and he took our house because it had a better view. We had less than a week to be out. I packed and unpacked again and thought we were set. I started to accumulate baby things. I applied my knitting lessons to baby clothes. I bought a sewing machine and remembered my grandmother as I made a layette from the pretty Korean fabrics I bought at East Gate Market.

For some reason I cannot remember now, we were ordered to move again and this time to the military side because there was no civilian housing available for us. It was a duplex. In the other half was a wife from California and two small children. The husband was away much of the time and I didn't get to know him at all. I tried to make the house comfortable but couldn't put much heart into it.

RIBBONS AND BOMBS • *I knew a lovely "older" woman. Dorothy was about* forty-five and her husband worked in the same section with Edwin. One spring day she invited me for lunch. I arrived to find it was a surprise baby shower. Everyone was dressed up in pearls and silk dresses but I, not guessing, was in my everyday clothes — a red bandanna-print maternity top that was very filled with the baby, with my hair in a braid down my back. The house was full of flowers and ribbons. One of the older wives came in a bit late, and after a few minutes, said that she didn't want to spoil the party, but she had just heard that the American Embassy in Saigon had been bombed, with many casualties. We ate the lunch and opened the presents in a somber mood. Every embassy is like a tiny piece of its home country. Inside the walls, it is the same as being in that country. It is one of the conventions that make international diplomacy possible.

I received useful presents and pretty things for the baby and for me. Four young friends, all mothers of toddlers, had gotten together a couple of months before and ordered a stroller from a catalogue. They had to plan ahead since an order from Sears came by ship and took eight to ten weeks. One wonderful, irreplaceable gift was a blender, with handwritten instructions for making baby food. The giver of this treasure, Pat, was about to give birth herself, and our little boys arrived the same week. She had an older child, and the best part of her gift was the experience she shared so generously. Some of the older wives gave me personal things — a kit with soap and cologne for the hospital stay, a novel. Most of the gifts were a lavish variety of receiving blankets, tiny clothes, and crib accessories. I filled the stroller with the boxes of baby things, feeling not very ready for motherhood.

Right around my due date, we were ordered to move again. The army needed their house back. We were assigned to a two-bedroom apartment in the embassy complex downtown — the best place I lived in Seoul, then or later. The apartments were small but had lovely gardens and were wonderfully located. I could walk to everything.

STEPHEN • *Stephen was born on May 12, 1965 in the 121st military hospital in Seoul.* I had considered going to a Korean hospital. It was just as well I didn't. He did not take a breath for eight minutes. The doctor did every sort of maneuver — slapping, tickling, pulling a fingernail over the reflexes of the foot, warm and cold water, blowing pure oxygen over the baby. A nurse positioned herself right in my line of sight so that I could not see him. Finally, without a sound, he took a tiny shuddering breath. They cleaned him up and hustled him into an incubator. I had a quick look, but I wasn't allowed to touch him. He was full term and perfectly formed, born after his expected due date, but he weighed only four and a half pounds. After a few days, I was discharged, but Stephen stayed in the hospital for three weeks. I didn't want to leave him behind. Edwin had arranged for a car and driver to take us back to the apartment. We crossed the center of the city and in a few minutes were back in our apartment. I took out the baby clothes and put them away again, refolded blankets that were already perfectly folded. My neighbor sent over banana bread. I liked it so well that while I had time on my hands she taught me to make it. I was allowed to see Stephen during visiting hours twice a day. Finally, he was released to us with the instructions to feed him enriched formula every two hours, night and day, and to return in two weeks.

Stephen came home and prospered. He was a small child until he was about five. His eyesight is poor, possibly from those eight minutes without breath, but otherwise he has no obvious lasting effects from his difficult beginning.

Koreans have a tradition of celebrating a child's hundredth day. The most dangerous days for the newborn have past. The child is given a name, and if a boy, the name is written in a family book. Many Korean families have books going back centuries. Edwin decided that we should celebrate Stephen's hundredth day with a party of one hundred people. The garden of the apartment complex was lovely for the August event. I bought tiny traditional boy's clothing in wonderful colors and with the brilliant Korean striped sleeves. I organized food and drink, flowers, tables and chairs. I engaged waiters and a woman to help me with the cooking. Invitations were sent. People from the embassy came as well as many of Edwin's business contacts. We had a receiving line to greet people as they arrived, Edwin and I shaking hands and bowing, Stephen sleeping peacefully in the stroller, which had a configuration as a newborn bed. I wondered who all these people were. The weather was fine, the baby beautiful, and the event went off without any major glitches. It was the largest event I had done up to that time. I was twenty-three, with a three-month-old baby. It was a little over a year since I had been a student at Hopkins.

In any weather but the wettest snow, I liked to put Stephen in his stroller and walk around the center of the city. I loved being his mother, and I loved being with him. I didn't have a car, and it was unsafe to take a bus. The buses were crowded and a high percentage of the population had tuberculosis — aside from the occasional suicide bomber. So I put Stephen in the stroller and went to the palace parks and walked all over central Seoul. I explored the city, saw the demonstrations, learned more of the language. Language courses for wives were short and concentrated on social amenities and housekeeping. I acquired much more by osmosis on my rambles and through my association with KFEA.

HARRY'S WARNING • *A year or so after we arrived, when Stephen was a very young baby, Edwin called me and said that I was to come to the Embassy. We had an appointment with his supervising officer, Harry. Harry admonished that while I could do little to help my husband's career,*

I could certainly ruin it. The work expected of me was a requirement of Edwin's job and not an option for me. I needed to change my behavior immediately. I was not to express my opinions in public, including among other wives. It would be better if I simply didn't have any opinions. I was to follow the instructions and the lead of the senior wife, and remember my place. It was fine that I was almost the only wife who had learned Korean, and I did a job pro bono with KFEA that was meeting official program objectives. Neither of those could compensate for my forgetting his warning. He used a crude analogy with electrical equipment, and said that he thought I was smart enough to appreciate his taking time from his busy day. Officially, this kind of reprimand is called guidance. I remember my shock and embarrassment at the scolding and sexually suggestive references. Edwin thought his boss had been helpful, and hoped I understood and had taken his warning to heart.

In the late fall, Edwin was offered the directorship of a small post in the south of the country. It was a promotion and a good opportunity for him, and in mid-winter we moved again.

KWANGJU • *We arrived in Kwangju in a snowstorm, and were greeted by the* office director, Mr. Kim. We looked around and went to sleep in the cold house. Overnight our breath turned into an icy haze on the windows. The first morning in the little house, I looked out the glass, onto the sad remains of a Japanese-style garden. An old pine tree twisted around the edge of a tiny pond. A rose bush had survived into old age, and a long cane had wound itself through scraggly, leafless azalea twigs as the vine had reached for the sun the previous summer. At the end of this serpentine stem, a few curling leaves were hanging down, and a single white rose was edged in snow.

Our three-room house in Kwangju had not served as anyone's home for a long time. It had been built for the Japanese colonial administrator in the thirties and came into American hands at the end of World War II. It had been used intermittently in the twenty years since then.

The house had a living room with wide glass doors to the garden and paper-covered sliding *fusuma* doors enclosing it from each side. Through one pair was a small room, maybe eight by eleven, that we used as our bedroom. Through the pair of doors opposite was a room with large windows on two sides; it held an old dining table and six chairs. Sliding *shoji* doors covered in white paper partitioned off one end, and the space was just as wide as the baby's wooden crib. The windows were warped and drafty. Stephen was six months old, and for that cold Korean winter he slept there in his snowsuit, with a thick quilt over him. The third, widest set of doors, opposite the glass garden doors, opened onto a long hallway that defined the house and led to the shoe-storing entry area. A long, lean-to addition was attached to this hall enclosing the kitchen, a room with a tub for bathing, and, toward the front end of the hall, a compartment with the toilet. This design has been in use in Japan for centuries. It can be aesthetically pleasing but does not provide for heat, as Korean houses do. The straw matted *tatami* had been pulled out and replaced with bare linoleum floors. The paper doors were full of holes. The kitchen was a new world to me, with its kerosene stove for cooking, unreliable well pump, stone sink, and a refrigerator left from before the Korean War. I was glad we had running water, at least some of the time. Most of the neighbors had just a yard pump, and many houses in Kwangju had only the water that was carried from the river.

Our sole source of heat was a very old space heater that burned number-two fuel oil, a kind of diesel fuel. It was a monster that stood in the living room, a big metal box about two feet on a side, three feet tall, with an exhaust pipe up through the roof. It was sort of a very big tin can that was over the fire at the bottom. Mr. Kim came to help us get oriented. First order of domestic business was to get a barrier around the heater so that Stephen, crawling around, wouldn't be burned. The office sent a carpenter who erected a heavy wooden fence around it. Mr. Kim explained that, despite the chimney pipe, this type of heater emitted carbon monoxide and advised us never to have it on while sleeping, or while Stephen was sleeping. I asked myself, "Why were people with a baby assigned to this house?" Mr. Kim further informed us that a man hired by the office stayed at the house all night to protect us from prowlers. Mr. Lee came and added to his responsibilities as kind guardian and handy man, the role of uncle to Stephen. Security was a different matter.

Stephen certainly helped me to get acquainted. His was the first stroller ever seen on the streets of Kwangju, or for that matter, in the whole province of Cholla Namdo. That first winter I suited him up, wrapped the plaid carriage blanket from my own infancy around him, and set out to discover the world. The first few times, the *hajimonis*, the grandmothers and elderly women of our street, came around the stroller, touching the carriage and the baby, commenting on his fair color and gray eyes, taking careful note of his arrangements, a little shocked that he wasn't carried in someone's arms. I could speak some Korean by then and was expanding my vocabulary hourly, on a steep learning curve.

LEARNING ABOUT FOOD AND WATER • *I walked everywhere with* Stephen in the stroller, creating eddies of astonishment and conversation wherever I went. The market was about a half mile from the house and I went often. After some experimentation, I settled on my favorite vendors.

Chickens arrived in late spring. The buyer pointed at a bird walking around, the vendor wrung its neck, and the buyer got to take it home. At eight weeks, they were dainty things, suitable for frying and stir-fry in the wok. At ten weeks, they were big as roasters. After that, until the next spring, there would be only tough old birds for soup and stewing. The kitchen was equipped with a freezer — we had a little generator to use when the electricity went out — and I was advised by Mr. Kim to buy at least forty or fifty chickens in the spring. Yes. Well. I created a sensation in the market by saying that I wanted the chickens without the heads or feet. And I wanted them without the feathers. Finally, all was made clear, a price agreed on, and the chickens were ready the following week. Fifty chickens make a substantial pile on the counter. Each chicken had to be cleaned, singed, cut up, wrapped, and labeled for storage in the freezer. Edwin contributed a supply of wrapping paper from the embassy co-op, brought back from one of his trips to Seoul. I bought little beef since most of it was from animals too old to work the fields anymore. Ocean fish came from Mokpo on the west coast, then half a day's drive away. A few months into my stay, the fish man asked with a big smile that I teach him English. He wanted to exchange lessons for shrimp or fish. Someone was just starting a mushroom farm in the mountains, and I made mushrooms with everything when I could get them. In winter, the only fresh vegetables were cabbages, carrots, turnips, and onions in varieties that were mostly new to me. The cabbages were a foot and a half long, twelve inches in diameter, mostly crisp, white ribs with a little frilly green around the top. These cabbages were the basis for famous Korean kimchee. Huge, cone-shaped, white radishes, more than a foot long, were the second staple. In the fall, these hardy crops were cut, interleaved with prodigious quantities of garlic, ground red chilies, and fermented fish sauce, and then layered in beautiful brown clay pots. Most houses had a pit where the pots were partially buried so that they would not freeze. This fall kimchee was the principle source of vegetables as well as seasoning from late fall until May. By then the kimchee was more than aromatic and so was every person who ate it regularly. Of course, foreigners who ate dairy products, especially rancid milk in the form of cheese, also had a distinctive and generally unpleasant smell. But we didn't worry about that since no dairy products were available outside of Seoul.

Spring was the hungry season. By late March, girls and women would crawl along the edges of the rice field irrigation ditches, searching for early dandelions, new wild grasses, and anything else that could be used to supplement the kitchen stores. Fields were fertilized with the animal and human wastes of the farm households. In English the containers, carried on bamboo shoulder yokes by the poorest workers, were called honey pots. Those fields did not produce much new food until May and June. The rice harvest was in October, and some farmers could not afford to eat their own rice but fed their families on a side crop of barley.

As the saying goes, necessity is the mother of invention, and was my culinary godmother. I started to cook then by using what was available, drying herbs in the summer, making some odd combinations that seemed to work out.

Edwin often invited business guests for dinner and an evening of conversation. There were no caterers or prepared foods, there wasn't a grocery store or supermarket. The first bakery, in the first tourist hotel, opened while I lived there. In Seoul, I had acquired a tiny cookbook put out as a fundraiser by the Benedictine Sisters of Peking, who moved to Japan after the Chinese Revolution. In a few sentences, with tiny line drawings, the book offered a range of northern Chinese recipes, mostly stir-fry. I modified it by what was available in the market and the Korean cooking I was learning.

Part of the kitchen routine every day was to boil water in a huge kettle a minimum of twenty minutes to try and prevent hepatitis and parasites.

The water was allowed to cool in the kettle and poured through a funnel into sterilized bottles. Mostly I used the Johnny Walker bottles left after office receptions. Their square shape made storage a little more efficient. Boiling water was poured over clean dishes in the drying rack. Everything we ate had to be boiled or peeled. No ice was safe, except for what was made at home from the boiled water. One million ameba can hibernate in an ice cube.

The embassy support staff, in their effort to make life a bit easier in the "boonies," sent a washing machine. An old-fashioned wringer washing machine would have been great. They sent a new, modern automatic machine, and it was installed next to the bathtub so that the water would drain there. There wasn't enough water pressure to run the machine. The drill was to fill it by hand with a bucket until it turned on, adding some boiling water from the kitchen to raise the temperature to tepid, then repeat for the rinse. When there was a shortage, I saved the water in the tub to use again. I hung the laundry outside or dried in the house during winter. The baby clothes and diapers were boiled on the stove in a huge, brass pot I bought for this purpose, and stirred with a very long ladle.

GUERILLA IN THE GARDEN • *In the mid-sixties, there were repeated* military confrontations at sea and many ground incursions between North and South Korea. Some of them become very serious incidents. Kwangju is the provincial capital and the largest city in the southwest part of the country. It is far from the border with North Korea, over mountains and difficult terrain, but not far from the coast. One night, there was a terrific racket and the sound of gunfire nearby. I raced to grab Stephen from his crib. In the morning, we learned that our neighbor had gotten up to use the toilet, attached to the outside of his house, and startled a guerilla who by happenstance was passing through the garden. The North Korean soldier, about eighteen and nervous, thought he was discovered and let off his gun, spraying the house next door with a line of bullets at the height of the baby's crib. Stephen moved into the bedroom with us, and we all slept on the floor for the rest of our tour.

Edwin was busy with his career. For two years, he averaged at least one night a week away from home on field trips and many evenings a week out on business. He came home for dinner at midday when he was free. He was good at his job, very committed to his responsibilities and his mission.

Five missionary families lived in their own compound and ran a small clinic. There were no other foreigners in the city of seven hundred and fifty thousand people that was without sidewalks, a traffic light, or television. All were to arrive during my time there. I was twenty-four years old, learning to live the diplomatic life, without heat or a shower, without a grocery store or clean water.

It was just a year and a half since I'd left Baltimore.

SOOK JA • *Sook Ja and I met soon after my arrival in Kwangju. She was a* Korean born in Japan, and after she graduated from the university, her parents had sent her to Korea to learn the language, the culture, and her family heritage. She and her husband had done the extraordinary, unconventional thing and decided for themselves that they wanted to marry. At that time more than ninety-five percent of marriages were arranged. Both their families were dismayed but, finding nothing very objectionable, eventually relented. By 1966 they had three children, the youngest almost exactly Stephen's age. The men wanted to know each other professionally. He was an up-and-coming politician, Provincial Minister of Agriculture, I think. His mother was a very famous Presbyterian preacher, as was his brother.

Sook Ja and I became friends soon after my arrival in Kwangju. It was not usual in Korea for people to invite you into their house. The outer garden walls were boundaries of privacy not easily breached. But she and I visited often. We called each other by our children's name, Stephen's mother and Kyung Hee's mother, or addressed each other as elder sister. We did not come to use our personal names until about ten years later. We talked many long hours, with the children near us. We also both had a lot to do related to our husbands' occupations.

YWCA • *Sook Ja was a deeply religious person and thought of her Christianity* as a liberating context for personal growth. Later, in the Eighties, in Canada, she wrote her doctoral dissertation on radical feminism as an aspect of Christian faith. Even as a young woman, she took positive actions to live rather than just talk about her beliefs. In Kwangju she asked me to join the board of the YWCA, a hotbed of feminist commitment. Every woman — about twenty on the board — was there because she believed that she had the means and the power to direct her own life and to influence community change. Korea was still a very patriarchal society, and it wasn't obvious or easy for women to be very active in public life, especially outside the sphere of their husbands' interest.

In Kwangju, men drove the jitney buses, and the bus girls collected the tickets on board. The girls also cleaned the buses and performed other services. Most of these girls had been recruited from impoverished rural areas. Sometimes the girls were indentured for a few years to get the families through hard times. They came to the city, lived in a company dormitory, in a room with sixty girls. They were paid very low wages for their ten-hour day, six days a week. After five years, when they were eighteen or nineteen, the bus company was supposed to provide a dowry. The girls were subject to exploitation, constant abuse, and harassment from the drivers. The girls were not entirely sympathetic figures. Uneducated, rough spoken, and dirty, most people regarded them almost as prostitutes.

One summer afternoon at the Y, the women met in a bare, dusty room with the sun slanting in through the open windows. We sat on folding chairs in a circle. The women spoke together very candidly, without the circumlocutions and elegance of normal, polite Korean speech. They asked direct questions and gave each other direct answers. The board discussed the possibilities to alleviate the bus girls' situation, and decided on a multi-pronged attack for social action. First, each of us committed to discuss this bus girl problem with at least one other woman. We also contributed one direct action. For example, the wife of the publisher of the city's main newspaper was going to get him to print a story. I was teaching a seminar to secondary teachers of English and planned to make this campaign the subject of a lesson. I also contributed what I knew of the Montgomery bus boycott. Another woman promised to bring up the subject of the bus girls at her flower arranging class. Her teacher and the other students, all well-to-do women, would talk about the girls during their three-hour class and find an action to add. A small team decided to enlist the girls themselves. They were afraid of taking action, even in the face of poor food, rape, beatings, and other mistreatment. They needed their jobs. No one on the Y board had ever been on a bus, but everyone would discourage members of her household from riding as long as the girls worked under these conditions. The women at the Y were outraged and meant to change this deteriorating situation. Remarkable and true, things did change. Over months, not years, this group of women overturned the system and a little humanity crept into labor conditions. As this campaign matured, our understanding of our roles as women and members of the community were evolving as well. Diplomatic wives were not supposed to make their opinions public and certainly were not supposed to take part in overt activities like this YWCA campaign. My part was small, and I am glad I was there to do that little bit.

CHUNG JA • *Over time, I became well acquainted with the teachers in the* seminar I taught. One of them had a very bright student who was about to drop out for lack of money to buy her required school uniform. The Korean government had recently made secondary school attendance compulsory, but the students had to buy their books and uniforms. They even had prescribed haircuts, down to the exact length of their bangs. Chung Ja was an outstanding student but from a very poor family. Could I employ her part time? And encourage her English? It was a great match. She came to the house in the mornings, helped me a little with housework, and mostly looked after Stephen so I could teach my class, attend the Y, and do my errands. (There were no babysitters or day-care facilities in Kwangju. Children were cared for in their homes by an army of available females.) I made sure Chung Ja did her lessons and had her lunch before she went to school around one o'clock. Our agreement was that she would stop work if her grades fell. She was fifteen when she started with me, an energetic girl, laughing with Stephen, full of jokes and smiles, quick to lend a hand wherever she could. Everything was easier once I knew her. Later on, she proved to be compassionate beyond anything you could have expected from a girl so young.

WATER • *Kwangju was chronically short of water. Our pump sucked at the* water table. The well was deepened, but sometimes the water was not there. In the two summers we lived there, water trucks cruised through the neighborhoods. Like all our neighbors, Chung Ja and I took two containers each, all that was permitted, and carried water into the house.

That had to last until the truck passed by again in two or three days. Every drop had to be used several times. I used Stephen's bath water for my own wash at the sink, then to wash the floor. Dishwater was used for the minimal toilet use we allowed ourselves. Laundry was minimized. Stephen wore diapers only at night, going bare-bottomed like all the Korean babies and toddlers.

Kwangju had a very small U.S. Army advisory group just outside the city at the Korean army base. The twenty or so American soldiers were rarely seen in the city, and the six officers went to a limited range of civic activities. In the summer drought, they were able to invite Edwin to shower and he went out there daily, but the invitation was not extended to Stephen and me.

Water is so ordinary in most of America that we notice it only in extraordinary circumstances. In the early fifites, in the midst of a drought, my family drove up to see the Croton reservoir. My father walked me across the dry, cracked lakebed toward the center where a little water was shimmering and evaporating before our eyes. In Kwangju, there was no reservoir, just the river, and it had run dry.

IN THE ATTIC • *The little Japanese house had the potential to be a nice home* but had been neglected for a long time. One of its strange characteristics was that in the evening there was frequently a sound, like a woman in high heels, coming from the attic. For a long time, I thought the sound was some loose bit of pipe or roof tile. One evening, I was alone in the house with Stephen when the ceiling shook. A two-foot wide section fell to the floor. I could see rats leaping around up there in the space between the joists and the roof. So many that the weight was finally too much to be supported by the old ceiling. Big, brown rats, jumping over the open chasm, separated from us by nothing more than air. I picked up Stephen and ran outside to find Mr. Lee, our night guardian. I woke him. He was sympathetic and left immediately for some supplies to close the hole. Good. On the other hand, he left us behind, alone with the rats in the ceiling. This was not at all good. It turned out that the whole ceiling had to be pulled down and replaced. It was going to take at least a week. In the process, the repair people could evacuate the rats that had made the attic their home for generations.

There was no way we could be in the house for this operation. In fact, I had to pack up almost everything for the duration of the repairs. Edwin took a week's vacation and we went to Hong Kong, the first of several trips I made there. It was interesting and very different from Korea. That story can wait for later.

PEACE CORPS • *The Peace Corps was planning to come to Korea and the* country director, Kevin O'Donnell, made a tour around the country. He asked me to write some training materials for the volunteers, who were then in Hawai'i learning the language. I wrote up a small manual, including the things that had been particular challenges in my own experience in Cholla Namdo. The volunteers used the manual in their preparations. Kevin then suggested that I participate and be the field resource, the person the volunteers could turn to when they needed something. The something the volunteers needed most often turned out to be a private bath (instead of the public bathhouse), a holiday meal, tea and chat in English about the frustrations and rewards of their jobs, a day shared when they had a spell of homesickness. One young married couple arrived very enthusiastic and seemed well prepared. In a month, the wife was depressed, almost unable to get out of bed, crying all the time, so homesick, and with such a case of culture shock, she had to be sent home. The husband was doing okay but went back with her. The plane to Seoul didn't fly every day, and I talked to the wife many times during the days they spent in Kwangju, waiting for their flight out.

The USAID (Agency for International Development) assigned a regional officer, a nice young guy, to support family planning programs and agricultural assistance. After a few months, he went back home, married his sweetheart, and they returned together to Kwangju. Even though AID was much less rigid and regulated for wives than the State Department, the young wife found it heavy-going getting used to both Korea and married life. I think she minded most the loss of privacy. In Kwangju, we were only a handful of foreigners, and we were all plainly identifiable by our appearance. Some people were isolated by less than adequate language capability. People were curious about the strangers in their midst. They sometimes felt free to do or say things you didn't expect. In Korea, for example, total strangers came over and rubbed or patted my pregnant belly when I was waiting to cross a street. This newcomer wife wanted to wear the clothes she chose, go where she pleased, and especially, not go where she chose not. It was not a happy beginning for her.

This wife was very publicly noticed when she began an affair with a Peace Corps Volunteer, a woman also new to Korea. In 1966, any sort of homosexual or lesbian relationship was formally and officially considered a security risk. People kept such relationships secret because they were likely to lose their job, or worse. Lyndon Johnson had a very longtime friend and aide who was outed maliciously and forced to resign instantly. In Korea, there was a generally accepted repugnance about homosexual relationships. These two women chose to abandon discretion. They found a little place and moved in together. It was the scandal of the decade. The AID officer was faced with a possible transfer and was distraught over this development in his personal life. The Peace Corps needed to address the issue immediately with the Volunteer. I was asked officially to talk with them both separately, find out what was happening, and try to help to calm things down. The AID wife really just wanted to leave and soon did. The Volunteer did not. She came to my house many times for lunch or tea or just company. I didn't have anything else constructive to offer her.

While I was in Kwangju and later in Taegu, my husband and I hosted an ice cream party every summer for the volunteers. Ice cream was not available anywhere outside of Seoul then. I made several flavors and toppings at home and we sat around, swapping stories and kicking back in the summer humidity. The State Department had a rule that wives could not earn money and so I was an unpaid volunteer. For a large portion of my Foreign Service life, I did not earn money, contribute to my social security, or have any financial independence.

SILK • *Kwangju was a very rural city in an even more rural province. The main* industry was silk. I went to the factory many times. Young girls with tiny fingers stood at sinks of hot water, pulling apart the silkworm cocoons. There were many very labor-intensive processes, all done by young women who lived in the company's dormitories. These were not as bad as the bus girls' conditions but not an easy life. At the apex of the hierarchy was the woman who wove the brocade patterns that Korea is so famous for. She stood on a platform in the best light and brought these exquisite designs from her loom. She alone wore colored silk. Everyone else was dressed in the company's cotton uniform smock. She had the additional responsibility to help identify and then train her own successor. The training process took about five years.

Basketry was done in every rural village and baskets were fabricated by hand in some small factories. The basket market was located on the edge of the city, and I used to go there sometimes with a friend. Nearly everything was made, sold, and bought by women. It seemed like all the men were busy at other jobs while the women carried on the life of the city.

FIRST LOOKS • *In Kwangju, I started to look at calligraphy. I had seen it in* Seoul and in museums before I left New York but in the context of the surroundings — architecture, street signs, newspapers, art, pottery — it revealed a vibrancy and depth that I had not experienced before. Through my husband's work, we often met cultured people who made calligraphy for pleasure, and we met artists who incorporated it into their work.

At about the same time, I began to inquire about the tenets of Buddhism. I had been interested in Buddhism in a casual way for several years. This was a chance to follow that interest. Korea had once been a Buddhist country but in a reformation more sweeping than Martin Luther's, the monks were pushed aside and a more secular Confucianism had dominated since the successful ascendancy of the Chosun dynasty five hundred years before my time. There were still many temples and libraries of Buddhist scholarship, but the religious aspects no longer controlled society. It had returned to something more like its earlier manifestation — as a philosophy and moral system.

SUNCHON • *Near the town of Sunchon we went to an old temple, Songwang-sa.* The temple was built alongside a small river, opposite a low cascade over rocks. Like most temple sites it had an old growth forest. The Korean forests had been cut down for lumber and charcoal during the Japanese colonial occupation, and what little remained was destroyed in the war. The exceptions were temple grounds, which had nearly the only old trees in the country. Nobody cut those and the ancient trees gave temple precincts everywhere a sacred and contemplative atmosphere. We waded in the stream and dipped year-old Stephen in it.

One ancient wooden building had not had much renovation for most of a century. The monk caretaker took us to the tiny building where old calligraphy was stored. The faded boards were still legible but covered with dust, and some were greenish with mold. The original forest had crept up to the temple itself, and some plants were establishing themselves in a few of the floorboards. Several years later, I went there again for my own research and the entire temple had been repaired, repainted, and reroofed. The old calligraphy boards were renewed. The undergrowth was tamed for gardens around the temple buildings, and the monastery itself was vigorously in service. It was a place for reflection and serenity and the quality of that first visit remains with me.

OMENS • *My husband grew professionally and did an excellent job for the United States.* He was fluent in Korean and was frequently asked to give speeches for special events, holidays, and meetings. He brought together people from academic life, the arts, public media, the private sector, and generally addressed the role of cultural representative in a broad and lively way. All of this took a lot of time, and he was away from home a great deal.

Aside from a minor infection Edwin had that spring of 1966, we were healthy, busy, and productive. Edwin enjoyed the variety of his professional experiences. He also enjoyed his personal freedom. During these years in Kwangju, I became aware that he was involved with other women. A Korean man we knew very well, meaning to compliment me, said that I was like a Korean wife, patient and understanding, accepting my husband's outside liaisons without fuss or commotion. I was so humiliated and confused. At one point, Edwin told me the same thing himself, saying that it didn't mean a thing, that he loved me, and that the sex was only recreational. I was a few months pregnant again, and he attributed my distress over this revelation to hormonal changes. He didn't feel that his behavior outside had anything to do with our life at home. I minded his behavior very much but didn't know what I could do about it. Edwin also had taken to using the Korean term for wife, *yobo*, instead of my name. I minded that, too, but it continued all the rest of the years we were in Korea. Korean wives seemed to accept this sort of thing. My mother had lived with infidelity for years. I was isolated, without financial resources, with a toddler, pregnant, and with the examples of the women around me and my own mother, I thought I had no practical choices.

AILEEN • *Life went on. Despite all the private travails, I did enjoy my activities* — the Peace Corps, the English teaching seminar, the YWCA — and I loved being Stephen's mother. He was a very lively toddler, so bright and cheery, and it was just fun to be with him. Although I thought it was a bit soon, I was looking forward to the new baby. The time passed and in December we went to Seoul to await the birth. The embassy lent us an unoccupied house, and in the new year Aileen was born in the 121st Hospital in Seoul, a perfect, beautiful baby girl.

The next morning she had a band-aid on her heel. The doctor came in and sat down next to my bed. This was certainly not usual military hospital behavior. He asked if I knew what syphilis was. Yes, a kind of VD. I really didn't know much. Dr. Lee said that I was infected and so was Aileen. That was impossible. I had not been with anyone other than my husband. It must be a mistake. No, it was a positive diagnosis and they would test Edwin that day. All of us needed to be treated at once, as this was not a very recently acquired infection. I was crying and holding Aileen. Edwin came at the visiting hour and said I must have contracted the disease from a dirty needle at the Kwangju missionary clinic and passed it on to him. As I was soon to learn, that explanation was not possible. Syphilis is transmitted through sexual contact. We were treated and recovered from the infection. We never spoke about it again.

Aileen was an easy baby, nursing without fuss and sleeping well very soon. She got a nasty diaper rash, though, and I queried the missionary doctor about remedies. I wasn't alarmed; after all, practically all infants get diaper rash. Hers didn't clear up. Her skin looked as if it had burns. The doctor told me to dry her clothes in the sun and stop worrying. I was taking Aileen to be seen almost weekly, and her skin problem was worse. Her color was poor, and she had trouble nursing. The doctor said to boost her nutrition with formula and fortify it with a little sugar. I needed to relax and stop worrying. But the baby was not well. I told Edwin we should get another opinion. Finally, the first doctor sent us to a Korean pediatrician and, a few days later, I went back to the missionary for the report. It seemed that Aileen was sick, perhaps very seriously. There were three possible diagnoses, all very bad, and she should go to Seoul. By this time her face was swollen, her skin was fiery and tender, and she moved slowly. She hardly cried.

I made an appointment at the military hospital and took Aileen to Seoul. Edwin stayed in Kwangju. On the plane ride up, the rough patches on her face began to bleed from the cabin pressure changes. I went directly from the airport to the hospital. After a wait, the intake nurse took one look, hustled us down the hall, and a military doctor met us in the room.

The doctor was a wound specialist. He sewed together guys who had been torn apart in Vietnam. Babies and their frantic mothers were not his specialty. After some preliminaries and his first examination, we met again and he said that he had called for a pediatrician. With about fifty thousand troops, maybe as many as seven or eight thousand dependents, there was only one pediatrician in the country for all those children, and he was traveling to another base, but had been summoned back. They tested. I waited.

The pediatrician arrived a couple of days later. He ordered other tests and called me into the office. He said that Aileen was very sick. The good news was that Creutzfeldt-Jakob Disease (mad cow) was eliminated. He believed that it was going to turn out to be leukemia. I could hardly hear his voice. He spoke as clearly, patiently, kindly as it was possible to do, and I could hardly hear him. He said that he was giving an order that I could come to his office at any time. Where was my husband? He should come to Seoul. Over the next day or so, this doctor explained the illness. It was not an automatic death sentence. He said there was medicine in Japan, although leukemia this acute in an infant this young was unusual. He had sent in the paperwork to requisition the medicine and have it sent to Seoul. Requisitions? Paperwork? Another day passed awaiting approval for the requisitioned medicine. That night around midnight, the hospital called at the home where I was staying. Aileen was on the critical list.

The next day, the pediatrician met me early in the morning. The requisition request was approved. The medicine was being sent from Japan on an emergency basis and should arrive within a couple of days. Meanwhile, he, the pediatrician, had to leave. His father had died overnight and he had to return home for the funeral. He would be back in about a week. The physician we had met at the first was back on our case.

For part of each of the recent days, a senior wife, Ruth, had come to be with me. A lot of the time Ruth simply stood nearby, ready to say a kind word or just take my hand for a moment. Along came the doctor now back in charge of Aileen. His words are still audible to me. Right there, in that yellow hall, he said, "I cannot be responsible for the baby's survival." Ruth stepped very close to me and wrapped her arms around me. I couldn't hear what she said. Her voice in that corridor was muffled, very far away, as if at the end of a long tunnel. Aileen had been moved into a private room, partly to make room for the equipment around her, partly, I suppose, to spare the parents of the other infants.

Edwin met me at the hospital the next day. Aileen actually looked a little better after the transfusions. The leukemia medicine had arrived. They were waiting for her to be strong enough to use it. Edwin sent me away from the hospital, to see Stephen, to rest a little. I didn't want to go but he was very firm. I took a taxi and when I got to the house, my friend, Renee, was at the door. I saw it in her face. Aileen had died as I left.

But death generally is not tidy, and there are many things to follow. There were the funeral arrangements. There was a phone call requesting that I go to choose a coffin. Impossible to do. It was almost impossible to breathe. We had to tell our families. Edwin decided that telegrams were best, and we composed a message. My parents called at once. They had reservations, were ready to come to Korea immediately to be with us. Edwin said that we could not deal with the extra stress of my family and to tell them not to come. I must have told them because they didn't come.

Stephen was two years old. He wasn't able to understand anything except all the distress around him. He cannot remember any of these events. Renee folded him into her family for the days we were there, and me, too. I stayed awake, watching him, wanting to guard him from the unnameable, unknowable.

When we arrived at the chapel, the white box looked so small. At funerals, there is a custom that each person put a shovel of dirt on the coffin once it is lowered in the grave. I couldn't, though, and instead, scooped up the dirt with my hands, and dropped it over the tiny white coffin. In another day or two, we went back to Kwangju. In the bedroom, Aileen's crib was empty, bare, nothing of hers, not clothes, not toys, not photographs, nothing, was in the house. Nothing. It was absolutely empty. There was nothing to touch, nothing to hold, nothing to fold and put away.

For ASKing

With no other proof but memory
Exists that moon blue eye, a black curl creeping over the edge of an ear
A smile committed to nothing more — or less — than that moment
Trusting an untrustworthy future.

Edwin said that he had instructed his chief staff member to remove it all. He thought it better that I not see reminders. For decades, I believed that no picture of Aileen still existed. I worked hard to preserve her image, consulting my memory often, preserving as much detail as I could. She was not erased. She was a person in my family, loved as the other children are, not as long but as well.

In Kwangju, there was no one at all to talk to candidly. Edwin went back to work, coping in his own way, occupied by his professional responsibilities. He was unable to talk about Aileen or any of the events of this fatal year. Gradually, a silence as opaque as glass block grew around all of this sorrow. It was unreachable, carefully avoided, crashed into occasionally in the dark, but never opened or examined, never shared.

SEA VOYAGE • *Home leave was coming up. Three years had passed since we* had left Washington. I packed for three different things. We planned to take a ship, the *President Cleveland*, from Yokohama across the Pacific. There was to be consultation in Washington for several weeks followed by home leave in New York for two months. After that, we would move to a new posting in Taegu.

I bought presents for family members. During the three years of our absence, I had sent snapshots and now I assembled photographs and slides of Korea to share our life with them. I said goodbye to my friend Sook Ja and my students, and attended all the receptions that were part of official departure. Chung Ja, the girl who had helped me so much, was almost finished with school. My farewell present to her was the fees for the following year so that she was certain to graduate. The movers came. We left.

The voyage was my first ocean crossing. I remember most the splendid nights, full of starry skies and phosphorescent seas echoing each other. I had not seen such darkness before. We started out from Yokohama with storm warnings, and by the first morning at sea, we were in a typhoon. It blew for three days, keeping most of the passengers in their cabins, including Edwin. When I walked around the ship with Stephen, the outside doors were locked but parts of the decks were glassed in. I could see the huge gray swells and sprays of ocean like waterfalls. Most of the ship was nearly empty, especially the dining room. Stephen and I were not much affected by seasickness. Finally, the storm blew itself out, the sun shone, and the air was deliciously salty. Once everyone recovered, the meals became absurdly long and luxurious, the wine and conversation at dinner about equally old vintage. I walked the decks, breathing the marine atmosphere, and watching the rare seabird. For as much as a couple of hours at a time, I regained some equilibrium, felt nearly normal. I had been living on twin levels, walking, talking, eating, taking care of Stephen, all as if the world were arranged in its customary form. Just under the recognizable surface, was the upside-down confusion and silent mystery that surrounded Aileen. Her name was unspoken, and I began to guard her memory, to sequester the minutes of her life.

HOME LEAVE 1967 • *Home leave presupposes a home to go to. Many Foreign* Service people had a vacation place or another permanent place. Some had a room waiting for them with family members. We returned to New York for the bulk of the leave to an apartment we rented near Flushing. We went to Washington for the consultation and then to New York for the leave. Stephen was two and a half, old enough to have a lively personality and considerable vocabulary—at least half of it Korean—and his grandparents all wanted to enjoy him. We seemed to be in almost constant motion. Edwin wanted to visit friends of his at the University of Illinois and then spend a week on the beach in Hawai'i. I was exhausted from all that had passed.

    The summer of 1967 was the summer of love, sex, drugs, and rock 'n' roll, the emerging counter-culture, and nonviolence invaded by violence. Demonstrations had been going on all over the country and all over the world. In October, a huge demonstration took place on the Washington Mall. Hundreds of thousands of people, maybe more than a million, showed up from all over the country to protest the Vietnam War. They stood and sat around the reflecting pool, listened to speeches, and addressed the government about something that mattered. This space is substantially reduced now, by both the contemplative Vietnam Memorial and the bombastic WWII Memorial. But in 1967 the crowds used the same space where Marian Anderson sang in 1939. The statue of Lincoln in the memorial, which has become a temple to most Americans, symbolically overlooked the whole event. D.C. police and National Guardsmen lined the streets leading from downtown to the Mall. I saw girls with arms full of flowers give them to the soldiers and police as they went down 14th Street. I was about the same age as some of them, twenty-five, slim, and with a long braid down my back. I walked along with Stephen in a little folding stroller. I saw people so angry with the demonstrators that they were almost incoherent. A woman came up to me as she walked out of Garfinkel's department store, and she whacked me with her handbag. I remember her most for the blue rinse in her hair and her vituperative fury, striking me as if I was personally responsible for the entire downtown disruption. Other people were so angry with the government or Lyndon Johnson, they also were almost incoherent. Most people, though, seemed to feel that if they could listen and display their opinion, they could influence events, and the war would end.

    Edwin had meetings. Stephen was in a little plaid stroller, and I walked down to the Mall to see what was happening. The density of the crowd was amazing, but even more was the sense of purpose and intentionality of the huge mass of people. The antiwar movement was underway, developing its tactics and methods. On that day, people of all ages and shapes and sizes and colors met with one agenda. Late in the day, after the speeches, the main crowd dispersed and a subgroup went to the

Pentagon. I went back to our apartment. Edwin was upset that I had gone to the Mall.

NO MORE TALKING • *In New York, I was surprised that almost no one was* interested in where we had been or what we had seen and learned in Asia. Families on both sides were happy to look at and have Stephen's baby pictures, but they had no interest at all in Korea. To them it was the place where the Korean War had happened. The differing attitudes about the Vietnam War were very divisive. It was as if the dissension on the streets was replayed in miniature in the living room.

My family was more politically tuned in than Edwin's, and my father was prepared to send my brother to Canada if need be. When the lottery came in, Bobby got a lucky high number, but their opposition remained steadfast. Edwin felt that there were many factors the public didn't know and that the antiwar movement was in error. He and I did not agree on the prospects or purpose of the war and had not found a way to talk about it. I grew up in an environment where political conversation and disagreement were interesting, a stimulating element of social discourse. But by 1967, that kind of civil speech was disappearing fast.

Absolutely no one in either family was willing to talk about Aileen, either. She had died just a few months before. Edwin and everyone else expected me to get over it.

While in New York, we visited, shopped a little, and prepared to return to Korea. We renewed our immunizations and visas. For several months, I had been packing: household goods for the move from Kwangju, luggage for steady travel with two-year-old Stephen, preparations for a new post.

TAEGU • *We arrived in Taegu in the fall of 1967. Our house was on the campus* of Keimyung University, a private Presbyterian liberal arts college. The house was very large, with four big bedrooms, ample living room, nice dining room, two functioning indoor bathrooms, and a huge kitchen with a very capacious pantry. The house had a very lovely but neglected multi-level garden with fifty-year-old roses and rose trees.

Such a large house came with some disadvantages. It seemed as if half the embassy officers in Seoul needed to make a field trip to Taegu, and they assumed we would give them hospitality. Sometimes in the front hall there was luggage from different guests who were simultaneously departing and arriving. The house was an unofficial hotel. I bought extra linens and blankets, more dishes and glassware, and kept a very careful calendar. The house and our life there required heavy maintenance. After much trial and error, I hired an older woman to help with the housecleaning and to babysit as well.

I became pregnant with Daniel in the fall. I saw a Korean obstetrician, Dr. Lee, and was determined to have the baby in Taegu. Except for the usual discomforts early on, the pregnancy proceeded without any special problems.

Edwin was in a similar but larger professional role and entertained at home frequently. There were no caterers to hire, and I developed an extensive repertoire of dinners and lunches that could be expanded or contracted depending on the number of guests and how much advance notice I had. Twenty for dinner the following week was not so bad, fifty the following day was a challenge. Edwin continued to attend many functions in the evenings. A family dinner hour was rare.

WAR THREATS • *Not long after we arrived in Taegu the U.S. navy ship Pueblo* was captured in North Korean waters. The crew was held and mistreated for a year. The capture was a major event that renewed hostilities between the North and South and inevitably involved the United States. All civilian personnel were put on a fifteen-minute evacuation notice. This meant that you had to be ready to leave with fifteen minutes' notice, with one bag per person, to be carried in your hand. We were advised to pack the bag and leave it inside the door of our residence. The plan was to remove all civilians, if possible by helicopter to Pusan, and then by ship to Japan. If an alternative were needed, civilians might have to travel to Pusan by bus convoy or something else. I packed a bag for Stephen with food items, a couple of small toys and books, a few extra diapers and clothing. Some of Stephen's items went in my bag, along with my clean underwear, a tiny book of poetry, a small pad and pencil, our immunization records, and passports. The bag for Edwin had his pipe paraphernalia, clean underwear, and a shirt. Everyone had a sweater, too, since it was cold so late in the year.

Taegu had a large American military base with many families. The day after the crisis began, a group of wives asked to come and see me. The American system designates the highest-ranking civilian authority as the ranking person, and that made me the ranking wife. I was twenty-six and had served only in Seoul and Kwangju. They wanted to know what information I had. Did I feel that evacuation was likely, imminent? What were the guidelines I received? We talked about the possibility of sending home valuables like photograph albums or silver. I shared what I knew. These senior military wives would use our conversation to try and give guidance to the rest of the base wives. All we could do was make a guess and hope that none of the players would lose control of the situation. The intense anxiety about imminent war diminished, but the crisis lasted a year.

KEIMYUNG UNIVERSITY • *Shortly after our arrival in Taegu, Keimyung* University, where we rented our house, asked me to teach English as a second language. I was delighted to do it. Once I became a faculty member, I met people there and was asked to teach a yearlong course in the history of the Mediterranean world from the Neolithic Revolution to the fall of Rome. I used the United Nations world history series edited by the brilliant Jacquetta Hawkes. With the help of a student teaching assistant, I taught these courses in Korean. I learned as much as I taught, maybe more. The students liked to stop by my house for conversation, and I held my office hours in the front room that I used as a study. The State Department did not allow me to accept my salary, so I designated the money to create a scholarship fund for women studying history and politics. Most scholarship funds were available only to male students. This redressed the imbalance a little.

One of the most interesting aspects of being on the faculty was the insight into the politics of research. Korea was a tight dictatorship. Many ordinary books were prohibited. A person could be arrested, jailed, lose a job, for the possession of illicit materials. I knew people who were beaten up and fired. I loaned many books, sometimes several copies of the same book. My only stipulation was that the book was to be loaned to another reader and then another. I ordered books from the States and bought books in Japan and Hong Kong. If I left one in the faculty lounge or lying on my chair when I left a meeting, I hoped it would not be there when I came back and it never was. Then and now, I don't believe ideas and knowledge have any value unless they are passed along, tested, argued about, and revised. I don't believe we are stronger or more likely to prevail by being ignorant. My friends and colleagues craved ideas, discussion, and intellectual argument. For a number of years, it was against the law. I was safe enough. They were the ones who took the risks.

A book seems to be the safest and most certain way to pass along information with the meaning preserved intact. The Internet is a great tool, but information is modified, deleted, and censored in a moment. Its transmission and reception depend on batteries, electric grids, and money. A book connects us to its contents in a physical and intellectual way. We hold the author's ideas in our hands, unmediated by anything except our own curiosity.

We continued to have a busy agenda with cultural guests, Koreans and Americans. The American Brass Quintet was visiting and staying in the house when we got news of the murder of Martin Luther King, Jr. in April 1968. I wonder how it can be that we so fail to see ourselves in another person, how it is possible to commit such violence against ourselves. But it goes on and on. The quintet adjusted their program, and the concert went on that night as a memorial to King.

KYONGJU • *Near Taegu, in Kyongju, is the large Buddhist temple complex,* Bulguk-sa and Sokkoram. It is an inspiring and thought-provoking place. I went there several times while I lived in Korea and returned years later for my research on ancient books. The architecture and philosophy are classical and beautiful.

Haein-sa (Temple of Reflection on the Smooth Sea) is one of the principal temples of Korea, in the Gaya Mountains. I visited there several times, including an overnight retreat, when I lived in Korea. I did not return until the 1980s. If you arrive on foot, you will see a fast-running stream with calligraphy on a stone. The main buildings are built around an open quadrangle. Approaching the principle temple, a long, broad flight of stone stairs about thirty feet wide leads to the entry, which is painted with traditional, multi-colored designs. At dusk, a monk strikes a bronze bell to send the name of Buddha out into the world on the wind. It signals the monks that it is time for their prayers. People from all over the Buddhist world come to Haein-sa to study. As they climb the steps and cross the patio at the door, the colors of their robes glimmer in the late-day light — gray and blue-gray for the home order, and others from Korea and Japan — deep red from South Asia, mustard-flower gold from Tibet and Central Asia, black from Europe and America, all blowing on the air as the monks pass into the temple.

At midnight, the largest gong, twenty feet tall and eight feet in diameter, is struck with a long, heavy log suspended with chains from a beam. The deep basso bell sends its vibration ahead of the sound itself. You can feel it on your skin before you hear it. The sound wave moves through the pine forest, unsettling the needles. They move a little and whisper as they brush against each other. Even the moonlight seems to tremble just a little.

Haein-sa was first built in 802 A.D. It is home to the great Buddhist library that houses the *Tripitaka*, the complete Buddhist scriptures carved onto 81,258 wooden printing blocks. The *Tripitaka*, in blocks and printed, has been on the monastery's library shelves since 1398. Monks and scholars go there from all over the world. The open windows are so artfully designed that they have kept the treasures safe from moisture, rot, mildew, fire, and other hazards for centuries. A modern facility was constructed, with attention to the most scrupulous conservation techniques, but a test block began to deteriorate immediately and the original library remains home to the collection. The monks, in their various colors and with their many languages, come to this source, perhaps the oldest in continuous use in the world.

DANIEL • *For the Fourth of July, two weeks before the baby was due, Edwin* invited three hundred people to celebrate our national day, with a buffet dinner and fireworks in the garden of our house. There were no caterers. My helper and I, with another relative of hers, chopped and cooked, fried dozens of chickens, baked for days in the July heat. Edwin always enjoyed his role as host. People often complimented him on his hospitality. The receiving line went on and on. My doctor arrived for the party and made me go right inside. When it became dark, I held Stephen up to the window to see the fireworks.

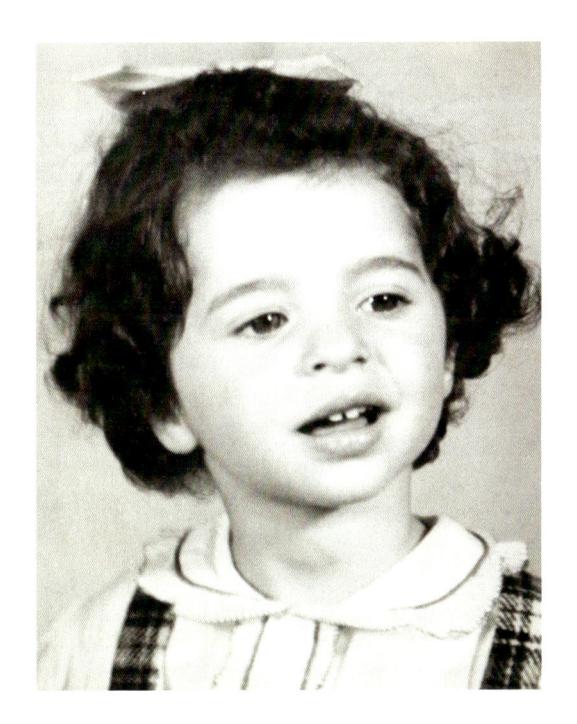

Age 3, New York City.

The cherry tree plate, painted at age 8, my first exhibited art, 1950.

Cherry Blossom Branch, Ink on paper, 26 x 12.5 inches.
I received my painting name for this work, Seoul, 1970.

Memories of the Ancients, Yang-dong, Korea, 1987/1998.

The Hand of Buddha, Ink on paper, 12.5 x 26 inches, 1970.

Working at Atelier Petit, Tokyo, 1976.

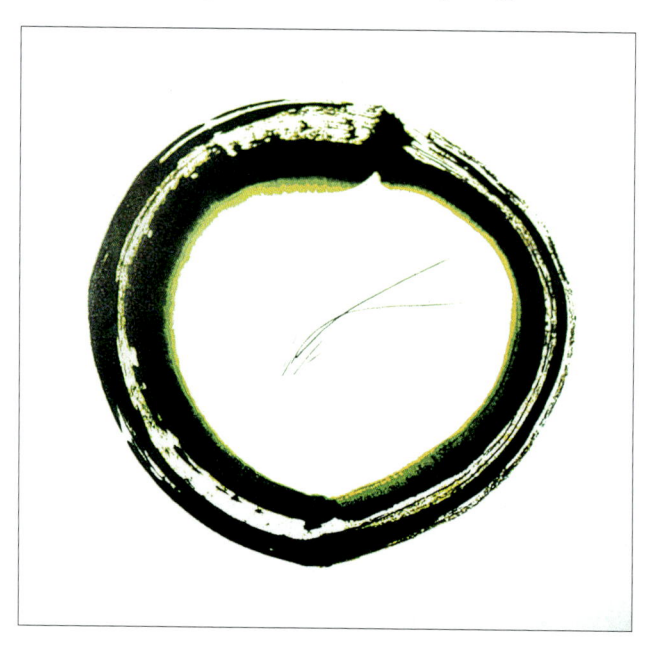

New Morning, Lithograph, 24 x 24 inches,
printed at Atelier Petit, Tokyo, 1976.

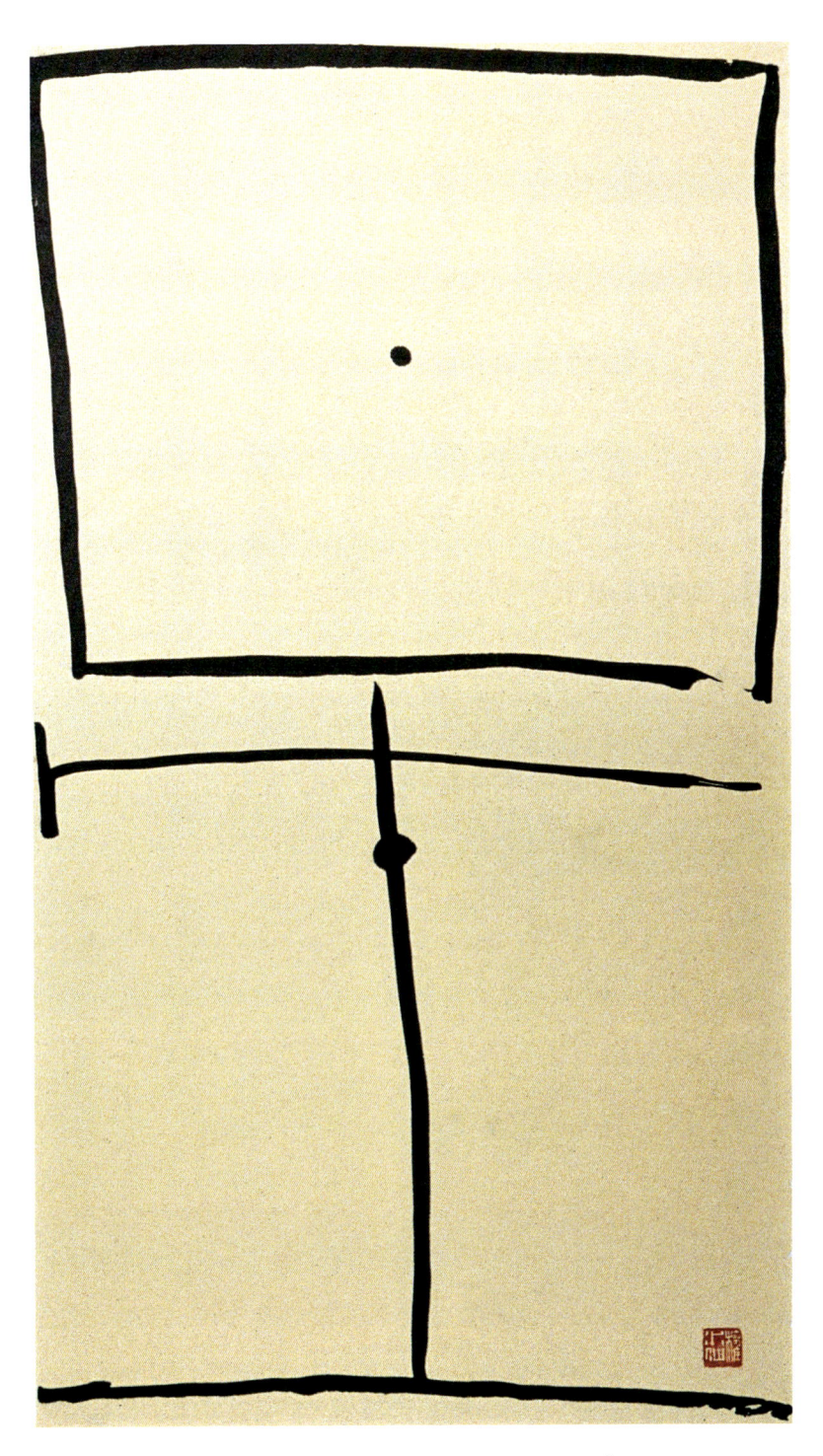

Hoshi (Star), ink on paper, 24 x 13.4 inches.
Exhibited with the *Sei Boku Kai* (Pure Ink Group), Ashiya, 1974.

One Picture of Two Trios, Ink on amate paper made by the artist, 16 x 20 inches, 1985.

Night Bird Serenade (Cliff poem), Ink and colors on paper, 1984.

In the garden, Tepoztlán, Morelos, Mexico, 1984.

Manzanas de Amadeus, Ink and pigments on canvas, 24 x 20 inches.

River in my garden at dusk, Tepoztlán, 1985.

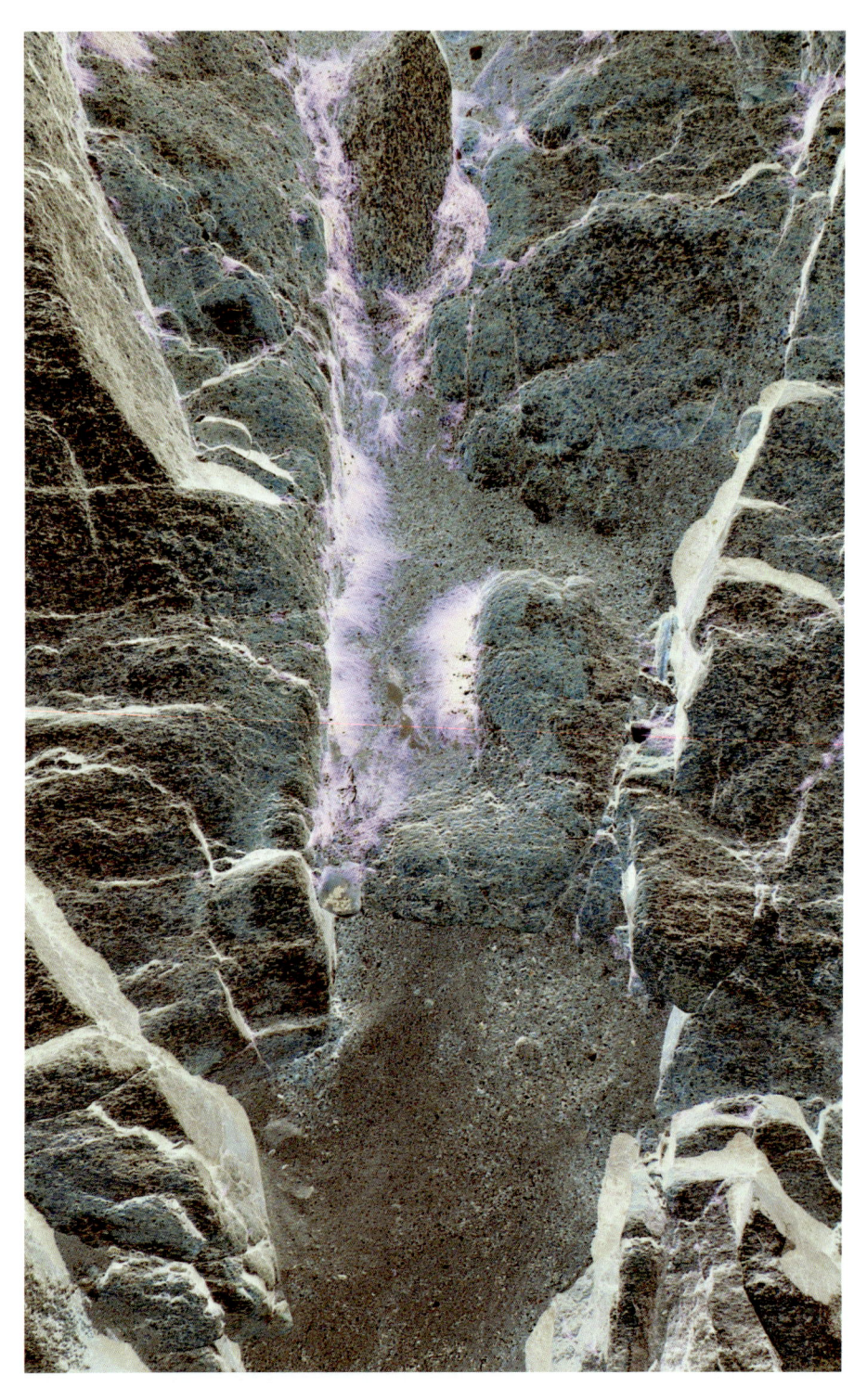

Tidal pool, Quiberon, Photograph, 4.5 x 6.5 inches, Quiberon, Bretagne, 2007.

French Fields, Oil on linen, 18 x 22 inches. Rochefort-en-Terre, France, 2007.

Water Lilies, Water color and digital painting,
9 x 12 inches, Santa Fe, NM, 2008.

Cut Fruit, Watercolor and digital painting,
9 x 12 inches, Santa Fe, NM, 2008.

Wielding a sledgehammer, Santa Fe, 1992.

The aspen bed, Santa Fe, 1992.

English Leaf, Photograph, 8 x 10 inches, London, 2001.

Wedding in our garden, 1997.

Breakfast spot on a bend of the Yellowstone River, Montana, 1997.

WaterLight, Kinetic photograph, 13 x 19 inches, 2010.

Despite my anxieties for this new child's well-being, everything went very smoothly and Daniel was born in Taegu on July 20. He was a big, hearty baby, cried and nursed and was altogether easy.

Stephen liked being the big brother. When Daniel was about four or five days old, I heard the little infant's cry start and then stop. I looked in on him. Stephen had the baby in his arms. He had lifted Daniel under his arms and was holding him against his chest. I disentangled them after a minute. He put his very worn and ragged blanket around Daniel and told me that babies need a blanket, not big boys. Even with the ordinary fraternal squabbling, they were good together all through their childhoods.

1968: ESCALATION ON ALL FRONTS • *All was not well in our family.* Edwin and I never spoke about any of the problems. If I brought up an issue, he said did I really think things were so bad, I was just tired, there was nothing wrong. Then he would bring me a present. He seemed to think it was all just my insecurities or something of that sort. However, he said that he needed to be able to discharge the tensions and strains of his work. He expected that if he was tired or under pressure, he had the right to take out those frustrations on me and even the children. I frequently had bruise marks where he grabbed me. I feared his moods. At the same time, I internalized the idea that his outbursts were my responsibility. If I could improve, do things better, be better, there would be no reason for him to become so angry. These attitudes are classic, but isolated as I was from any resource, I did not know it. There was no one to talk to or turn to. Though it was masked in public, the disharmony between us did not go away.

There was also violence in the United States all through this period. The antiwar movement was growing in strength and ferocity. Riots were a regular feature of the news. Protest movements were growing all around the world. In 1968 the streets of Paris were barricaded. Students rose and were crushed in Mexico. Federal troops in Mexico occupied one of their southern cities for the next fifteen years. Korean authorities cracked down on dissent and banned teachers, journalists, and playwrights.

In 1968, the year started with the Tet Offensive in Vietnam. President Johnson announced he would not seek reelection. America cascaded into a frenzy of fire and fury. All the calls for calm were futile. Things got worse and worse. Robert Kennedy was killed in June. Everything seemed to be disintegrating militarily and politically. In November, Richard Nixon was elected president. It seems that we haven't yet fully recovered from 1968.

POINTING • *I had had some exposure to Buddhist philosophy and tried to study and learn about it in a more orderly way. I practiced meditation and thought about the principles as much as I could understand them. I began, like all students, with the idea of being present, especially in my own life, and with the practice of of direct pointing. This practice guides us to be awake, mindful of the reality in front of our eyes. This idea is very simple and powerfully difficult to achieve. I began this practice in the mid-sixties. I continue to find it a useful guide as well as a perfect goal.*

The summer of 1968 marked four years since I had left Baltimore and Johns Hopkins University.

SEOUL 1969–1970 • *Edwin was offered a promotion to a more senior position* in Seoul. I said good-bye to neighbors, friends, colleagues, my teaching at Keimyung University, packed up the boxes and the children, and on a hot summer day we moved again.

We returned to Seoul in the summer of 1969 and again lived on the civilian side of the Yongsan housing compound. Daniel was a year old, a chubby, healthy baby, with blue eyes like crystalline candy, and curly brown hair. Stephen was four, always busy, about to start nursery school a few mornings a week. I was twenty-six, a mother and Foreign Service wife. I knew my roles well but had little idea of who I was or who I might become. I was busy, though.

I had not had a car since I used my father's Chevy Impala in my college days in New York, and I was agitating for one. Edwin didn't drive and a car was not crucial to him, but that summer we finally bought a third-hand Plymouth from someone who was being transferred. I met Myrt and Larry that summer in Seoul. They lived a few blocks away. We have continued our friendship for forty years.

Over the previous five years, I had done some writing for Korean publications and for the *Women's News*. I had written a few times for the *News* when it was just starting up as a mimeographed, stapled publication, on our first tour in Seoul, and had sent pieces from time to time from Kwangju and Taegu. The *Women's News* had evolved into a slick cover, monthly magazine, with articles on all aspects of Korean culture. It was professionally printed, with a distribution in the thousands. The editor-in-chief asked me to work with her. I enjoyed the writing and learned something about editing and deadlines. I stepped in as editor-in-chief for my last year in Seoul.

The USIS (United States Information Service) conducted a workshop for university and secondary teachers of English. This workshop took place for two weeks once a year. It was a major activity, with presentations by specialists in many fields, and it was prestigious for teachers to receive the invitation to attend. I had been teaching steadily and had had varied experiences, when I was asked to manage and conduct the program. It required about eight months' preparation and became a nearly full-time activity as the conference approached.

There were a lot of occasions for official entertaining, with plenty of drinking. Waiters usually have water on their trays now, but not then. I used to ask for tonic with lime, to distinguish it from the vodka and gin tonics with lemon. I was becoming a good cook, which I enjoyed, and a good caterer, which I liked less. By this time, I had devised a system to keep track of official events, citing dates, occasions, guest lists, expenses, menus, subjects discussed, and so on. The government reimbursed expenses at a very inadequate level. I think you could claim up to a dollar per guest for a reception and three dollars for dinner served. A wife's services as events planner, linguist, cook, hostess, secretary, information reporter, bookkeeper, and public presence were not reimbursable. Spouses received no social security credit, and still were not permitted to accept financial compensation for professional work outside the embassy.

A wife also remained subject to formal review by her officer-husband's superior (and much of the information still was gathered from the superior's wife; that was part of her job). Every aspect of her life was commented on: how she dressed and brought up her children, her language skills, cultural adaptability, personality traits, relationships within the embassy community and the local one, what activities she followed to further American interests. Canada, Japan, and some other countries recognized the nature of the spousal role. Some gave the wives a choice: not travel to post, stay at home with the children, have a private life with stability and continuity, or accompany the officer to post, participate in an official capacity, and receive recognition and some form of compensation. A peripatetic life has many rewards, but they come at a very high price.

PICKING UP A BRUSH • *On our return to Seoul, we were hardly unpacked* when I started painting lessons with Park Se Won, the chair of the Fine Arts Painting Department at Seoul National University. He was a well-recognized traditional painter working in the Chinese southern school style, and he took a few private students. I was fluent in Korean by then, and I had been gradually developing dual interests in calligraphy and Buddhist philosophy.

Professor Park started off by demonstrating the correct stance, posture, and arm position for the brush. He demonstrated the grinding of ink, adding water drop by drop and rubbing the ink stick against the inkstone until the well was filled and black as velvet. He demonstrated the painting of a horizontal line. Every two or three weeks, a new line was added: horizontal, then vertical, diagonal, and curved. Professor Park demonstrated simple flower paintings, trees, bamboo, and, ultimately, landscapes. I had thought of the twisting trees and sheer, rocky mountain faces in typical Asian painting as stylized or idealized visions, but after living in East Asia for a while, I understood that the traditional paintings are realistic interpretations of actual places. Professor Park asked for trust, fidelity, and practice. I wanted to give all three to this study.

SEEING THE FIRST LINE • *I practiced every day. From the first, this method* of learning, that is, imitation based on trust in the teacher, made sense to me. It echoes the way dancers learn, and young children. It was possible to slow down enough to see what I was doing. Unless my attendance was officially required elsewhere, I usually practiced at the dining table while the children were having their naps in the afternoons. Very soon after starting painting lessons, I saw a line. The brush crossed the paper slowly, hovering at the surface. The fine mulberry fibers pulled the ink from the brush at the plane where the fibers were felted down into the sheet. Everything slowed down. Ted Williams, the Red Sox star, described the ball on a fast pitch as slowing down so that he could see it, even the stitching; and feeling he had all the time in the world, he hit it perfectly.

My line was my epiphany. When I saw the line and the space inside of it, I saw a place of silence, first in the line and then in myself. It became possible to imagine an alternative to the noise and violence of the world as I had experienced and observed it.

Much of my young adult life felt like an impersonation; I wore a mask, played the roles required by whatever circumstances I happened into, my identity unclear. With a brush in my hand and in the silence of the line, I found myself to be real.

Park Sun-saeng watched my progress and gave me the guidance I needed. The following spring, in a coincidental echo of the cherry tree I had made as a child, I painted a branch of cherry blossoms. It was qualitatively different from what I had been able to do before. Park Sun-saeng said that it was time to sign the work. In Korea, it is the custom for the teacher to choose the name the artist will use, a name that implies the artist's character and style. My teacher chose Seol Gyae, meaning Snow Valley. The name suggests an austere, solitary place. It is full of literary allusions and implications, a big name to grow into.

Shortly afterward, Edwin and I took another excursion to Hong Kong with the children. We saw the Tiger Balm Gardens, took the tram to Victoria Peak, and went to the beach at Repulse Bay. I went to some shops specializing in Chinese art materials and bought powders for paints: Chinese indigo, *Shin kiang* yellow from petrified tree branches, Japanese red from Mexican cochineal, ink sticks with lovely designs embossed on the face, and two sticks of jade the size of my index finger for my new name. I brought those jade blanks back to Korea. A carver, a specialist in making *hanko*, designed two beautiful companion name-stamps. Each has a tiny figure on the top, and on the printing surface the pair have the mirror image of the characters for the name, one positive and one negative. Imagine making these works of art fit the meaning of the words and the style of the artist, in reverse, so that they will print correctly, all on a stone surface half an inch square.

THE WAR WENT ON • *We felt very strongly the presence of the war in* Vietnam. Korea sent two battalions to fight, and they went to very difficult sectors. The soldiers proved to be tough and resourceful fighters. Public opinion was divided but not expressed openly, as Korea was in the midst of a tight dictatorship. They had a theory that economic democracy came first, empowering people, creating opportunity and political democracy would follow in time. Korea is the only country I have heard of where this theory was applied and actually seems to have worked. In the late sixties, however, the economic side was just getting underway. Political control permeated all aspects of public life.

The same kind of restrictions applied to Americans in Korea. We were not permitted to express personal political views in public. It was discouraged even within the embassy community. The strictures were clear and overt, although not expressed as formal policy. I felt the same as I had all along. I am a pacifist. I had studied and written about American involvements in Vietnam and other places as an undergraduate and graduate student. I had seen the great demonstrations in 1967 and '68. The commotion and messiness of dissent at home were very evident to us, ten thousand miles away. More of us opposed the war as the years wore on, and more of us spoke about it. As in America itself, the embassy community was not of one mind.

Our tour came to an end late in the summer of 1970, and I packed up again, children, boxes, and all. As we were leaving Korea, my husband received his next assignment. He was to be stationed at Hué, in Vietnam, with home leave and a short language course before departure. I think he believed that the war was a necessary evil and that we couldn't just leave and let chaos prevail. He would not speak against the government he served. In the end, of course, America left under much worse conditions. Chaos and suffering were the norm for a long time after. We traveled under the cloud of disagreement and unhappiness, kept submerged under the guise of false normality.

Six years before I had been a new bride, just leaving my studies at Johns Hopkins. Physically I moved from Baltimore to Washington, to Seoul (five houses and apartments), Kwangju, Taegu, and back to Seoul. I crossed the Pacific Ocean four times, saw San Francisco, Hawai'i, Hong Kong, Okinawa, Guam, and Tokyo. I had become a wife, mother, teacher, speaker of Korean, sometime writer, and had picked up a paintbrush. When I left in 1964, the Vietnam War had been escalating for several years and it seemed like it would have to end. Six years later, President Nixon and Henry Kissinger didn't seem any closer to ending it or to having any intention of ending it. I had given birth to three children and two were going back with me.

ANOTHER HOME LEAVE • *Edwin was in Washington to have consultations* preparatory to his assignment to Vietnam. The official policy was that a limited number of families could go to a safe haven in Asia, Thailand, or the Philippines, in exchange for the officer accepting a longer assignment. There were already too many families in Bangkok and Manila, and he was turned down but he kept trying to arrange the family safe haven. At the safe haven, the family was "on the economy," which meant finding their own housing, without allowances for school or medical care, and without the protection of diplomatic passports. It was an economy inflated and stressed by the proximity of the war and the large number of civilians who were in residence because of it. Edwin was adamant that he wanted us to be nearby where he could travel easily and see us more often.

Home leave was even more difficult than the previous time. We rented a small apartment in Manhattan for two months. Our time with relatives in New York was tense and inharmonious. His family was very anxious for his safety. Our life was so different from their experience that it was hard to find any common language. The children were our main topic of conversation. Visiting my family presented even more difficulties. Everyone in my family was outspoken and antiwar. That fall of 1970 my brother was twenty. He had become immune to military service through the lottery. My mother was nervous and blamed every problem on the threat of the draft and the war. Dad was still involved with Cammy. Relations between my parents were as acrimonious as ever.

FIVE

Annandale

WHILE WE WERE IN WASHINGTON, we searched for a house to buy. Neither one of us had ever lived in any kind of suburb. Edwin thought it would be the best environment for the boys. It was a kind of ideal life he had long imagined. We contacted a real estate agent and looked around the Virginia suburbs, deciding on a house in Annandale, off Sleepy Hollow Road. The street was barren but in back of the house a quarter acre of woods was bordered by a little brook. I can only recommend that before anyone signs a contract for a house in the suburbs, he or she should be required to produce a driver's license. In persuading me to live in the suburbs, Edwin made the commitment to learn how to drive. That never happened. In any case, we gave our down payment and moved there in January 1971.

My husband wanted this house very much. He said that if he were to be killed in Vietnam, we would have a nice place to live. I think he meant well, and it made him feel that he was fulfilling his role as provider for the family. He also continued to insist that the children and I go to a "safe haven" in Asia, and he worked relentlessly to make that happen. When his short course in Vietnamese was finished he was sent to a French language course, although by then French was irrelevant in Vietnam. It did give him time to advocate for permission for us to go to Thailand, which was eventually granted.

Meanwhile, Stephen started public school kindergarten and Daniel went to a sweet co-op nursery school three mornings a week. My parents came to visit a few times, always with a lot of tension between the men. Mother came by herself from time to time, often when she and Dad were at an especially incendiary point. She had never liked the idea or practice of motherhood, but she enjoyed being a grandmother and the boys enjoyed her, too.

I bought one of the best cars I have ever owned. It was a little Alpine Sunbeam, called a Cricket in the U.S. Just large enough for our family, it was sunny green with a stick shift. It was a joy to drive and ahead of its time. It took me everywhere.

Culture shock is the confusion, missed cues, and anxiety that a person feels when entering a new and unfamiliar culture. The worst culture shock I have ever experienced was right there in Annandale, Virginia. I was more disoriented arriving in Virginia than I had ever been in Korea. It took me a while to get used to suburban living. It was never a good fit. I tried to cope with these varied stressful circumstances: Vietnam, Edwin's upcoming assignment, the move to somewhere in Asia on the one hand, and suburban family life and the political environment on the other.

By 1971, we were preparing to leave for a new post, my husband for Danang (Hué had been demolished in the Tet Offensive, requiring a change of assignment) and the children and I for Bangkok. We took the long series of immunizations, including the horrendously painful series of rabies vaccinations (rabies was very prevalent then in Thailand). We listed the house with a rental agency, contacted packers, gave the children's winter clothes to Goodwill, shopped for necessities for our new life, called in the movers, and packed our bags. Parents came to say good-bye. I sold the Cricket back to the dealer. Stephen's first grade class gave him a farewell party. We secured our visas and reservations. On the morning of our departure, my husband put the luggage in the rental car and left for the office to pick up the tickets, intending to meet us at the airport. I was going to make sure the utilities were off, lock up the house, and drive over to National Airport with the boys.

GOING NOWHERE • *A little later, the phone rang.* He said to quickly call the telephone company and be sure the phone was on so he could call me back. Ten minutes later, I learned that the Danang assignment had been canceled, and we were not going anywhere. The house was completely empty. I spent the next few hours on the still functioning phone, turning back on the utilities, canceling the rental listing (fortunately the prospective renters had not yet signed the lease contract), extending the car rental, and generally doing what had to be done for life to be resumed. Exhausted by the events of the recent weeks and hours, we went for a few days to a little resort out in Shenandoah. It was beautiful in the clear air and blue skies of early fall. Confounded as we were, we could hardly appreciate it. We didn't know if we would stay in Annandale or be reassigned elsewhere. Should Stephen go back in school? Should we continue to rent a car or try to get back the one I had taken to the dealer just two days before? Since leaving Korea, we had spent more than a year in constant motion, most of it without any definite knowledge of where we would be in a couple of months' time. We returned to the house, rented some furniture on a weekly basis, and waited for our future.

I had been growing up during the years in Korea and left feeling that I was competent, professional, and respected for my capabilities as teacher, editor, and participant in civic activities. I had picked up a brush and ground ink. Much as I loved being with my children, it wasn't a complete life for me. Now, in Annandale, I was occupied with domestic necessities to the exclusion of almost everything else. Edwin went to the office on the bus line about six blocks away, but for absolutely everything else he needed transportation in the family car, and I was the only driver. Edwin was an avid golfer, and many weekends I dropped him off at the course and returned for him after the "nineteenth hole." I still had the set of clubs he had given me in Seoul but had no aptitude or taste for it. The clubs stayed reproachfully in the closet.

The marriage was laboring under all these stresses, and we had other difficulties. Over time, even perhaps from the beginning, it had been evident to me that our sexual tastes were not alike. Perhaps because our sexual experiences were so different in kind and degree, our expectations were not in harmony. By the early seventies, this difference was acute. Some of Edwin's practices were uncomfortable, even painfully disagreeable to me. I could not help but think of his experiences with other women during the preceding years. I did not manage to change myself enough to change my life then.

Suburban Washington had an evolving culture in the early seventies. I became acquainted with the neighbors and mothers from the nursery school. One woman I was very friendly with had two children, one Daniel's schoolmate, and the other a new baby. By taking work home, juggling child-care, and with a supportive husband and family, she managed to preserve her career at a major Washington law firm. Another mother at the co-op school was a physician, managing to maintain a part-time practice and care for her family. Several others were politically active. With the future so uncertain, not knowing from week to week where I would be, I could not join the women who worked and by inclination would not join the ladies who lunched. I had little leisure and little relief from the anomie of my situation. Alienated, isolated physically and emotionally from family and friends, I was despairing and lost. I did not make any journal entries or write the long letters I had sent for many years.

I took the boys to the Washington museums as often as I could, about once a month. It was a major undertaking, with driving, parking, a stroller, and all the impedimenta that such outings with a toddler and five-year-old required. Not much time for study or contemplation.

Government employees and their spouses were not supposed to support political candidates or even donate to their campaigns. I did join the League of Women Voters and found the style of consensus-building and mutual self-education to be interesting.

I had learned about gardening in my various houses in Korea, and worked in the Annandale garden as much as I could. In Seoul, I had been painting most days at least for a few hours. In this house there was no place to do it. I had my beautiful colors and brushes and tried to practice. I took things out, used the little dining room for an hour, and then put everything away again. A few acquaintances from Korea days had moved back to the D.C. area and when I saw them they seemed happy, and I suppose they thought the same about me. I had developed an ability to compartmentalize my feelings, to act the necessary part as the situation required. In public, at least, I appeared to be all right.

I was profoundly lonely in a way I never experienced before or since. I was separated from the person I had become in the last six or seven years, and was not yet the person I was going to grow into. It is a cliché to talk about the despair of the suburban housewife because it is so widely experienced as true. I didn't have confidence enough to put first things first. The years in Korea were my young adult life, and I felt that almost all of it was gone. I started to do yoga around this time and found the contemplative focus helpful but difficult to achieve. A box of glass bricks appeared to surround me. I was visible but dim, unclear, and distorted to myself.

We were assigned to Washington for the immediate future. A great deal of our time was spent thinking about the next assignment, considering possibilities as they arose. Officers are assigned for "the good of the service," but there were no prohibitions on advocating for a post you wanted. At one point Edwin wanted to go to a West African post. We had dinner with acquaintances recently returned from that post. They had been in the service about fifteen years. He was a very successful officer. As the men chatted about the important political and economic issues, the wife told me about her survival system. They had eight children, named alphabetically. She liked babies and didn't like the diplomatic life. At each new post she became pregnant. A baby could mean up to about a year of freedom from most career-related requirements for the wife. A new baby was her price for accepting a new post.

As for the post itself, we learned that there were logistical and school issues as well as health concerns. Logistics were covered by a cooperative effort among the diplomats of various countries, who took a communal shopping list on their trips to Brussels, Rome, or London and brought back supplies like thread, band-aids, writing paper, and potatoes. The post was an excellent career opportunity and there was also a monetary differential, paid because of the hardship conditions. We could send Stephen, then seven years old, to boarding school in Rome or leave him at one of the excellent boarding schools in the U.S. I thought I could cope with the logistics but was adamant that I was not willing to part from my son. I offered instead to stay in Washington. For the first time, I refused to go. Edwin was determined not to go without me.

Other possibilities emerged. Finally, there was a perfect fit in Osaka. My husband was assigned to a year of Japanese language school. Wives still were not entitled to language training at the Foreign Service Institute, although I was assured that there were classes at post. I was glad to go to Japan.

I had learned by now to look carefully at various aspects of a post and take nothing for granted. After living in Korea and visiting Japan several times during the sixties, I thought I had at least an inkling of how it would be. The school for the boys, Canadian Academy in Kobe, was reputed to be excellent, health care was available, and you could even drink the water.

The year of language school passed. In the summer of 1973, the house was sold, I packed up again, said good-bye again, and left Annandale without regret.

SIX

Japan

WE ARRIVED IN OSAKA and went immediately to visit our future home in Nishinomiya, a small city between Osaka and Kobe. My predecessor was packing up and making her farewells. She found time to share some information and show us around the house. All of us had slept off the jet lag during a week in Tokyo when Edwin had consultations, and so had energy for exploring while we waited to move in. In that first week, we went to the top of Rokko-san, and I registered the boys at school. From the bus stop we climbed four wide flights of stairs up the mountainside to the front door. Canadian Academy was in a picturesque location overlooking the Inland Sea and the harbor.

Long distance we had agreed to purchase our predecessors' car, a little gray 1967 Datsun Bluebird. It had no heater to speak of, but everything else was as good as Japan ever made. I drove it around Japan for the four years we lived there. It is probably still on the road.

On a hot summer afternoon, we moved to our new house. We stepped through the door in the wide wooden gate and entered the walled garden. It was a delicious mixture of short palms, tall pines, and bamboo set in a lawn inside the wall. There was a two-seat glider that the boys immediately and permanently commandeered for their games.

The house was white stucco, two stories with a terracotta tile roof, built for a merchant in the 1920s. It was a gracious house, with a music room off the living room, a dining room seating twelve, a large kitchen with a pantry and butler's pantry and bar, but no butler in our time. There were four bedrooms upstairs. For a while the boys wanted to sleep together, so we had a guest room and a room for me, used also as a second guest room. The house had many nooks and crannies and a tiny house behind it that in the past had been for servants. It was wonderful for hide and seek. We also inherited a big white cat, Shiro-chan, from our predecessor's child, a girl about Stephen's age.

The Kansai region of western Japan swelters in the summer. It is more humid even than Washington. Many afternoons Stephen and Daniel, then eight and five, played complicated, lengthy games of their own invention. Eventually, they played in a mixture of Japanese and English language between themselves and with the Swiss boys who had just moved in next door. We became acquainted with the Japanese medical system right away when, in our first week in the house, Stephen's knee and the window had an unhappy meeting. A few stitches and a lemonade were all the treatment required.

The children started the school year at Canadian Academy at the end of August. I accompanied the boys on the train to Kobe and stayed as they boarded the school bus there. At the end of the first week, shy Daniel, just starting kindergarten, said to me that they could go on their own from then on. Didn't I know that schoolboys didn't have their mother tagging along? Stephen was supposed to look after Daniel and he did, until the train arrived. At that point they parted company until the afternoon return. After a little while longer, I stopped meeting the train. They were confident to come and go, and their orbits included shops and the homes of friends in the neighborhood. One day when they wanted to go somewhere, in the ordinary parental way I said, "We'll see." Stephen quickly answered, "Mom! 'We'll see' means almost no! Say almost yes!" I think I did.

In Japan, on the first day of school each year the children are sent home with earthquake disaster information: where they will be taken in case the school is destroyed, how to plan a family meeting place, measures to take in a catastrophe. Earthquakes are an almost daily reality in Japan. Houses are deliberately built with spaces between the lath, and sections are not firmly attached so that they can separate with minimal damage. Bamboo is often planted around the foundation so that the strong web of roots will reinforce the structure.

A few weeks after we moved in, our first significant earthquake shook the house. The boys were upstairs and I was in the kitchen. I ran into the hall and saw that the staircase had separated from the wall. I edged the boys down and we went outdoors. Once the aftershocks died down we called a repairman. He explained the system and showed me where the wall had been repaired repeatedly for decades. It worked as it was supposed to, with no harm done.

On quiet afternoons, I often took a bath in the deep claw-foot tub. In warm weather the window was open, brushed by a pine branch. Otherwise the world, in Nishinomiya at least, was at rest. Around two o'clock, the music of a flute drifted over from the house next door where the grandfather played in his garden in the afternoons.

One note from a bamboo flute
Resting on the air
Like a swallow on the porch rail

I had not had Japanese-language training in Washington and started some lessons at the Kobe consulate. The teacher designed the lessons for a wife, with the subject matter mostly revolving around cooking, shopping, and so on. When I started calligraphy I stopped the consulate lessons.

CALLIGRAPHY: A NEW LINE OF INQUIRY • *Weeks after arriving in Japan,* I had a calligraphy teacher, Tanino Shigeko. She was two years younger than I, twenty-nine when we met. She and I arranged for her to come to the house on Wednesday mornings to give me calligraphy lessons, which continued for two years. Her gifts to me were many, and she opened the way for me to find one of the most satisfying parts of my life.

Shigeko-San was the best person for me to meet. I had started painting in the guest room upstairs and showed her some of the work. My earlier ink paintings of bamboo and trees became the first basis of our relationship. She considered me an artist. Our Wednesdays were passed entirely in Japanese. She demonstrated, talked a little, guided my hand. We started going to exhibitions together and often had lunch to talk over the work. And then to talk about whatever there was to talk about. My language capacity grew with this encouraging regime and so did my painting.

Shigeko-San went on a trip. In her absence, I experimented, writing my first poem in Japanese, in calligraphy. Over the next months, I tried many things. I attached the brushes to the kitchen broom handle and covered newspaper with large characters. For brushes, I tried crumpled paper, handfuls of pine needles, a mop. At the same time, apart from the calligraphy practice, I set myself the task of painting bamboo studies every day as an exercise to understand both the plant and *sumi-e* (brush painting) more deeply. As the year progressed, I gradually removed everything extraneous, finding the essential qualities, until a simple spray of stalks with a few leaves seemed to sum up the flexible strength of it. I followed this practice and felt well acquainted with bamboo. It took a year before I began to sign my work, using my name-stamps. My painting name is pronounced Sekkei in Japanese and has much of the same feeling that it has in Korean, with references to classical literary imagery. It is a poetic name in Japan, and I worked hard to grow into it. The year's experimentation and practice contributed to my eventual style in calligraphy, which turned out to be spare and simple. Later the same values came to characterize my poetry.

Calligraphy as an artistic form is sensual, aesthetic, tactile, and literary. The brush and the paper have a relationship that is moderated by the artist's intention. I could see the ink being pulled onto and into the paper. I learned to be aware of the feel and smell of grinding ink, to see the lake of blackness spread over the black landscape of the grinding stone.

In Nishinomiya, time seemed to lengthen out. When I was painting I made a world of my own. I was very busy with the rest of my life, official responsibilities and family. I studied a little of Buddhist philosophy. We were friendly with a Buddhist monk, Sato-Sensei, who was a senior monk at a nearby temple. He and his American wife had children about the same ages as Stephen and Daniel, and we visited together from time to time. Sato-Sensei was an artist of considerable reputation. He spoke with me and guided me for a while. I found ideas that resonated then and have remained part of my life. I am most influenced by the precepts to do no harm, to aspire to point directly toward reality, to have forbearance in the face of suffering and difficulties so that these difficulties can be recognized and alleviated. Through this practice I started to develop mindfulness, awareness.

OUT IN THE WORLD • *I met the mother of one of Daniel's classmates at the* school. We enjoyed each other's company and went to a few exhibitions together. I invited her to my house for tea. In the course of her visit she asked about my painting. I showed her some new work. She said that she hoped I would allow her to bring her husband over sometime, as he would enjoy them as much as she had. I mentioned it to Edwin and said that I wanted to have them over soon.

We invited them for dinner along with another couple, and as the evening progressed, she reminded me that we were going to look at the paintings. Her husband was as interested as she. He was the chief officer of the Mitsui Bank in Kobe, which was being remodeled and, as is normally the case, it had a large gallery. Would I like to show my work there for the inaugural exhibition coming up in a couple of months? I told him that I painted for myself, not as a professional artist. He was still eager to have my work, maybe even more so. Rather stunned, I agreed to the exhibition. We shook hands and he invited me to the bank to see the space. I had no concept of what it might take to produce an exhibition for a gallery, never mind one in a prestigious bank.

Many people helped with advice and logistical assistance. The bank sent out the invitations. They made sure the press was there, as this was an event for the bank as well as for me. They arranged a very generous reception. I had never installed an exhibit and soon enough was sent away so the experts could do their work. I returned to a show elegantly hung, with flowers arriving and people bowing to me. The show was very well attended. The reviews were good and a few pieces were sold. It was a wonderful, serendipitous beginning. I did not know then that this was going to be my work. I only knew then that painting made me feel like myself, whole and at peace.

Meanwhile, Shigeko-San had taken a few of my lesson sheets to her *sensei*, her teacher, in Nara. She belonged to a group of disciples and protégées of this artist and wanted him to see the work I was doing. Their intention was to create a modern calligraphy based on a return to the root meanings imbedded in the characters. Their group was called Sei Boku Kai, the Pure Ink Group. They invited me to participate in their next exhibition in Luna Hall in Ashiya, a nearby city. I exhibited two pieces with them, both single large characters in the modern style with traditional framing. They politely chatted with me about the work, theirs and mine. I had a feeling of fellowship despite the gaps in my language skills. I was improving but not yet ready for full-scale discussions of the philosophy of art.

KYOTO • *Kyoto is about an hour from Nishinomiya by train. Like everyone else,* I had a train pass and I used it often. Many Tuesdays I went to the Hankyu Line station just after the boys went to school. With one simple change, I was in Kyoto by ten o'clock. I got off at different stops and explored the city. I went into little traditional shops, museums, all sorts of places. The people of Kyoto have a distinctive accent, derived from the eras when the court was there, before it moved to Tokyo in the late nineteenth century. As I learned new vocabulary, sometimes I incorporated this pronunciation and so wound up with somewhat inconsistent speech. In my observation, people are about the same everywhere, and Japanese people are as kind, helpful, and modest — and as thoughtless and arrogant — as people anywhere else. Supposedly, the Kyoto people are the most snobbish in all Japan. But on those quiet days when I walked in a store and asked about a piece of pottery, the shopkeeper usually explained what was valued and why, and then let me handle and admire a piece as long as I wanted. The galleries were interesting. Minami had wonderful contemporary art. Away from the hubbub of the openings, it was easy to find a lot to look at.

Sato-Sensei had a friend in Kyoto who owned Gallerie Kan. He thought I should go to see him. On the street level at the site of his ancient home was a tearoom with light lunch food. The second floor was a beautiful, spacious gallery. Above that was an open room with banquettes and a floor covered in gray carpet and piles of pillows. There were happenings and an open salon where, in the evenings, artists dropped in to talk to each other, or sometimes to read poetry or an excerpt from a play. I was invited to have an exhibition in the gallery for April 1974.

Again the gallery was a wonderful host, preparing a beautiful reception, making sure the press was in attendance, and inviting many artists from the whole region. Many people I knew came to the opening. The articles that appeared over the following week were flattering. Guests came regularly during the weeks the show was up. I was happy to return to Kyoto several more times and stay in the gallery, available to anyone who might come by to see the show.

In Japan, most people did not use their personal names, but it was common among artists and other bohemian types. People I knew personally usually called me Susan or Susan-San. The opening reception was crowded, and I as the artist was supposed to be talking to the guests. Unfortunately, one went up to my husband, and instead of addressing him by his name said, "Oh, so you are Susan-San's husband!" Edwin was greatly upset by this lack of proper recognition and what he seemed to feel was a lack of respect. Within minutes, he had my coat and my arm and we were on our way home.

It turned into a terrible evening. I was angry to leave my event. We argued. Once home it became worse yet. Upstairs, he threw or pushed me so hard it damaged the door. The marks were slow to fade.

MEANWHILE, BACK AT THE FOREIGN SERVICE • *My husband's usual* schedule was to leave before seven in the morning and, if he was coming home for dinner, return around seven-thirty or eight in the evening, in time to say good night to the boys. Many evenings each week, he had a program or reception to host or attend. He required me to attend many of them. So many that I finally limited official events to three times a week and refused to leave the boys on weekends. I made it work but it had a high cost.

I started wearing my "uniform" for functions: a long black skirt with a turtleneck and a necklace. For summer, the change was to a long white linen skirt and short-sleeved top. I have never had a major interest in clothes, and this outfit served me well for years. One exception was my New Year's dress. I bought some beautiful wine-colored ribbon silk and made a high-neck, short sleeved dress that fell in one line from neck to floor with just barely enough ease to dance in. I wore that dress every year in Japan and still have it. It is waiting to be a quilt some day.

We had a great many guests from the United States, cultural figures who had done significant work, as well as some friends and relatives. One of my favorites was Louise Nevelson. She was a very large presence, and wore dramatic clothes and huge hats. She was best known as a sculptor, using found objects to create her assemblages. She told me that she had come to it because at one point she was so poor that she couldn't afford to buy anything, and picked up cast-offs along the street for material. In the week she spent in Japan, I hosted her part of almost every day. She wanted to attend a geisha party. Geishas are very highly trained entertainers who have a lot of skills aimed at insuring their male clients have a wonderful time. This time Louise was the guest of honor and I went, too. Louise had been a dancer early in life. At seventy-five, she was straight and elegant, and very graceful. The sumptuous dinner, served on an endless supply of tiny plates, was accompanied by various forms of entertainment, music, dancing, jokes, and stories. Louise stood up and started to follow one of the geishas in her dance. The geisha responded, making clear what she was doing without compromising her movements. They danced together for several minutes, Louise more and more into the movement and spirit of the hour.

I met John Gardner and his family when they came and stayed in our house. He and his wife, Joan, had two children who were a little older than my boys. All of them were very blond and fair skinned. John was about forty then and had recently had great success as a novelist after several years as a university professor. He was a very dynamic person and enjoyed the limelight, enjoyed being outrageous. In addition to the usual mass reception and other events, we invited several Japanese authors and critics to dinner at our house. John was charming and willing to talk about books and writing as long as anyone cared to listen. Most of the party was sitting on the living room floor after dinner. The conversation veered off into art, and John asked what I was working on. We began to draw, as if each sheet was the next page of a story that was all pictures. He took my sheets and I kept his. We wrote occasionally and had a few telephone conversations after I returned to the States. In 1982 when I was living in Fairfax, he called and said we should get together. He said that he had been ill, and was thinking of getting married again. We made a date but, he was not well and couldn't make it. He died shortly afterward.

Life in Japan was very crowded with strangers who, however interesting, took up a lot of space and time. I was the cook and caterer, hostess and bookkeeper, by now with a pretty efficient system. Sometimes events were planned in advance, but sometimes my husband called from the office to say we were going to have seventy-five people for a cocktail reception or thirty people for dinner the next day. As in Korea, the reimbursement schedule was pitifully inadequate in high-cost Japan. At the end of two years, we were out-of-pocket the equivalent of one year of college for one of the boys.

Stephen and Daniel were flourishing at Canadian Academy. Both of them were learning Japanese along with their program in English. I volunteered at the school. The student body was a mixture of about half foreigners and half Japanese, many of whom had been abroad. It was very difficult for Japanese students, having lived out of the country, to be reintegrated into the school system, and so they often found their way to Canadian Academy. It was a good choice for Daniel and Stephen. They grew to feel confident and independent.

A favorite treat on Saturday morning was for the three of us to take the train to Osaka, to the San Ban Gai, the huge underground shopping mall beneath downtown Osaka. We went to Kinokuniya bookstore where each of us chose a new book, and then to the Cardinal café for lemonade. Edwin met us there when he finished his morning's work at the office nearby.

DANIEL TO THE RESCUE • *In October 1973, the world experienced the first* oil shock, when the OPEC (the petroleum cartel) countries cut off the world supply of oil. Within days in Japan, there were shortages of home-heating oil and gasoline. As the crisis continued, the co-op supermarket where I shopped for groceries was soon out of cooking oil, detergent, and paper goods of every kind. All plastic household goods disappeared. Buckets, food wrap, and drinks that were packaged in plastic bottles were not for sale. Meat and fish, usually wrapped in plastic, were available only by order and were wrapped in newspaper. The newspapers themselves became thin to save oil. Everything that had to be transported from anywhere became very expensive or unavailable. The embargo continued until March. It took time to manufacture and deliver all the things we had previously taken for granted. The economic impact was enormous and so was the effect on everyday living.

One essential item was toilet paper, and it was one of the first things to be rationed by the stores. Very soon there was none to buy in supermarkets or department stores. Daniel, age five, saved the day for us. He loved mint ice cream, and the only place to buy it was the little neighborhood pharmacy on the street between the train station and our house. He could go to the store by himself to buy ice cream, and sometimes I added another item or two. The pharmacist was taken with him; she always had a conversation with this blue-eyed foreign child when he went in the store. They were on very good terms from the moment they met. Daniel had stopped in the pharmacy on his way home one day and reported to us that the pharmacist had toilet paper behind the counter for regular customers only. He was a regular and so she sold him, from under her counter, at astounding prices, this precious necessity.

The same heating oil company had served the house since 1926. We were their regular customers, and so they delivered tiny amounts of heating oil a few times. We made our own rolled-newspaper logs and burned them in the fireplace, defrosting ourselves for a few minutes. We wore many layers of sweaters and conserved everything. We washed quickly, Asian style, using a bowl of water at the sink in the very cold house. No one had a leisurely hot bath or shower for the duration of the embargo.

In the United States, President Carter encouraged energy conservation as a matter of national and economic security. He addressed the country wearing a sweater, and ordered the thermostats turned down in the White House. Solar panels popped up everywhere. A great variety of programs supported innovation in solar and wind generation. Almost all of them were immediately dismantled when Ronald Reagan took office.

GOING AROUND • *I traveled around Japan, sometimes with my family*, occasionally with friends. Between Japan and Korea, the Japan Sea, called the Eastern Sea in Korea, is filled with hundreds of islands. Amano-hashidate, a section of the Japanese seacoast, is a mythic jewel. The four of us went to a *ryokan* (traditional inn) there, heard the Japanese creation stories, steeped ourselves in a stone lined *ofuro* bath, and walked along the empty beaches.

With friends I drove to Tamba, Tachikui in Hyogo Prefecture. We visited the great hillside kilns still operated by the descendents of the original Korean potters who settled there in the Kamakura period. And to Bizen to admire the brown, tactile ceramics made there. I went to several old castle sites. Most were fairly recently rebuilt after long neglect or bomb damage. With a friend I took the *Shinkansen*, the bullet train, to Okayama, looked at the black castle and strolled through the Korakuen garden with its water paths and swans.

Amidst all the pleasures of life in Japan in the seventies there were also some aspects that were unsettling, even repellent. The most popular comic book, sold and read widely, was titled *Rapeman*, and every story included the graphic depiction of a rape, which was not always even the principal crime depicted. Saturday morning cartoons usually had at least one scene showing a woman being stabbed in the breast. On the bus, little boys were seated while their mothers stood with packages in their arms. I monitored the kids' television viewing. They had a television allowance, to spend watching whatever programs they chose, within the parameters of what I thought was wholesome fare. Strip shows — straight, gay, or lesbian — were off limits for my six- and nine-year-old sons. They started piano lessons with a wonderful, enlightened music teacher, Kuneda-San. Stephen had a hard time sitting still to practice, although he spent many hours practicing baseball skills. Daniel took to it and continued music lessons through his early high school years.

The boys were big baseball fans. Just a short train ride from Nishinomiya, the Hankyu Braves played before huge crowds. We went often, each season. The Oji zoo was just a couple of stops in the opposite direction and we went there often, too.

They loved the Takarazuka Theater, with all female actors and a dual bill, one part a sentimental Japanese story, such as *Cho Cho San* (*Madama Butterfly*) followed in the second half by a Radio City Rockettes-type of show. The actresses were national stars and stayed in character outside the performance. Those playing male roles always appeared in trousers and short haircuts, but were feminine nonetheless.

The Kabuki theater, an older tradition, had very elaborate productions with the most gorgeous costumes, wigs, and headpieces. In the renderings of traditional stories, often lasting four or five hours, men played all the roles. They also stayed in character. Those who specialized in female roles wore softer clothing in public, and spoke in masculine but delicate voices. Often the roles were passed down from father to son for generations.

The Noh drama was an ethereal theater event, but its mysterious beauty was not for children. The Bunraku puppet theater, however, was a great treat. The puppeteers, clothed all in black, were on stage and, in effect, invisible to the audience, who were caught up in the traditional dramas. The live productions in theaters were attended as much by adults as by children. A serialized version appeared on television and my boys were addicted to it.

Even more, they loved the sumo matches, with the long ceremonials and matches lasting only seconds. Sumo was a national obsession. My boys kept dutiful records: They knew the wrestlers' names and stats, and followed them through the newspapers and television shows. Even the Emperor attended the New Year's *basho* (tournament) in Tokyo. Traditionally, no head could be higher than the Emperor. He had to sit at the top of the arena, above the cheapest seats. The Empress accompanied him. After the preliminaries, he would turn to her, and she would take his glasses from her handbag, a human gesture between people who lived a very constrained life. The Empress was a very talented artist and, against all tradition, she allowed her work to be exhibited in public once or twice. After we moved to Tokyo, we were invited to the annual diplomatic summer garden party at the Palace. It was a formal, rare opportunity to meet them, if only momentarily.

The twentieth century was a dynamic one in Japanese history. Japanese women were no longer as restricted as before the war, but, despite the constitutional guarantees, equality was nowhere in sight. A major political campaign, "Pink Power," was organized to give divorced women the right to see and visit their children. Children belonged to the father's family. This was one of the most severe disincentives for women seeking a divorce, no matter how difficult their circumstances.

Sometimes it was hard to reconcile the contradictions between the crude and ugly public depictions of women, and the elegant, admired, and widely practiced arts of flower arranging and calligraphy. The refinement of

Japanese culture, practiced in the tea ceremony, temple architecture, garden design, and pottery was in sharp contradiction to the coarseness and vulgarity of popular culture, with its emphasis on pornography and violence. In Tokyo one New Year's Day morning, I walked through the new snow to a neighborhood temple in Akasaka, and watched the white prayer papers fluttering over the doorway. On the way home, I was confronted with hawkers inviting me in to the "sex-u show-a."

As Kyoto was in such easy proximity to Nishinomiya, I was able to visit the temple and palace gardens there in every season. Although I knew the aesthetic principles of Japanese garden design, I hadn't known that these gardens were so emotionally and psychologically fulfilling. The art of garden design was very significant and widely practiced in Japan.

The gardens of Kyoto are in three major styles. A landscape garden, with trees, water, hills — natural or imported — and flowers for every season, is intended to remind the viewer of the natural world, and sometimes even of a specific place outside the realm of the garden itself. It is the style that most nearly approximates western landscape design. In Kyoto, Konchi-in, at Nanzen-ji Temple, is in this style. It has winding, shady paths and a little lake, and invites the visitor to move along its paths to lovely views and charming resting places.

Tofuku-ji Temple is one of the main temples in Kyoto and was founded in 1236. It is designed for walking along paths of sand with stepping-stones. It is famous for the centuries-old moss and trees. It is especially known for its autumn foliage and graceful footbridges, where you pause over the slow streamlets and see the moving reflections of your own face in the reflected red foliage.

Ryoan-ji Temple has many trees surrounding the exquisite and simple buildings. In the L-shaped space formed by the walls, the gardens are sand and gravel set with huge rocks mostly buried under the surface, so that you feel their strength rather than see it. The *karesansui* (dry landscape) style is contemplative and abstract. Monks rake the gravel as a meditative activity. One day an elderly, wise man will rake the gravel as active contemplation, showing the way through his concentration and calm action. Another day, a young monk, seventeen or eighteen years old, rakes the garden, learning as it changes slowly but constantly.

I was often in these gardens alone. In the quiet of these evocative places, I began to intuit the change that lies within permanence, that something, even ourselves, can be one thing and, at the same time, be in the process of becoming something else.

THE RED INCIDENT • *The Red Army was a terrorist group that had caused* a lot of damage and discomfort in the Japan of the sixties. Early on, the public was sympathetic to some of their goals, but as they became more radicalized and extreme in their behavior, the public increasingly rejected them. I was told how alienated they were from basic Japanese values. One time, as police chased them through a neighborhood, the Red Army cadre ran through a house, trampling over the tatami with their shoes on. The idea that a Japanese person could run over the straw-matted floors of someone's house with his shoes on struck people as such barbarity that the story was repeated for several years. Even firemen shook off their shoes before crossing tatami. The Japanese authorities pursued the Red Army vigorously. Finally they seemed to be permanently out of the Japanese islands. Still, we never completely forgot the threat of terrorism. There were many groups with various styles of violence.

One morning when I was waiting for the train, I noticed a man on the platform. It was well after rush hour, and there were few people waiting. It wasn't surprising to see him get off the train at the end of the line in Kobe, as that was the principal destination, but a little later I saw him in the Sogo Department Store. I decided to leave without completing my errand. Walking on the street, I was sure I was being followed. I thought to go to the consulate, a few minutes' walk away, but across a park. In my mind, I went over the techniques taught in the antiterrorism course that I had been required to take on our last home leave. I stayed on the busiest streets, watching this person pretty steadily. I began to make my way back toward the train station and, by luck, saw a neighbor I knew slightly. Normally, we would have just said hello and gone on separately, but I attached myself to her without explanation. We took the train together to our station. The same man followed. By then I was very uncomfortable. Once inside my house, I phoned the consulate and was speaking to the security officer when the gate bell rang. One of the boys ran to the gate and opened it before I could stop him. I left the phone open on the table and rushed to the door. The same man who had followed me all day came through the garden and stood in the doorway of the house.

The man showed me a wallet with a badge, and began to explain in Japanese that he was with the police. Someone had been assigned to tell me that morning that we would have unusual protection, but the message did not reach me before I went out. It seemed that the Red Army had made a direct threat against my children.

The year before, in 1972, elements of the Red Army Group had attacked Lod Airport in Israel. One of the attackers survived and was sentenced to life in prison. To secure his release, the bomber's confederates were threatening to kidnap my boys. The Japanese police and American Embassy security considered the threat credible. Red Army elements had been located moving through Japan, heading toward Kobe and Osaka. While it was possible that some other family might have been the target, we were the most likely. By the next day, the police had set up camp in our back garden. They came with communications gear, and a trailer where they slept and had their meals. They set up roadblocks at each end of our street, letting through only known residents. As everywhere, foreigners were a lot of trouble to the police, and the Japanese wanted no incidents, especially involving children.

I wanted to take the boys back to the States. Edwin felt that choice allowed the terrorists to win. We could not give in to terrorist threats. It only encouraged them. The Japanese officials would have been glad for us to be out of harm's way, or at least to keep the children out of school, until this threat was over. Edwin made the decision that we would stay. It was decided among the police and security officials to keep as normal a schedule as possible. The main change was that I drove the boys back and forth to school, and we did not go anywhere unnecessarily. The usual procedure for security is to vary the route and the times of travel, but the boys had to be in school at fixed hours. There were police boxes, little mini one-man stations, at regular intervals in every Japanese neighborhood. Each one was assigned to watch over us as we passed by in the car. I'm sure they breathed a sigh of relief when we left their zone of responsibility.

I didn't want Stephen and Daniel, just eight and five, to be frightened by thoughts of kidnappers. I tried to make all this activity into a kind of game. Years later, as adults, they told me that they had not realized the circumstances at all, and had thought the police encampment had been very interesting.

After about three weeks, the threat was considered neutralized. The terrorists had moved hundreds of miles through Japan from Kyushu toward Nishinomiya before they were captured or escaped. I understood that the episode was closed, but did not get over it for a long time.

RETURN FROM THE SURREAL • *By the summer of 1974, life had returned* to normal. My mother came to visit for a few weeks. She had recently retired, and at sixty, she meant to fulfill her desire to travel. As a gift for her retirement I took her to Hong Kong for a few days. I had been there previously and liked the city. Mother took some time by herself, hired a car and driver (one of her favorite things to do), and toured around by herself for a day. She had a winter coat made at one of Hong Kong's famous shops. They roll out bolts of cloth, measure you, do two fittings, and have the clothing ready overnight. We weren't in a hurry, so we gave the tailor two days. On our previous, trips Edwin had had suits made. I wasn't a big shopper but liked a store called Dynasty. I bought a silk robe that I had for many years. Mother's visit passed smoothly. We always stayed in contact. From the time I left New York, I was a good correspondent. Once we went abroad, I set aside an afternoon every week to write to Edwin's family and my own. I kept it up for more than twenty years, describing our surroundings and experiences, the people I met and the events of the day. None of the letters were saved, so many details are lost now.

The celebrations for the Bicentennial of the American Revolution began in 1975. We commemorated the battle of Concord and Lexington with a party. We encouraged people to come as some figure from the American Revolution. A French couple came in full-scale eighteenth-century costume. They barely made it through our twentieth-century door, she in her wide skirts and he, as Lafayette, in his tall wig. Funny British friends came in casual, very red jackets, and announced energetically that the Redcoats were coming! The kids made a fort in the garden, where they marched around being rebellious colonials, enlisting the other children in the cause. It was rare to invite families together, and I think the Japanese guests were a bit nervous but had fun. I made all sorts of historical

American food, which was a novelty to everyone. The menu included corn pudding, hush puppies, molasses pie, Virginia ham, New England beans, spiced cider, and many more old recipes.

We knew many artists and writers then, and enjoyed the more informal ways they adopted. A few, like Shingu, the sculptor, became almost friends, and we visited their homes with our children. Shingu's little girls were around Daniel's age. We spent some very happy Sundays at their weekend place in the country.

At one point, the Deputy Chief of Mission, the second ranking person after the Ambassador, asked me to take on some personnel matters. I was the senior American wife then. (The wife's status was still determined by the husband's position.) There were some issues that needed attention. A couple at the consulate had become involved with a British couple, swapping partners, leaving the children to stay where they could. Those children sometimes stayed overnight with us when the four parents wanted to have their privacy. I didn't think it was any of my business, but they were not at all discreet and their unconventional relationship had become known all the way to Tokyo. I didn't like this task, and felt that as they were in Kobe, and part of the consulate there, it wasn't up to me to set them straight on suitable behavior abroad. I had some conversations with the American wife. Kobe was her first post, and she hated being there. The loss of privacy, the language difficulty, and the absence of family, all troubled her and she had not found anything to do. Soon they left the country. Later on, the same DCM asked me to start keeping track of the activities of the women at post, outlining their service contributions to the mission. It was the beginning of official recognition of the roles played by spouses in the Foreign Service. Later, the Forum Committee, formed by Foreign Service wives, made a systematic study, formally described the economic and personal repercussions of existing policies, and presented the case for the status of wives to Congress. But that was still years in the future.

I was busy with official diplomatic activities, official and private guests, children and a household, learning the Japanese language and getting familiar with the culture, and coping with the traffic and terrorists. I tried to paint every day.

Contradictions were not confined to the world outside. Inconsistencies and bafflements were right in my own household. Osaka was a wonderful post for Edwin. He enjoyed it and was good at it. Nishinomiya was one of the best places I lived in the Foreign Service. The boys had a good school, friends, and physical freedom (except during the terrorist episode). I was studying calligraphy and painting, exhibiting my work, and getting nice feedback and reviews. Sounds ideal, if you leave out terrorism and the cost of living.

But these external advantages did not translate into loving harmony between Edwin and me. For one thing, we never, ever spoke about Aileen. Although she had died five years before, and I had recovered from the intense grief that lasted for a long time, I did not want to forget her. She was my child, not a blot to be erased. I thought about her and wanted to talk about her and this enormous event in our lives, but there was no way to share any of it.

We didn't spend a lot of time together. Edwin had an abundance of activities that kept him away from home for long hours. He had the respect of his associates, and loved his role in Osaka and the perks that went with it. He enjoyed the interesting people and programs that were his responsibility. He sometimes forgot that at home he was not the director and we were not staff. There was tension between us over decision-making, and sometimes his will was challenged. This tension increasingly extended to the most intimate aspects of our lives. Our continuing differences in sexual taste became more intense. He wanted me to adapt myself to his preferences and around this time became even more insistent about it.

VISIT TO KOREA • *We decided to make a family trip to Korea. We did some* sightseeing and visiting around Seoul and went on to Kwangju. No one had replaced us, and we stayed in the same little house we had lived in a few years earlier. As was the custom, Edwin was hosted at a massive dinner in a restaurant, which did not include the boys or me. At these parties in Korea, the guests usually eat and drink a great deal. Edwin indulged heavily and became ill. He was in bed then for two or three days. Toward the end of our stay in Kwangju, when he was recovering, several people came to say good-bye. The man who had been, and was still, the head of the office was chatting with me. As someone else had said years before, he complimented me on my patience and tolerance, saying I was like a Korean wife in understanding my husband's inclination to enjoy other women and spend so many evenings away from home. I was as embarrassed as I have ever been, and felt, again, very humiliated to have received this kind of compliment. There was no place or time right then, but on our return to Japan I raised the subject with Edwin. It was a very short talk without any resolution.

DINNER IN KOBE • *Early in 1975, I received a phone call from the wife of* the CIA station chief. His job was not a big secret, although we were very discreet and never talked about it. She was inviting all the consulate wives for dinner, just wives. Most all-female social events were in the daytime, but no one declined. We had what seemed to be a normal evening, unusual only in the absence of men. After the meal, with coffee in the living room, our hostess started to cry and her troubles spilled out. Her middle-aged husband was seeing a young and pretty Japanese woman, and making no pretense about it. This was not a surprise to most of us. Consulates and embassies are very intimate communities where many things of a personal nature can become widely known. She had told him she wanted to leave Japan and he refused. How could this be? She could just buy a ticket and go, couldn't she? No, she couldn't. In the seventies credit cards were in use but not so easily available, and she didn't have her own card. Like all the rest of us that evening, her checks came from a joint checking account, which, in her case, had very little money in it. The government would have issued the ticket she was entitled to, but the officer, her husband, had to request it. She had to wait until his tour was finished in a few months and travel home in the "normal" way.

Credit cards are very useful and also symbolic. In the modern world, to be independent, a person needs both money and credit. Foreign Service wives, with the prohibition on earning money and the nomadic life, rarely had credit of their own before the late seventies. No one at that dinner party did. The acquaintance from Kobe called me in Washington a few years later, reporting that her husband had decided to live with his Japanese girlfriend. She was now divorced, had a job, and was happily settling into her own apartment.

MOVING ON • *We had been sent to the Osaka post for four years with a home* leave in the middle. Edwin was promoted and offered a more senior post in Tokyo. Instead of the four years we had expected, two years into our time in Japan, I packed up and prepared to move to Tokyo. At one of our farewell parties in Nishinomiya, for the first time I heard Shigeko speaking English. (We had started using our given names at the Ashiya exhibition.) Her English was excellent. In the two years we had known each other, with our long lessons, lunches, going together to exhibitions, and my exhibiting with the Sei Boku Kai, I had never heard her say even one English word. I asked her why she hadn't told me she spoke English, since my Japanese had been minimal when we met. With a smile, she said, in Japanese, "We didn't need it, did we?"

On our way to home leave, we stopped in Tokyo for consultation. A house was designated for the position Edwin was going to be taking on. We would be moving into it before the new school term began. We flew back—no more ships—for a brief visit in New York, a Washington consultation, and then six weeks of home leave.

YET ANOTHER HOME LEAVE: 1975 • *My brother had recently married*, and we met Barbara. They were living in a little attic apartment in Flushing, deeply in love, as newlyweds should be. My brother's adolescence had not been any happier or calmer than mine. Now with Barbara's love and confidence, he was beginning to have a much better life. She is a lovely woman, but even if I didn't care for her, I would love her for the life she has helped my brother to make.

In Washington, President Ford had taken office after Nixon resigned. The Watergate scandal had taken two years of energy and confidence away from the political system. Vietnam was finished with the ghastly evacuation of the embassy in April, and politicians in Washington were very busy pointing fingers and assigning blame away from themselves. It was easy to lay it all on Johnson since he was dead by then. That's what seemed to be in style.

The public acrimony and distrust of the recent several years created a corrosive atmosphere. No one could act creatively to reestablish an open dialog. After all the assassinations in the sixties—Medgar Evers, John Kennedy, Martin Luther King, Jr., Robert Kennedy, Viola Liuzzo,

James Chaney, Andrew Goodman, Michael Schwerner, and many more—after the deaths of more than fifty thousand Americans and two million Vietnamese by 1975, you would think everyone had had enough. But the Vietnamese turned on themselves and so did we. Our social fabric was worn very thin.

Fever

Hot faces
Hot words
A fever of hate
A fire in the blood

Shoot hack rip rape
Slash burn bomb

What else can you do?
What else can we do?

Our family visits were strained. The disagreements about the war and politics in general were so vehement that it was all but impossible to remember that we were supposed to love one another.

We headed back to Tokyo, with a stop at the golden Grand Canyon and a few days of recuperation in Maui. Unhappiness lay just a little below the surface. There was an increasing, steady undertone of dissatisfaction for both of us, masked by the busy-ness of returning to Japan.

TOKYO • *We came back to find that another officer had appropriated our house.* He was a bachelor, with no greater responsibilities than Edwin, but possession and lobbying were more than nine-tenths of the game. He had moved in. I would not have agreed to leave Nishinomiya to live in the embassy apartment house, but we were there. Edwin told me it was done; we had to live with it.

The Tokyo embassy apartments were built in two phases. The first two buildings, Harris and Perry, were older, with two-storey apartments, small rooms, and no soundproofing at all. The apartments were designed so that two two-bedroom units could become a one- and a three-bedroom by removing a closet partition—and any possible sound barrier—between the bedrooms. They had a little character, though, and were very nice by Japanese standards at the time they were built. Later on, Grew House was added, with larger, flat apartments, better closets and kitchens, and no charm whatsoever. Grew was intended to be mostly for families with children. In all the buildings, generic government furniture was in place and employees had weight allowances for their personal effects. Since then all those buildings have been torn down or sold.

The grounds were luxurious and very well tended. There was a tennis court and, in summer, an outdoor pool. A few spots in the gardens were lovely. In the fall some of the trees were wrapped in bamboo, like arboreal overcoats, and were very sculptural in the snow.

The worst problem about living in an apartment house owned and operated by your employer is the complete lack of privacy. All your neighbors are the same people you have to work with every day. Spousal arguments, misbehaving children, extracurricular affairs, all come to the notice of colleagues. Gossip is inevitable. If you don't want to gossip about other people, that becomes an item, too. During my two years in Tokyo, at least three different men left their wives to begin new relationships with younger Japanese women. Times were changing and female officers were able to marry. A husband accompanied one officer, and for a while he stayed home with their child. Although he was new to the service, an embassy job soon turned up for him but not for the many wives wanting to work. We were prohibited from having employment in the Japanese economy although many did so discreetly. Discreet is a relative term, though; all of us knew which wives among us had part-time jobs teaching English.

We stayed in Perry House until an apartment became available in Grew, a two-bedroom next to the elevator. How were we going to accommodate two school-age children and all the entertaining that was expected in this position? And a corner for my painting? After a couple of months someone left, and we moved to a larger, quieter apartment. I kept my painting equipment on the floor of my clothes closet and used the dining table as my studio.

The Grew House apartments were laid out so that bedrooms shared common walls with adjacent apartments. Our headboard backed up to the headboard in the apartment occupied by Edwin's boss and his wife, three inches away on the other side of the wall. Almost everything was built in and there was no way to move the furniture. Joan, living in the next-door apartment, and I tried to laugh about, it but we were breathtakingly aware of how ludicrous this was. Sound carried, as it does in most apartment buildings, and when the windows were open you could hear every sound, almost every breath.

The boys attended Nishimachi School, a wonderful progressive school founded by Hane Matsukata. She educated the students based on an ideal of trust, respect, and excellence. The previous spring while the boys took the entrance exam, I had been interviewed extensively. The school was a community and parents were expected to share the values and aspirations being taught to their children. It was a place of achievement and harmony. Stephen and Daniel regard it as their happiest school experience. I volunteered there, taught some art classes, and had fun with the children.

The air in Tokyo was terrible, the sky so polluted it seemed green sometimes. Stephen had a lot of allergies that turned into asthma. I took him to a specialist in Yokohama at the naval base. There were still many soldiers wounded in Vietnam who could not be sent back to their homes. Some badly burned or disfigured men took years to recover. Some of them were still at the main hospital in Yokohama. For a while, I visited and wrote some letters and listened if they had anything they wanted to say.

HOKKAIDO • *Hokkaido is a large island in the far north. Edwin had business* meetings in the capital city, Sapporo. I went along, glad to have the chance to see this part of Japan. It was conquered and incorporated into Japan in the eighteen-seventies. It is a cold place, with snowy mountains and birch forests. It makes you think of a Canadian or Russian province, especially in the winter.

One of the culinary marvels of Sapporo is hairy crab. A group of local people invited us for a traditional meal. We had dinner in a restaurant that had a fireplace that took up a whole wall. They served tubs of these crabs. Everyone wore a white-cotton bib. Mine came down to my waist. The piles of shells grew and grew. We cracked and picked and ate and drank. It was almost addictive, nearly impossible to stop, until we were exhausted by pleasure.

The original people are the Ainu. They look Caucasian and often have blue eyes, wavy hair, fair skin, pronounced facial bones, and many genetic and cultural distinctions from the Japanese. The traditional Ainu crafts are similar to the indigenous crafts of North America. I bought a shawl from a weaver. The wool is longhaired and very soft, the weaving pattern often mistaken for a Native American style, even in New Mexico. The colors are similar to the traditional Hopi colors, and the pattern looks a little like the geometrics of the Navajo. The Ainu baskets are reminiscent of those made in western North America.

With cold forests the dominant feature of the landscape, longhaired animals are very common. I found excellent handmade calligraphy and painting brushes, and still use them more than thirty years later. Good brushes are a joy to work with and an investment for more than a lifetime. I think you make better work with good tools and materials. I can still be seduced by a beautiful brush. When I see one of these Hokkaido brushes standing in a coffee can in the studio — also an artifact from my past — I always want to start something, even if only a single line.

Seduction

Offering exactly what you want
And making it impossible
For you to refuse it

METAMORPHOSIS • *I returned to teaching for a while and gave some courses* at Tokyo Bunka Gakuin, an art college. I made two trips with a friend to Mashiko where I met and briefly spoke with Hamada Shoji, the great twentieth-century potter. I went by myself to Kamakura to see the great Buddha. Another friend, Kimiko, was a native of Yokohama. She told me stories about the city, of the conditions in the thirties, the fire bombings in the war, the Thought Police arresting her briefly for wearing a western style skirt instead of the approved padded pajamas. Mao was not the first to enforce discipline and authority by trying to control what people thought inside their own heads.

Despite everything, I was making art and had exhibitions and invitations. When a prominent gallery asked me to do a show, the embassy's chief executive heard of it. He forbade the exhibition because I was not allowed to work beyond doing charitable activities. I was not about to give up this precious opportunity without a fight. Edwin told me that if I persisted, the embassy would have the Japanese government revoke my visa and I would have to leave. I answered that I would leave rather than surrender. We went back and forth until I came up with an idea. This exhibition was a cultural activity and was in furtherance of Japanese-American cultural relations. That made it acceptable. Everyone saved face. The show went ahead. I hadn't spent the past twelve years in Asia for nothing.

Printmaking in Japan is an old and very sophisticated art. There were many exciting innovations in technique and aesthetics in the seventies and the prosperity to support a large thriving art world. While I kept on with calligraphy I went to the Atelier Petit to make prints. Gaston Petit is a French-Canadian priest who had been sent by his order to Japan. He is a wonderful artist and founded an atelier for printmaking. I worked there, learned something of lithography, and met many printmakers. I joined with three other women for a show of our prints at Gallerie 412 in Tokyo. The following year, I was invited to participate in the twenty-second annual Print Exposition of the College Women's Association of Japan. This was a major event in the print world, and I felt very honored to receive their invitation. I also had a one-person show at the American Center. In the spring of 1977, I was very pleased to have a one-person show at the Mikimoto Gallery in downtown Tokyo. For all of these events, the work was well received and generally had good press commentary. Several magazines did feature stories. I was well launched as an artist.

The last Tokyo show was very large, more than forty pieces. It was a summary of my work in Japan, with a few early ink paintings, abstract and traditional calligraphy, some prints, and my first abstract paintings, all on paper. The exhibition was well attended, with good sales, and good conversation. As was my habit, I went to the gallery on several different days to be there and greet anyone who might come by. An old man in traditional clothes came in when the gallery was otherwise empty. He walked around slowly with his hands behind his back, considering each piece, and then he sat down on the bench in the middle of the room. We started talking. He was interested in how I had arrived at the calligraphy style I used. I asked about his own work.

He reached inside his brown kimono and pulled out a tiny face, hardly bigger than his thumb. He was a maker of masks for the Noh Theater, and this was the maquette for a new mask. He had been working on it for several years, studying the play and the character. The actors wore one mask for the whole performance, and it had to reflect the role's personality and transforming action. On the face of a great Noh actor, the mask would suggest sorrow, joy, anger, kindness, delight, and despair. The mask was wood that had been polished and partially or fully painted. My exhibition guest was carrying around the tiny maquette, considering it in various circumstances, finding out if it encompassed all that the character needed. It was to be used for a century or two, and he took his time in making it. He liked one of my small calligraphies and took it with him.

It was time to leave Japan. We had the usual round of farewells, the packing, the planning for the journey, and the reassignment to Washington. When we left for the States, I thought I would go right on being an artist. I imagined having a studio, or at least a room for my materials where I could work every day. The boys were growing up. They would be in school and have their activities. I loved being their mother, being with them, enjoying their company. We had a lot of fun together. Once the household was established in Washington, it would be time for me to pay more attention to my work.

SEVEN

Fairfax

NISHIMACHI, THE TOKYO SCHOOL, HAD A SISTER SCHOOL, the Washington International School, in the Georgetown neighborhood of Washington. It was run on the same principles and with the same program as the school in Tokyo. To me it seemed sensible to let the boys continue in a system that was so positive and that they were used to. I wanted to look for a home in the city, but Edwin's insistence on suburban life prevailed through many arguments. We bought a house in Fairfax, in the Virginia suburbs. I really should have known better. The first time in Annandale had been a mistake. I was not suited to this style of living. With still only one driver in the family, it was a foolish choice. We moved in before school started in August. We had four bedrooms, half an acre of lawn to mow, and room for company.

We visited New York, of course, and our parents came to see the new house. Relations between my parents were as they always had been. When Bobby had married a couple of years earlier, Cammy was still there, still waiting. She thought that finally she and Dad would divorce their spouses, and the two of them would have a life together. Instead, he asked her to continue on as they had been for over twenty years. When he told me the story, he said that he was heartbroken when she refused but that it was too late. He would not make good the commitment that had existed between them for such a long time. She broke it off completely and finally, and retreated from the field to repair her life with her patient husband. Twenty years of futility.

But it wasn't too late for him to go out with a variety of women, and he continued to have brief affairs until his mid-eighties. He and Bobby enjoyed a close relationship and shared an avid interest in business. Dad continued to manage his financial affairs and had several jobs. He liked and needed to work. Mother had her activities, books, meetings, and travel. They only fought when they were together.

Edwin's parents were more sedate people, and they enjoyed life a great deal more. In their families, large gatherings were frequent and we saw them then. They came very rarely to Virginia.

The antagonism between my husband and my father was always palpable. They could not have a civil conversation for two minutes. After a while, my father stopped coming to visit. I found myself exhausted by all these Byzantine family relationships. I wanted to get settled and get back to work, to painting.

Stephen and Daniel were in seventh and fourth grade in 1977. They had some cultural adjustments to make to life in the Virginia suburbs. They were used to a school environment that was very quiet and where children were respectful of each other as well as of the adults. Polite children in Japan do not look directly into the eyes of their teachers, and in Fairfax one of Stephen's teachers interpreted this as his being inattentive. Adjustments were made and in a few months both boys were getting on well. They found friends at school without too much difficulty. Stephen got involved with basketball right away in middle school. Daniel stayed with tennis and asked to continue his piano lessons. They did fine in terms of grades, but the education was not as deep or as sensitively presented as at Nishimachi School. I volunteered at the elementary school and did some nice units, including field trips to the National Gallery and other museums. In a short while, I was teaching in the after-school arts enrichment program for Fairfax County, which I continued for several years. Some children came term after term. It did not pay much, but I made enough for my studio supplies. I had nice neighbors and made a good garden at that house. One year for Mother's Day, the boys gave me rose bushes and a note that said the bushes came with "digging service."

ROME • *I went to Italy for the first time in 1980. Edwin had some NATO meetings* in Greece and Italy. Although I had studied European history, art, philosophy, and politics in college and graduate school, I had never been there. I had a day or two on my own in Rome. I spent the time wandering through gardens and the city streets in the misty rain. I sat on marble benches and made drawings. I was surprised at how calm Rome seemed, not like the frenetic imagery of the movies. Edwin met me there. I accompanied him to a few receptions, and we went to some of the famous landmarks.

At the top of the Spanish Steps, the church was being renovated. At the bottom of the steps is a piazza with an English café. In the nineteenth century the area was very popular with English tourists. Multi-storey houses line each side of the long staircase. In one of them is the room where Keats lived and died. Keats was twenty-six years old, in love with Fanny Brawne, ill with tuberculosis. On the recommendation of his physician, he went to the warmer climate of Rome to try and survive the winter. Destitute, lonely, and very cold, he rented the attic of this house. The room is about seven feet wide, with a low ceiling, and with a small window opening right onto the upper steps. In 1980 the whole building was a low-intensity, romantic shrine to him. I was in Rome about a week. We made one or two day trips, and it was time to go back to Virginia.

DEADLOCK • *I worked alone in the studio and tried to keep growing my skills.* My studio was either the small guest room or the kitchen table. It seemed that we took up the whole house for family needs. All twenty-seven hundred square feet of it needed to be cleaned and outfitted, but there was no place for me. Finally, I hired a Chinese immigrant carpenter, who partitioned off a little section of the furnace room. I had, if not a whole room, at least a space of my own, with a door that closed. It was the size of a large walk-in closet, a little less than seven feet by ten feet. I paid for it with money from a picture that I sold. In the next few years, I did a few more exhibitions, including two solo shows, at the Fairfax Council of the Arts and Gallery Amerasia in Washington.

The work was not growing and neither was I. My husband, my parents, even friends, said that this was a nice hobby, but I had no real talent. They couldn't see me as an artist. The work just didn't look like anything you expected to see in a Washington gallery. I'd had invitations from a few galleries and juried shows, a few sales, and a bit of favorable press, but I did not have confidence to find and follow my own path. Eventually, in an act of desperation, I destroyed every painting I had made in Fairfax and a few more. I burned them one by one in the fireplace.

Those years in Fairfax were very difficult. I grieved and was deep in sorrow in almost the same way I had been when Aileen died. The loss of identity was acute, especially just as many women I knew were finding themselves freer to fulfill their hopes. I still wanted to try salvaging something from my marriage, suffering as it was from the same years-old, unresolved issues. We were growing less content with one another with each passing year. There were nights when I stood in the kitchen, watched the clock, and wondered if I could bear to live five more minutes.

One night I stood there counting the squared boxes on the wallpaper. The wall was gray with pale yellow lines in a sort of double grid. I counted the squares and watched the clock and waited for five minutes to go by.

Knife in hand, I thought of my sons sleeping thirty feet away. I watched the clock for five more minutes. The canisters were lined up on the counter. The napkins were in a yellow holder on the yellow table. The refrigerator hummed. The hand of the clock stuttered slowly, one second at a time, toward five more minutes. The boys slept on.

The window was dark. No moonlight was in the garden. Five minutes passed again. The first faintest light began to be visible outside the window. My feet were disconnected ice at the end of legs that hardly belonged to me any more. The grief of even one more day was insupportable.

How much I loved them. In the end, leaving them to suffer such a legacy was more awful to me even than my staying to live one more day. I watched the clock for five more minutes and five more, and the night passed. Unknowingly, innocently, they saved my life. I put away the knife and my tears, and began the second half of my life.

I could not put painting aside and could not continue. My struggle was private, inward looking, and futile. For many years, I had read and thought about Buddhist philosophy. The first lesson back in the Korea days was about looking clearly. In Japan, I had read more deeply and had some conversations with wise teachers. Over the years I had heard and read many iterations of this concept of direct pointing. It means, I think, that we must look at something or someone clearly, drawing aside the obscuring veil of our own expectations and recognizing what is actually right in front of us. Not what we hope or fear, not what we expect or believe, but the thing itself, clear and accepted as such. This particular tree, right here, is not the idea of a tree, but itself. This was and continues to be the central principle for me in my work as an artist. Now, after more than forty years of drawing toward an understanding of this concept, I think it is an essential way of living. In Fairfax, I was beginning to apply the principle of direct looking to my own life. I didn't much like what I saw and didn't know what to do about it. I watched. And I waited.

THROWING A LIFELINE, HOPING THEY COULD CATCH • *Some refugees* from the Vietnam War had been resettled in the U.S. but most were stranded in camps all over South Asia. Laotians and Cambodians were caught up in the mess. Things boiled up to a crisis of huge proportions when large numbers of desperate people climbed into the flimsiest crafts and tried to sail away from the excesses of the new regime. Some people walked from one country to another. Families were separated. In this time of the "boat people," I wanted to do something. Four friends and I formed ourselves into a mini-organization, named ourselves the Coalition for Asian Refugees, and went to work. We learned how the system functioned, and didn't function, and how it could be made to work. Senator Harold Hughes from Iowa was one of our guides through the bureaucracy. He cared deeply about the people in so much trouble and helped us learn what we needed to know. The best organizations were Catholic Charities and Jewish Philanthropies. Both these old time groups knew about displaced people and knew how to help. The refugees arrived with nothing, almost literally just the clothes they were wearing. Sometimes they were sick, always sick at heart. We learned how to search for one individual person in the sea of refugees spread over five or ten countries. We asked only that when we said good-bye the resettled people do the same for someone else. Eventually we five resettled more than forty people. It was a lot of work and many hours and was just a tiny drop in the bucket of misery that spilled out of what used to be Indochina.

TURNING POINTS • *Both boys had bar mitzvahs while we lived in Fairfax.* For Stephen, now becoming Steve, the lunch party was in our garden and for Daniel, in a nearby park with a historic house. They were family parties attended by about one hundred people, and the boys had fun once the service was over. I was not religious but felt the boys should have a basis for making a choice of their own about religion. Edwin had a sense of tradition and wanted to please his family.

Meanwhile, Edwin was keeping an eye out for a new assignment. He continued to work fairly long hours and traveled occasionally, but was home more regularly than he had been when we'd been abroad. He played golf and mowed the lawn. He was often angry. He and Steve had many strenuous arguments. Daniel usually kept out of the way.

There was never the possibility that Fairfax, or anywhere else, was going to be a permanent home. Eventually, Edwin was offered an attractive position in Mexico City. It had a lot of advantages, including an interesting cultural life and a good school for Daniel, and learning the language would be easier. Edwin started Spanish language training in 1981 and went to Mexico just after the winter holidays. I stayed behind to let the boys finish the school year. Daniel was going to graduate from middle school and Stephen from high school.

Daniel had been placed in a school for gifted students. He was talented in mathematics and still kept on with his music. Through a program at Johns Hopkins University, he was awarded recognition as the highest achieving student in language arts in Virginia in a nice ceremony at the Science Museum in Richmond. In his last year he opted to take Spanish and arrived in Mexico with a working knowledge of the language.

Stephen was in the throes of college applications. He was an excellent student and set his sights high. The fellows and I took a few car trips to tour universities, Cornell, Williams, Colgate, and the like. He decided on William and Mary in Williamsburg, Virginia. Our gift to both sons was that they would have no student loans and be able to start their adult lives without the burden of debt. As late as the eighties it was still possible to send your children to college without mortgaging their future or your own.

It was a unique period in our lives in that the boys and I were together as a trio while their father began his new post. I was preparing for the move but also, after two fallow years, I began to paint again. I planned to continue in Mexico. By this time language training was offered for spouses and I took the ten-week intensive course, the maximum available.

Things were changing in the Foreign Service. Women were much more often employed and spouses were declared to be independent individuals, not subject to official direction and review. You couldn't help noticing that this official recognition came exactly as a fair number of spouses started to be the husbands of officers.

Edwin came back for the graduations and returned to Mexico City. The three of us packed up, readied the house for the future renters, and took the train to New Orleans. We slept overnight in compartments, looked at southern scenery that was new to us, and had a great time. New Orleans was fun, with the jazz bands parading through the streets. We stayed in a hotel that had been a grand French home in the distant past. Stephen, seventeen, was intrepid and led us on our explorations. Daniel bought his first print, a Mississippi river boat, and still has it in his collection. From New Orleans we flew to Mexico City and the next iteration of our peripatetic life.

EIGHT
Mexico

IT WAS JULY WHEN WE ARRIVED IN MEXICO CITY. Edwin had leased a lovely old house in the hillside *colonia* of Las Lomas, on a street bordered by the huge Tecamachalco gorge. The owners lived next door. I became friendly with Malena and Luis right away. We arrived during the rainy season with the monsoon pouring down late most afternoons and continuing through the night. It was chilly, and I bought some wool Indian blankets while we waited for our household goods to arrive. This was the first time we had been allowed to bring our own furniture to post, and it was nice not to have the institutional drabness that had prevailed in the embassy apartments at other posts.

The house was vertical, with a few rooms on each of the six floors and the garage underneath. The stone-faced entry hall, twenty-seven steps up from the street, was seventeen by seventeen feet square, paved in Mexican marble. Daniel and his friends had many parties in that room.

It was perfect for teenage dancing. Half a flight up, the large living room was lit from outside by a wall of small-paned windows. They reached almost to the twenty-foot ceiling. Another flight up, the large family room was next to the dining room, which seated fourteen. There was a breakfast area, and a kitchen to store and cook all that food. Behind the kitchen was a functioning washing machine, although you had to climb two narrow flights of outdoor stairs to hang the clothes out to dry on one of the roofs. The next flight up was occupied by two very high-ceilinged bedrooms, which shared a bath and dressing room. The front one had a little balcony and a secret panel in the floor. During the worst days of the Mexican Revolution, families hid their daughters in spaces like that. This house wasn't that old but was built in the style of about 1920. Each of the two floors above this had another bedroom and bath. Most of the floors were terrazzo, marble, or bare, polished wood, very sensible in such a dusty place. We needed to wash the floors every day. I was lucky that my neighbor was able to recommend someone to help. We distributed ourselves through the house. Edwin had chosen one of the uppermost bedrooms as ours, and Daniel made his choice among the rest. Stephen was there only for a few weeks until he left to start college, so he didn't do more than set himself up for the summer.

Life was arranged in Mexico City to depend on the presence of someone at home all the time. Answering the doorbell at the gate on the street took several minutes as you traipsed from one of the many upper floors, down the twenty-seven garden steps and back up again. The gate had to be opened for the propane gas delivery and utility meter readers. The newspaper deliveryman was paid in person. The garbage collection was at irregular hours, and you were not permitted to leave the trash on the street beforehand. A milkman rang his bell as he passed through the streets — usually fresh milk was not sold in the small supermarkets.

Juanita was a very competent housekeeper. The air in Mexico City was terribly polluted. The State Department officially classified it as hazardous. They calculated that each two years there shortened your life by six months. The Mexican government sometimes closed the schools in the winter because the pollution was so pervasive it made children sick. They kept a bird in the zócalo, the main plaza, as an indicator, like the proverbial canary in the coalmine, except that this was outdoors on the street.

Periodically the bird died and was replaced. The smog made everything filthy. We washed the kitchen counters just before cooking and the table before each meal. All those floors were mopped every day, not because I was a fanatical housekeeper, but because the gritty, black junk accumulated that quickly. And we breathed it in every day.

We spent the summer acclimating ourselves. Daniel prepared to start at the American School, where about half the student body was Mexican and the school day was bilingual. We explored the city and got acquainted. By chance I had some Mexican cousins that I had met only once as a child. It was a wonderful coincidence. We became very friendly and had many happy times together. They told me stories of the city. Lily taught me some of her recipes, and Jacobo put up with my halting Spanish with his charming smile. The family was large and I enjoyed being with them on many occasions over the next few years. The best surprise was meeting Perla, the wife of my cousin Isaac. She was making textiles and feeling her way tentatively toward being an artist. On the first day we met we fell into friendship and have loved each other ever since. We always have a lot to talk about, but we don't need many words to understand each other, even if a long time passes without being together. I have been very lucky in friendships, and it is one of the central satisfactions of my adult life that several women and a few men have built these precious relationships with me.

In 1982 Mexico City was huge, approaching twenty million people. It sat on layers of civilizations, and archaeologists were uncovering some of them right in the city center. When the Templo Mayor was opened next to the cathedral, they built boardwalks for the public to walk around and follow the excavations. Some subway stations were Aztec sites, with glass windows revealing the ancient walls. Large parts of the city were built in the Spanish colonial period, but underneath were Aztec remains, and under that the civilization the Aztecs had conquered. The museums are filled with ancient treasures, Olmec, Aztec, Mixtec, giant stone heads, textiles, delicate gold. Museums dedicated to folk art, modern sculpture, corn. No matter how much time you had, it would be impossible to see it all.

Tenochtitlán, a major pyramid complex, is right in the city. A long flight of stairs is aligned with the boulevard. Each step is a few inches deep, too shallow to rest more than the ball of our modern feet. The boulevards are planted with roses and monuments. The architecture is extremely varied, with ancient, colonial, and nineteenth century existing side by side with the very contemporary, usually with an energetic harmony. It was very exciting to be in this Latin environment for the first time. There was always more to see as long as you could keep breathing the air.

Our life took on some of its usual contours. Edwin was a senior officer by this time with substantial responsibilities. There were a lot of official events to attend and host. I limited my participation to no more than a few evenings a week. With Stephen off to the university and Daniel involved with high school life, I had time and wanted to concentrate on making art and learning Spanish.

Edwin's work continued to require his attending and hosting many events. By this time I was efficient at entertaining. I had not learned to like large receptions and parties, with everyone standing around, looking over my shoulder to see if anyone more important than someone's wife was available. Nevertheless I was skilled at negotiating these events. Dinners were better. Sometimes there was real conversation and the opportunity to encounter a new acquaintance. I attended very many of these quasi-social working events my first year in Mexico. Daniel was in high school, busy with friends, school, tennis, and piano lessons, and life seemed to settle into its customary shape.

At two o'clock one winter morning, Stephen called to say that the freshman dorm at William and Mary had burned down. Everyone was out and safe, in pajamas, being cared for by the Red Cross. We were limited to just two minutes. The university needed all two hundred students to call their parents before the news hit the morning television programs. I was able to make reservations and went to Williamsburg that day. Stephen was somewhat in shock, like all the students, but otherwise fine. He had had the presence of mind to put on his glasses as he evacuated the building and so at least could see where he was going. The Red Cross had arranged for emergency clothing, local merchants opened their stores to the students, and the university did its best to house and counsel the students.

The students were able to get out in time because of one stroke of good luck. Someone's grandfather came to visit and didn't like the fact that all the smoke detectors were in the halls. He had insisted on installing one inside his grandson's dorm room. The fire spread undetected throughout the building, between the wall studs, the spaces acting like chimneys. The unofficial smoke detector signaled smoke coming through the boy's vent. He awoke and sounded the first warning. A few minutes later the whole building was completely engulfed. Without that extra minute or two many students might have been trapped inside. When I went with Stephen the next morning to look at the remains, it was amazing. Only part of the exterior brick walls was still standing, hung with huge icicles from the fire hoses. Almost nothing of the interior remained. Steve's bicycle, still chained to the bike rack, was a semi-melted, twisted sculpture encased in ice. I stayed for several days, saw that he was recovering, kissed him good-bye, and returned to Mexico City.

IN THE STUDIO • *I had set up a studio in one of the extra bedrooms and* started painting again. I met other artists and became acquainted with the art community. A few galleries began to show my work and I was invited to participate in some nice exhibitions. The Museum of Technology asked to organize a survey exhibition, including whatever old pieces I had on hand, to suggest the trajectory of my work. A major corporation purchased a large piece for its Latin American headquarters. A prime time arts television program invited me to appear, filmed my studio, and broadcast the program several times. I had a major show in Guadalajara. Many other fine opportunities opened up for me over the next three years.

The work was evolving and so was I. Previously almost all my work was painting on paper, in a fairly small format. Except for some of the calligraphy, all my art had been figurative and deeply influenced by my years in Asia. In the last months in Fairfax, I had tentatively started new work and now in Mexico, I was experimenting more boldly, trying out new materials and techniques, combining old and new ideas about as fast as I could make the pieces.

One day I drove out to a large artists' supply store and bought a tall maple easel with black iron wheels and balances, which I still use. I was on a course of change and growth with few of the doubts I had suffered previously. The energy I had in the studio extended into much of the rest of my life in Mexico. Artists like Armando Villagrán, Carmen Padín, Federico Calderón, and many others became part of my circle of friends. They invited me to their studios. I was welcomed into their homes and shared a little of their life in Mexico.

HEAVY BREATHING • *There were two exceptions to this happy change.* One was that I began to have breathing problems. I saw the embassy doctor several times. He said that many people were having the same symptoms, from the extreme pollution. He had sent several people back to Washington recently because of it. I tried various medications and regimes but it got worse as time went on. It became so bad that I had to rest partway as I climbed up to my bedroom. I developed asthma and could hardly walk a block without wheezing and chest pain.

The second exception was that my relationship with Edwin, which had improved, was declining rapidly. He had always been possessive but his jealousy became the stimulus for almost daily recriminations, without any basis in fact. I had always been faithful. His temper was explosive at home and I tiptoed around every possible issue. As a present for him, I bought a little print from an artist I had met recently. Edwin unwrapped it, saw the signature, and threw it across the room, suggesting I had a relationship with this man. I couldn't avoid everything and didn't like feeling that I needed to think so carefully about everyone I saw and everything I said. We tried some small weekend trips with Daniel and by ourselves when Daniel wanted to sleep at his best friend's house. The weekends were all right but trouble was back as soon as we returned to everyday life.

While we were in Mexico, Edwin's mother died. I was astounded when he did not permit me to go to her funeral. Even today, I cannot understand it. It was so lacking in respect, so inexplicable. I loved his father, Dave, and wanted to be there for him. Edwin's sister, not knowing the circumstances, never forgave me for this tremendous omission.

Meanwhile the doctor suggested that I leave the city because of my respiratory problems. I went to Acapulco and stayed for a few weeks at the vacation home of a friend. Her apartment was on a cliff high above the bay, with a gentle warm wind blowing all the time. In a few days I felt better and in two weeks I seemed restored to health. I was walking and working, and returned to Mexico City feeling fine. The asthma and breathing problems immediately returned. The doctor said he was going to require my permanent evacuation from Mexico. That entailed taking Daniel out of school where he was nicely settled in, and the two of us going back to Washington. Edwin could not accept that I leave without him. We looked for alternatives.

A PLACE IN THE COUNTRY • *In Mexico City, the mountains trap the dirty air.* It falls on the city and stays captured on the valley floor. In the eighties, twenty million people needed cars and buses to get around. They needed to burn some form of carbon for heat in the winter. They built and rebuilt, releasing the dust. At least two million of those people did not have modern sewers or running water. Chemical debris mixed with the dust. Lead from the gasoline, carbon monoxide, sulfuric acid, nitric oxide combined in the high altitude air. No wonder the canaries died.

Over the mountains, in the smaller cities and towns, the air was clear. We took out a map and drew a perimeter to include choices within an hour or two of the city. Tepoztlán was one of those.

I drove there to see what it was like.

I stayed in the new, white hotel and spent a few days catching my breath and looking around. My friend Elena knew an artist living in Tepoztlán. She sent him a note. He knew of someone with a guesthouse that might be available. When I met Roger, he was a bit laconic in his description but called his acquaintance and made an appointment for me to see the guesthouse. Paula, the owner, explained her rules and we came to an agreement. I planned to move into the guesthouse as soon as I could.

Paula's tiny guesthouse was six streets from the zócalo. It was near the end of a narrow dirt lane lined with stone and adobe walls six and seven feet high. All over Tepoztlán, the street walls were covered with bougainvillea and vines — intense reds, fuchsias, pinks, even orange — uncontained by the property lines. The gates and doors that punctuated the streets were usually the same blue, occasionally green. A few non-conformists chose other colors. All were brilliant in the high altitude sunshine.

Back once more in Mexico City, I found that I needed very few things — painting materials, some books, sheets and towels, not much more.

City clothes were not needed nor wanted. I did want my tape player and a radio. I used to love to hear all the faraway shortwave broadcasts that come over the air at night. I don't know why the radio is so much better at night, but I am very glad that it is. In Tepoztlán, on Sunday nights you could hear Willis Conover's jazz program on *The Voice of America*. News came from Canada, South America, and Asia. There were dramas on the BBC, and music from everywhere, all accompanied by crackling static, high-pitched whistles, and the romance of night-time flights of fancy. I am still an inveterate listener. Unfortunately, the Internet has all but eliminated the snaps, crackles, and pops.

From the beginning, painting was at the center of my life in Tepoztlán. I was breathing, walking, sleeping, and painting. Health returned. I stayed away from the city. Once in a few weeks, I drove back for some brief errand or event. Afterward, I gratefully returned to my little house. As I became better acquainted with my rural neighbors and weekend artist friends, and came to know the village, I felt more and more that I wanted to stay.

My landlady was not a very congenial person and a few times people warned me to be cautious around her. In the spring dry season she let the water cistern run dry. The little house became very uncomfortable. I had to haul water from the public tap, which ran only a few hours a day. Friends offered me showers and sympathy and advice on where to move. Roger again came to my aid and arranged for me to see the house of his friend Margot. As I entered the gate and crossed the stone bridge I thought I had entered paradise.

Of all the memories, the expansiveness of that time in Tepoztlán resonates in my memory. For the first time, I chose to use my life as seemed right to me. Out of habit stretching back to my childhood, at first I felt guilty to be so free, so comfortable. No one — least of all me — expected me to ever abandon the iron corset of responsibility just to be happy. I laid it aside for a while. Eventually, I felt bound to try to stuff myself back into its contours.

THE LONG RIDE • *And so, one summer day, I put my bags and boxes back in the car. In the rearview mirror, I saw Octavio standing in the shade at the edge of the veranda, his old hat in his hand, watching me drive away.*

The car crossed the village slowly, skirting the zócalo. The day before I had given back my post office box key. It was not a market day and the zócalo was quiet. The midday toasting at the tortillería was starting and sent a breath of its sweet smell through the open car window.

The car turned left onto the high street leading away. Two streets up the hill I passed the corner of Roger's street. On the next block I noticed that someone occupied the upstairs apartment that had been rented the year before to the anthropologist.

I passed the low iron fence of the Church of San Miguel. At the end of the summer that fence would be braided with garlands of wild orange zinnias from the hills above. For now, though, climbing roses twisted through the spikes. Once I passed the jacaranda trees, I had to accelerate, turn up the entry ramp, and enter the highway.

The highway was in good condition. The state had recently mowed the verges and repainted the white dividing lines. The traffic was light. Every car passed me. The curves and vistas were all familiar. I didn't stop at Tres Marias. Before the toll booth the road makes a long horseshoe turn around the edge of a deep barranca. The little stream at the bottom was a thousand feet down and the zigzag of the sierra was two thousand feet overhead. Many afternoons in the summer rainy season, rainbows — doubles and even triples — crossed the entire space in perfect parabolas. I pulled off onto a skinny space on the shoulder and ate the snack Carmen had put on the seat of the car — Doña Elvira's tortillas with fresh cheese and an avocado.

Once past the tollbooth, the traffic picked up. The road descended into the haze. La Malinche stood still and snowy over the entrance to the Periférico, the highway into Mexico City.

NINE

Detours

I RETURNED TO WASHINGTON ALONE and rented a small apartment downtown. I took it for a few months and didn't know what would happen after that. My sons went together to the College of William and Mary to start the school year. Edwin arrived and with hope and good will we bought a hundred-year-old row house in Capitol Hill, a few blocks from the Library of Congress and the Folger Library. The house in Fairfax was rented and shortly after our return the tenants bought it.

At the same time I rented a studio for myself. It was the hayloft of a carriage house, now converted to a garage. A long flight of wooden steps, overhung by a magnificent magnolia tree, led up to the studio entry. It was a great space. The owner was about to refinish the floor, but I persuaded him to leave the old wood alone and use the money for skylights, which he did. It was a nice long room with a square alcove off to one side. I had an old yellow sofa, left from the Annandale days. An antique china closet I had brought from Mexico was just right for paints and all the small containers that clutter up every studio. With my sturdy easel and a drawing table I was ready to work.

In the summer, before I left Mexico, I had been invited to do a large exhibition in Mexico City. My old friend, Margaret, wrote a very nice catalogue essay for it. Shortly after I left, in September, a major earthquake reduced much of the city to ruins and, of course, the exhibition was canceled. My friends and relatives mostly lived in older buildings. They were all right. Newer buildings, however, were prone to collapse straight downward. When I visited a year later, some streets were still buried under mountains of rubble.

I met Rebecca soon after I arrived in Washington. She had recently formed a business to represent artists and craftspeople. Most of them were from Eastern Europe where she and her husband had served in the Foreign Service. We developed a good relationship, and she sent my work to various exhibitions, venues, and commission competitions. Her outlook was that we should each concentrate on what we did best: my job was to make art, hers to know what to do with it.

One day I walked into the Library of Congress and found that an acquaintance from Korea had become the head of the Korea Division. I was interested in ancient books and papermaking, and he facilitated further study at the Library. After I had been working at the Asia Division for a while, I was permitted to look around the storage areas. I saw boxes donated in the twenties and thirties, with their original shipping tags intact, never opened. Some of these boxes were catalogued as "Gift of…" but the contents were unexamined. It takes a lot of money to open, decipher, and catalogue materials so that they are usable for scholarship and research. The Library was then in the process of digitizing the catalogues. After that the librarians were hoping to be able to get to the thousands of boxes in the attic.

I met many people at the Smithsonian and the Freer Gallery of Asian Art. I was curious about some of the identifications and labeling of some ancient works at the Freer but felt they were the experts and I was an interested bystander. I had a number of conversations about paper and ink with the curator. One day, I was told to call the Korean Embassy and make an appointment with the cultural attaché. Because of my work at the Library, I had been nominated for a grant for travel and research on ancient Korean paper and books. I needed to fill out the paperwork so that the process could be completed. I was already selected, I was told, and when did I think I wanted to leave? By April I had my new passport, a visa for Korea, and the project was underway.

KOREA ONCE MORE • *The International Cultural Society of Korea was the* host organization. They made all the travel and hotel reservations and provided me with an assistant who helped with translation as needed. I went to many parts of the country, and the ICSK facilitated access to curators, museums, and collectors everywhere. One part of the research was at Hein-sa, the temple with the library where the great Tripitaka is stored. It consists of more than fifteen hundred Buddhist scriptures. Approximately every century, war permitting, the whole sutra is reprinted from the eighty-one thousand carved wooden printing blocks. The newest printing project was being planned when I visited in 1986. The preparations and execution took several years.

All the monks and nuns of this order must have work to earn their living. A nun, Young-dam, was going to make the handmade paper that was needed for the reprinting. Her father had been a papermaker. In the past it was very unusual for a woman to take up the craft, but he had taught her and they had worked together. She loved the freedom she had as a nun, to do the best work she could without the need to consider a husband or children, or how much money she earned. We spent a day talking and laughing in the courtyard of the convent.

I walked around with my assistant. She was surprised at the lightness of the atmosphere at the temple, the beauty of the buildings, and the surrounding forest. She told me she had never been to a temple before and had thought it would be very gloomy and boring. I was glad that I had seen Hein-sa so many years before, when it was a much more remote place, with fewer tourists. I was glad, too, that the order and the government together had committed funds and energy to keeping this great treasure for a future as long as its past.

With the help of the International Cultural Society, I had been in touch with many people I had known in the sixties. The Society arranged a luncheon with my old teacher, Park Se Won, and a number of cultural figures. He was very well known, and his work was often given to state visitors.

Several past friends called me when I was in Seoul, and I had wonderful meetings with them. I was able to see some of them often enough to feel that we had almost reestablished our relationships. A few of them planned a reunion, rounded up everyone they could find, and we met in a restaurant for long reminiscences, and much catching up. I found so much affection and good feeling stored up for me.

In the course of my research in Korea, I thought about the connections made with paper. Korea produced such excellent inks that they were exported as tribute to China, and the court signed scrolls and paintings, "made with Korean ink." Many aspects of Japanese culture have origins, distant and not so distant, in Korea. The tea ceremony, the *koto* (a stringed instrument) and its music, astronomy, Tamba pottery, Zen (Seon) Buddhism, and many other cultural assets arrived in Japan from Korea. I thought there were superb opportunities for original research. After I returned to the U.S., I mentioned these possibilities in scholarly circles. At that time not very much real estate, that is, museum space, scholarly grants, project funding, etc., was given to Korea. Usually it was subsumed under either China or Japan. All that has changed with the emergence of prosperity and modern life in Korea.

During the research grant, I documented everything with photography as well as written notes. I took many dozen rolls of print and slide film wherever I traveled. In some cases they were the very scenes I had photographed previously and serve as a record of the astounding changes in the country. Modern, prosperous, educated, respected Korea is not much like the mostly rural, desperately poor country I first encountered in 1964. Those twenty years were a pivotal and historic time.

The photographs taken during that trip became the center of my work for the next several years. When I returned to Washington I gave some talks at the Smithsonian, the Folger Library, and at a Dard Hunter Museum conference by video. The Library of Congress and Smithsonian staff invited me to give a slide talk. Since nearly all my subject materials were in private hands, it opened up some positive avenues of study and inquiry. The discussions afterward were very detailed and lengthy, and I was glad that my work proved to be useful. I received a query from a museum in New Orleans and another in St. Louis that said they had heard about my work from someone on the west coast. There was a major exhibition of *5,000 Years of Korean Art*, and in San Francisco I did a short television commentary at the opening.

The Library of Congress had just received a grant to conserve a very early Mexican document, the *Harkness 1531 Huejotzingo Codex*. The document is the account and transcript of a civil trial and contains parallel Nahuatl and Spanish texts. It is very elaborate, with many drawings, and is of enormous value to scholars. The Library Conservation Department was embarking on a major effort to save the crumbling and disintegrating treasure. By a string of roundabout events, I received a phone call inquiring if perhaps I might be available to talk with them. I lived nearby and went to the Library within a few days. We had a long discussion and examination of the codex. They asked if I could consult with them. I gave a slide talk, and we arranged for me to give a workshop and teach the Nahuatl (Indian) papermaking techniques. I donated some of the *amatl* (ficus) fiber that I had brought back from Mexico. They used my agate stones and other implements to make new paper that resembled the old in content, acidity, and weight. The conservators were successful and acknowledged my contribution to their project.

NO VIEW FROM THE STUDIO • *I worked in the studio, making poetry and* visual pieces. I made some unique sheets of paper, about thirty-five to thirty-eight inches high by about six feet long and used a great variety of materials on them — ink, colored pencil, watercolor, pastels, conté crayon — to make abstract remembrances of Mexico, homage to poets I liked, sometimes just rhythmical forms suggested by the texture and grain of the sheets themselves. They were like sanctuaries from my everyday life.

The return to the marriage, on the other hand, was a disaster for me. The old issues were all unresolved, unacknowledged. I went back to acting a part, presenting an acceptable exterior surface just to get through the days. Edwin went back to his old behavior, too. Promises to seek counseling, to be calmer and less controlling were forgotten or suppressed. I couldn't let him come to the studio. I needed that small place to be as quiet and tranquil as possible. He was concerned with every detail of my day. Nearly all the time I was bruised somewhere from his grabbing and holding me so tightly. Nothing was right. I lost confidence in my studio work and myself. One horrible day, once again I burned a large pile of work in the fireplace at the house. In that period of internal and external crisis, I felt that the most central fact of my identity had neither meaning nor validity.

I turned away from my art and tried to rethink my future, of having a profession in architecture, library consulting, or another means of redirection and escape. I was forty-four years old. Once more, I felt that my outer life was a masquerade concealing the inner anomie and alienation, the loss of autonomy.

Steve and Daniel were away at college. One Thanksgiving they were in Washington and my beloved Aunt May came for the holiday. She and I spoke on the phone from time to time and were as loving and close as ever even if we didn't see each other. The boys enjoyed her almost as much as I did—her wry, drop-dead humor and gentle loving enriched the weekend and our lives. My parents still fought their old battles. They didn't come for that holiday because Dad and Edwin could not stand to be in the same room together. I could only too easily imagine my life becoming one long war of attrition. Something had to give.

BUILDING A FUTURE • *Since my girlhood, I had imagined building houses.* I decided to study architecture to fulfill this old dream, to create a way to support myself, and to remove myself from an intolerable situation with my husband. I was more than a little afraid of him by then. His behavior was erratic in private. I could not predict what he might do or what might upset him.

I investigated schools, took the Graduate Record Examination (at age forty-five, out of school for twenty-three years), and applied to a few universities for the master's of architecture program. I received offers of teaching assistanceships and scholarships. My choices came down to three. The University of New Mexico was in Albuquerque. Shortly after returning from Mexico, we visited friends in Santa Fe. I got off the plane in Albuquerque, smelled the air, saw the Sandia Mountains, in the southern Rockies, and knew I wanted to be there. The high desert atmosphere and exquisite scenery of New Mexico appealed to me even more than the architecture I saw there. I think I imagined it might be a little like Mexico.

Virginia Tech was the most interesting for the work they were doing with an early emphasis on renewable energy, for the wonderful setting in Blacksburg, and for the department chair, who spent the day with me, and offered me support right there on the spot. The third was the University of Pennsylvania, the most prestigious institution, in the middle of Philadelphia. Edwin was very insistent that I should choose Penn because he was able to get to Philly easily on the train and the others were completely out of reach. The old pattern was continuing. I chose Penn.

The University of Pennsylvania campus is in the middle of West Philadelphia, adjacent to a very rough neighborhood. I traded my Washington studio for a small apartment about fifteen minutes' walk from the campus. It was stimulating and very interesting, both for the courses and for the experience of returning to be a full-time graduate student after such a long time. Some of the work was challenging and I enjoyed studying, as I always had. The program was for a combined degree in architecture and landscape architecture. I worked hard, began to make friends with some of my fellow students, even went out for a beer with them on a few Friday nights.

School Days

First of September

Girls' hair blowing across their eyes
Boys proudly wearing t-shirts a little too small
Men with glasses and important briefcases
Women with babies and books and seriousness on their laps

Promising lawyers, cool enterprisers-
Passionate zoologists, precise French speakers-
All dreaming

Couples and trios and quartets sit on the grass
Leaning toward and then away from each other
In a friendship-making dance

They talk about death and art and freedom and sex
And what kind of pizza to get

Penn is also home to a research group called the Pre-Columbian Society. While I was in Philadelphia I gave a talk about Nahuatl tribute and prayer papers and compared them with Mayan papers. The society members were eager to hear about the codex in the Library of Congress. A lively lunch discussion followed.

Edwin was always popping up to Philadelphia on the train. He sometimes called and sometimes just showed up. It didn't matter if I had to study, prepare for a charette (a competitive, collaborative, essential element of design work), or just needed some quiet time to read. Almost every weekend and sometimes during the week, he was there. I had to shop and cook, make conversation, be a wife. It was a fiasco.

Before I started at Penn, the Department chair had told me that, because it was a little late in the application period, I should enter the program, pay the very high tuition, and in the succeeding years I would receive financial aid. In the middle of the year, I had a review with the head of the School of Architecture. I was doing well academically. He was complimentary about the designs in my portfolio. I brought up financial aid. I was more than a little chagrinned when he said that if a student didn't receive financial assistance in the first year, it was not likely to happen at all. I had paid for the first year with money from pictures I had sold but there was not much left. There was no possibility that family funds could be used and I could not borrow such huge sums.

With the combination of circumstances as they were, I resigned from the program.

NEW YORK INTERMEZZO • *Edwin retired from the Foreign Service and* accepted a job with a foundation in New York. We moved there but never managed to settle in. The job was not a success for him. New Mexico had been on my mind since my first visit. Over the next year, I went to Santa Fe several times.

I used what I could of the time in New York. I was a volunteer at the Metropolitan Museum of Art, about five blocks from our apartment. I wandered through the museum at least a few times a week. One of the most memorable shows was in a small, pass-through hallway gallery. The pages of Cezanne's late notebooks were framed and hung so that you could see the evolution of his thinking as he moved toward abstraction near the end of his life. The same allée of budded trees was drawn over and over. You could see how Cezanne stripped away the extraneous to leave only the form and beautiful line. I went to see it several times.

The Museum of Modern Art was still on 53rd Street. There was a broad ivory marble staircase to the first exhibition floor. It turned about halfway up. As you looked up toward the top, Picasso's *Guernica* exploded in your face, fists shaking at the ruin from the sky, everyone screaming so viscerally you could hear them in your head. When you thought you had recovered from that shock, walking around the corner you found Matisse's *Red Studio*. Red everywhere but then the blue sea is just beyond the open window. The twentieth century was summarized in one magnificent painting after another. At the end of the huge gallery waited the Matisse *Bathers* and their lapis lazuli blue sea. And that was just the first room.

I walked in Central Park and the Cloisters and along the rivers. There were dozens of museums, and I went to a lot of them. We went to concerts and plays and went out to eat. We carried on the surface of the good life in New York without any sense of permanence or belonging.

We had a spacious apartment on 87th Street, but the small bedroom designated as my studio was more an overstuffed storage room. Stephen and Daniel were moving through their academic careers and came to New York only for holidays and term breaks. They were beginning to find their way out in the world. I saw my parents more than I had for years. They argued a little less only because as they grew older they had a little less energy. Edwin and Dad liked each other no better than they had earlier, but they found it possible to have a short family visit. Bobby and his family lived in Great Neck. We saw each other occasionally but our lives did not intersect very often.

When I had left Washington, my friend and mentor in the Asia Division suggested I call on his counterpart at the New York Public Library. I met him shortly after I arrived in New York. We had a pleasant talk for an hour and he gave me a copy of his own new book. Right then and there he offered me a desk in the Allen Room, Room 112, the main library's research room, to continue my research on ancient paper. I worked there and benefited from the library's resources and the wonderful help and support of the professional staff. From time to time I needed materials in the Rare Book Room and began to consult there on some identification issues. The Library invited me to deliver the Cam Memorial Lecture. They invited scholars from the entire metropolitan area and a few people came from Yale and Princeton as well. My friend Jean came from Washington. She is a paper expert and author herself and it was great to have her there. I was prepared for fifteen or twenty minutes of questions at the end of the talk. After almost an hour of questions, our hosts suggested it was time to go.

I met the Chief Librarian of the Asia Division at Columbia University. She took me to the basement and showed me the collection of *chekkori*. These large paintings usually are elegantly executed inventories of scholars' writing rooms, showing their collections of books, writing implements, and furniture. They use a primarily red palette and are stunning works of art. Columbia has a large collection but at that time no funds for conservation. The priceless scrolls were wrapped in dry cleaning bags to protect them as much as possible from the humidity of the steam heating pipes directly overhead. The librarian and I had a long afternoon's conversation about both the art and the conservation issues.

While I was in Washington reorganizing my nonartist future, I got a job as a diplomatic escort, accompanying official cultural visitors to the United States. I accompanied cultural grantees, university professors from Thailand and Ecuador, an Indian journalist, a Philippine artist, an East European Minister of Trade. Their visits were to facilitate educational and business objectives and to give them some familiarity with American life and customs.

Edwin had been very successful in the Foreign Service but he and the foundation were not a good match. He was asked to resign. He was devastated. I had a couple of escort assignments but he did not look for another position. The economic recession was beginning. New York was undergoing a severe downturn in the real estate market. The residents of our apartment building had voted for a very extensive renovation and a concurrent huge increase in the maintenance fees that made our apartment very expensive. Without Edwin's salary we found it very heavy going. There was no reason to stay in New York. We put the apartment up for sale and after a few months had a contract. We decided to move to New Mexico.

We packed up and said good-bye. The movers loaded the boxes and furniture once more. We stayed overnight in my cousin's apartment across town. Daniel went with me to Santa Fe while Edwin remained in New York to conclude the sale.

TEN

Santa Fe

IT WAS SUMMER IN THE LATE EIGHTIES. Santa Fe was less busy then, but the great changes in the plaza, the population, and especially the suburban sprawl were already underway. Tourists were there in profusion for the summer attractions: the Chamber Music Festival, the Opera, Indian Market. Daniel was spending the first of many summer vacations in Santa Fe. We looked around the city and waited for the movers.

A day or two after we arrived, Edwin called from New York. "Disaster," he said. The co-op board turned down the buyers. In cooperative buildings the residents own the whole building together and have the right to refuse to sell a share, effectively meaning an apartment. They don't have to give a reason. After Watergate, Richard Nixon was turned down by an east side co-op board and went to live in New Jersey. Despite a lot of last-minute maneuvering, the board was adamant and the sale did not go through. Edwin remained in New York. In Santa Fe, again through a friend of a friend, I went to stay in a little guesthouse on a llama farm. A few days later Daniel left for Massachusetts, and I looked for a job and a place to live. Edwin continued to stay in my cousin's apartment. He phoned me every night. There was a lot of phoning in our history and there was about to be a lot more.

The furniture had arrived in Santa Fe. I needed to find a place to live as quickly as possible. A lucky chain of circumstances brought me to Park Plazas, a large subdivision on the south side, and to a small three-bedroom townhouse with a little garden. I signed the lease and moved in at once. During this week my cousin called. She said that Edwin was still in her apartment and had overstayed his welcome. I needed to tell him to leave. He was reluctant to go. My mother loaned him a cot and some miscellaneous housekeeping items. He returned to camp out in our apartment on 87th Street.

I was offered another State Department assignment, to escort a European Minister of Trade on her official month-long visit. Could I leave within a day or two? I left everything in boxes, packed my bag, and was on my way.

If possible, every visitor has the opportunity to see one national park. The experience is usually a highlight of the trip. After this minister met with members of the business community in Denver, for example, we went to Yellowstone National Park. The escort must be a cultural interpreter, easing the way, explaining as necessary, but not imposing personal views on the experience of the visitor. The escort also facilitates appointments, drives to points of interest after more formal business is concluded, keeps accounts for funds, makes reports on the outcomes of the various programs, whether they were helpful to the foreign grantees and to the community and institutions visited. The escort is responsible for ensuring that the visitor shows up, on time, and ready for the appointment. I escorted one grantee that did not allow anyone in his hotel room, even to make the bed, and did not order any food in restaurants. All his meals for the first several days were only the food I shared with him from my own plate. The minister above did not want to bother with local people unless she saw that they were of immediate practical utility to her agenda. Local people support the grantees through their efforts and their taxes. The escort must negotiate the territory so that everyone benefits from the program.

WORKING IT OUT • *In October I returned to Santa Fe. I had bought a car* right after arriving in New Mexico and was very glad that I had it. I could not afford to buy a car again for 150,000 miles. While I was on my escort assignment, Edwin had been insistent, as usual, on my staying constantly in touch with him. On my return, by phone, he was adamant that we couldn't afford the uncertainty of my assignments. I must quit the State Department and get a job with regular income in Santa Fe. He said he was too depressed to send out his résumé. He was staying in the empty apartment in hopes that another buyer would appear — in the most depressed real estate market in decades. My name as well as his was on the New York mortgage. Bills had to be paid. I could never know in advance when or how many assignments would be offered during the course of a year, but if I was available, I could expect four or five over twelve months. It was intensive work, seven days a week, with a lot of paperwork in the aftermath. The grantees were interesting and varied. I saw a lot of the country. Mostly I liked it very well. But I bought the idea that certainty — that elusive condition — was more valuable, and embarked on a job search.

Santa Fe had, and still has, few opportunities to stumble onto a great job. Some statistician calculated that there are more restaurant servers with PhDs in Santa Fe than anywhere else in the country. It is a place where you build a network and create your own opportunity. Of course, that takes time. In the meantime there is a lot of low paid drudgery available. In a few days I had a job, my first and last taste of retail clerking, at a store on the Plaza. The manager herself had recently been promoted from clerk. One of her first acts was to remove the stools behind the counter. She forbade anyone from sitting down during paid hours, whether there were any customers in the store or not. The martinet manager scolded everyone in turn, always suggesting how replaceable each of us was.

The staff of the store could make a cast of characters in a novel. There was the single student with two children who went on to graduate from college and become a politician. The mother from Pojoaque whose son had just returned from several years in Florence, sick with AIDS, and wasting away in front of our eyes. The middle-age, recent divorcée with no job history and no credit but a lot of beautiful clothes, coming to the store every day as if she were going to lunch at the Pink Adobe restaurant, swathed in her silver jewelry and perfect makeup. This job paid only about half of my previous income. Very soon I was doing the Santa Fe regular, looking for another part-time position to supplement my income.

In a matter of several months, I went from being a moderately recognized artist, then a researcher with my work respected and accepted by preeminent scholars, consultant to two of the world's foremost libraries, and a diplomatic escort for cultural visitors, to working as a retail clerk being paid barely more than minimum wage. I moved from an apartment on New York's Upper East Side to a small Santa Fe subdivision house, then to a tiny guesthouse. In writing this paragraph, I realize that possibly my most basic attribute is the capacity for change.

ESPAÑOLA • *In October 1989 there was an ad for a bilingual teaching position* in Española, about forty minutes north of Santa Fe. The local school board had received a grant under Title VII, bilingual education, to create an arts program for early intervention for high-risk children. The initial five teachers were to design the program during the current year and implement it in the following. The pay was meager but very helpful, and the work was something I cared about. The planning period was somewhat disorganized but we accomplished what was necessary. In the fall I began teaching after-school classes in two schools, Española and Hernandez Elementary, commuting from Santa Fe, and working around the schedules of the schools and the store.

One of my colleagues told me of a position that was opening the next fall in her school, the junior high. The principal interviewed me and proposed me for the job. Following an interview with the school board, I was offered the position. I was brought in under a New Mexico program called Distinguished Scholars in the Schools. I had to pass the National Teachers Exam before the term started and take some education courses. I did both. I began in August 1990, a couple of weeks before the students arrived.

Teaching at the junior high was something new for me. I had lived through my own and my children's adolescence, observed youngsters in Mexico, Korea, and Japan. None of that prepared me for Española Junior High. The noise and physical disorder were not conducive to learning. There was little of the necessary sense of shared endeavor between teachers and students, or between administration and teachers. There was a very high level of violence in the community, many parents on drugs, many children being raised by grandparents because the parents were either not willing or not able to care for them. The youngsters mirrored the behavior around them.

The resources were meager. I made it my habit to bake cupcakes on Sunday evening and have a bake sale in school on Monday to pay for needed supplies. I wasn't the only one. Every winter one of the English teachers sold lemons with salt, very profitable, although terrible for the enamel on teeth. She used the money to put on a play and to take the students to a play every year in a theater in Santa Fe.

The principal asked me to be innovative and creative. I made a unit about paper airplanes. They had to fly and be beautiful. The Gulf War started around Martin Luther King, Jr.'s birthday. Many kids drew Saddam Hussein and George Bush shaking hands or used peace symbols in their projects. We made sculpture out of the folded sprocket strips of computer paper, huge murals on giant paper rolls from the hardware store, anything I could think of that didn't cost much. I made a game of noise, with students taking turns leading the loudest possible drumming with hands on the tables, learning to lead and to follow, improving coordination, and beating away some of their restlessness.

At lunch, though, I often ate in my classroom and listened to Bach or Mozart. Gradually, the students began to come in during their free time after eating lunch. They talked quietly or read, using my room to avoid the fights in the chaotic schoolyard. They often asked me to play "the guy who hummed along," Glen Gould playing the *Goldberg Variations*. In class, while the students had a quiet task, I read poetry aloud, very softly. There was no requirement that anyone listen. It was not schoolwork and yet the students began to ask me to read, and to choose poems. Wordsworth and Donne turned out to be favorites.

Española is in a beautiful setting, with particularly splendid views of the mountains. It has a lovely stretch of the Rio Grande running through it. The town did not reflect its surroundings but had many ramshackle buildings, a paucity of community resources, and a kind of despair that was not easy to lift. None of my students had ever been to a museum. None had ever been to the Santa Fe National Forest or the great mountain parks. I wheedled a couple of field trips from the principal, who was a good guy but overwhelmed by the school's troubles and an uncooperative school board.

All of this did little for kids with major problems. One of my students had been attacked in the schoolyard and raped by a student while several other boys held her down. The rapist was receiving counseling and was there in class with her, passing her in the hallways, laughing at his exploit. She often acted out her feelings with aggressive behavior and rude speech. She was considered by several teachers to be a hopeless case. Eventually the court declared her to be incorrigible and sent her to a sort of reform school, very tough and harsh.

Another youngster came to school with circles under his eyes, his homework often not done. His mother was an addict. He awoke early to feed and diaper his baby sister, got the next sister off to school, managed to get through his own school day, and then rushed home again, knowing the baby had not been fed or changed since he had left in the morning. He was thirteen years old, trying to be a man. He was very angry with his mother.

An art class was not going to do much for these kids and the dozens more like them that I met. About all I could offer was a few quiet minutes and to listen if they had something to say.

To carpool with my colleague Paula, I left my house on Santa Fe's south side around six-thirty in the morning to be at her house a little before seven. We got back about five o'clock on a regular day, six-thirty on an after school day. Once in a while, especially on the way home on Fridays, we treated ourselves to tea and a shared muffin at the Tesuque Market. In the spring we decided to walk in the Santa Fe National Forest and began with the lowest trails. Each week we started at the next higher parking turnoff. By August we started at the ski basin parking lot at twelve-thousand feet. It was walking for pleasure, a calm respite with easy conversation.

Steve had joined the Foreign Service. After his initial training I went to his induction ceremony in Washington. I was glad to have the time with him. We all went to Daniel's graduation in Massachusetts. He decided to take a year off from his studies and moved to Alexandria, near Washington. The following year he began work toward his doctorate in mathematics in Chicago. They both were establishing themselves in new trajectories.

I could not paint during this period, but on as many Sundays as possible I ground ink and made calligraphy on newspapers. For those few hours the black ink of simple poems swirled over the newsprint. I lost myself in the line.

It was five long years since I had left Tepoztlán. I tried not to think about it and never talked about those halcyon days.

Meanwhile, during my stint in Española, Edwin was flying back and forth at unpredictable intervals, calling from New York almost every evening to tell me about seeing his old friends, the restaurants he found, the occasional theater, whatever he was doing. He always mentioned mopping the floor of the empty apartment where he was still sleeping on my mother's cot. He emphasized how our finances were stretched thin and refused to allow me to purchase a washing machine. Paula urged me at least to buy a washer without the dryer. It would be cheaper than all the quarters spent in Dirty Joe's Laundromat machines. More importantly, it would give me a little free time. I had no extra energy for arguing with Edwin. In light of all the larger issues, this might appear to be a small thing but the washing machine meant a lot to me.

In New York the realtor relayed offers for the apartment. She dealt with Edwin because he was there. He turned down several offers over many months, each less than the one before. The market kept falling. Without that New York expense I would have been all right, but with it I struggled and watched my savings evaporate. I called the realtor and told her to let me know directly when there was another offer. Finally there was a contract, very low but real. To complete the sale I had to send a check to the closing. I was determined that when we sold the apartment I would arrange a final divorce. Meanwhile, except in a legal sense, we were no longer a married couple.

ELEVEN

Turnaround

DURING THOSE YEARS IN THE EARLY NINETIES, I began to establish myself in Santa Fe. I expected to live here the rest of my life. I got my driver's license, registered to vote, took out a library card. I loved the Southwest Room of the downtown main library, with its oak tables, leather chairs, and beamed ceiling. The light from the street streams in through high, small paned, territorial windows. The reading room has a slight electrical hum and the soft sound of readers turning their pages. Now we have added the tap of laptop keys. I read the *Santa Fe New Mexican* newspaper, including the sometimes daffy letters to the editor. I began to follow a little of local politics. I went to the museums. The Palace of the Governors on the Plaza had been in use for centuries and now was the history museum. It is a wonderful old building and in a few contiguous rooms gives you a feeling of Santa Fe's Spanish past. It had been the residence and offices of the Governors. Lew Wallace, when he was governor, sat in the front room overlooking the Plaza, and wrote *Ben-Hur*.

Next-door is the Museum of Fine Arts with a wealth of New Mexico painters and the lovely Saint Francis Auditorium, where the Chamber

Music Festival delights us every summer. The Festival was only a few years old then. Sheldon and Alicia, the founders, still ran it as an intimate expression of their ideals. I volunteered and heard twelve or fifteen concerts every summer. I've supported the Chamber Festival ever since. One of my early volunteer gigs was on the TLC (Tender Loving Care) committee that assisted the artists during their time at the festival. I met many people, local and visiting, and it helped me to find my way.

Steve was in Tijuana for his first Foreign Service post. I spent a week with him in a part of Mexico I had not seen before. Away from Avenida Revolución and the border, Tijuana was a normal, modern Mexican city along the Pacific coast. He was seeing a nice girl and was enjoying his first assignment.

I volunteered with the Santa Fe Symphony. They performed on Sundays at the old Sweeney Center, which had been the high school gym before the new high school was built. I dressed up, by Santa Fe standards, and ushered at the concerts. These activities gave me a sense of real life. I felt that out there somewhere, I had a future, even if it was still obscure.

SUNDAY AFTERNOON AT THE SWEENEY • *One Sunday afternoon, at a concert, an attractive woman introduced herself.* We chatted a bit in the lull before the concert. She told me that she had recently separated from her husband and had taken a new job in Taos, eighty miles north of Santa Fe. After a few minutes' conversation, she said she wanted to introduce me to him, that "he would just love me"— love to meet me, I supposed she meant. We walked over to the door. A tall man in a gray suit was taking tickets. We said hello and shook hands in the ordinary way. The lights blinked their warning, and we parted to take our seats.

Those ninety seconds were enough.

That afternoon RD could see me from his seat but I couldn't see him. He has told me many times that he watched me all through the concert.

RD • *Two weeks later I was grading schoolwork in the evening. The doorbell rang.* I thought it was my next-door neighbor, the violin teacher. The tall man stood there in a leather bomber jacket, leaning against the doorframe. He said hello, in three notes, one eyebrow raised a little, wondering if I knew who he was. I was surprised to see him there. We had not exchanged phone numbers in our ninety-second meeting. He had done some research and put himself right at my door.

RD was a nice-looking man, in his mid-fifties, smiling in delight at least partly because of my consternation. We chatted briefly, offering each other bits of our current lives. He was newly arrived in Santa Fe from Ohio. He was teaching art at the School for the Deaf. I don't remember what I told him about myself but I do remember being embarrassed to be grading papers in an old flannel shirt. Too soon, I had to finish my homework. We wrote down our phone numbers and said that we would visit another time, which we did.

Soon afterward, on a rainy night, we went to a store on the Plaza for ice cream. The details seem clear even now, twenty years later. We ordered raspberry sherbet, then sat in a booth, and talked for a long time. He told me that his life had taken some rough turns. He had come to Santa Fe on a whim to try and find a new beginning, a common scenario in this city. He and his wife both expected that they would soon arrange for a mutually desired divorce. He talked about his life in Ohio, making sculpture, teaching deaf children, designing and building houses. He had three grown children. He asked if I wanted anything else. Then he went to the counter and ordered a second scoop of sherbet for himself. I don't think I had ever seen anyone do such a thing. I never had considered that if I wanted that second scoop I could just have it. That simple gesture was a true mark of his generosity—to himself as much as to everyone else.

We saw each other more frequently, becoming acquainted, becoming friends. One afternoon I took him to some of the downtown landmarks. The cathedral, built in the French style by Bishop Lamy, was being renovated. We walked around a bit and sat down on a bench in the back, outside the sanctuary. I noticed his hands. They were small for a man six feet tall. He sat half turned toward me, one hand open over the end of the wooden armrest, the other on the back of the bench. Perhaps from a lifetime of using tools, his knuckles were starting to twist a little, oddly graceful. He reminds me that I asked him, "You're not a Republican, are you?" He echoed, "You're not religious, are you?" With our mutual negative confirmations, we could go on letting our friendship develop. I do have Republican friends, but I haven't fallen in love with any of them.

Another day, we took a walk along the Alameda, the riverfront, both of us with our hands in our pockets, a half a yard apart. We walked and talked, very conscious of each other. The tension kept us just far enough apart that we could not possibly accidentally touch.

Around this time he moved from a shared house arrangement in Santa Fe to a tiny house in La Mesilla, near Española, on a horse ranch that bred Arabians. In front of the house a fence crossed the middle of a small pond. The other side was Santa Clara Pueblo with a magnificent view of Black Mesa and the Jemez Mountains. The pond was full of wild water lilies, cattails, and reeds. The house itself was one room. There was a kitchen smaller than a closet and a strange bathroom with steps up between the shower, the sink, and the toilet. There was very little heat from a single propane space heater with a huge chimney. But there were plenty of mice. He moved his piano, and a few pieces of furniture. I helped transport a large pile of suits, ties, and city shoes from Santa Fe. He built a skinny sleeping loft over one end of the single room, under a row of square windows that didn't open. And he built a skinny wooden ladder to get up there.

We kept on visiting and talking for some months. We ate together once in a while. He invited me out or I cooked something simple. We told each other more of our stories. He had several undergraduate and graduate degrees in architecture, engineering, arts education, an MFA and an MBA. He had been building homes in Ohio. The same awful eighties that ate up my resources had destroyed his building company when the housing market fell apart.

One evening he had been visiting at my house, in what was becoming usual but not taken for granted. As soon as he arrived home he called me. He had something more to say. Over all these months we had talked about everything that interested us, past and present. But never in all those months had we even alluded to our relationship, which interested him considerably. He said we were having what seemed to be an immaculate affair, a love affair except that we had not yet shared even one kiss. We agreed to meet for a little while the next morning at Cloud Cliff Bakery on Second Street. Naturally, we talked the subject over with our muffins and decided to go on an official date

For our date, we drove up the Cibola Forest Road to the Sandia Crest above Albuquerque. It was a perfect day. Where the road used to make a turn we pulled off next to a distinctive rock formation. We could see across the West Mesa past the volcanoes, to Mount Taylor. We got out of the car to admire the view—and each other. We stood there for a long time under the trees with our arms around each other.

It took us a little more time to become lovers. He is a gentle and thoughtful man in this as in the rest of his life. We had a lot of fun in that loft.

MOVING ON • *That spring and summer I was looking for a new place to* live. It needed to be quiet, beautiful, affordable, and available. Edwin was not resigned to the end of the marriage. I had waited to arrange the legalities until he seemed to be back on his feet. He had taken a position as escort comparable to the one I had given up a few years before. Our sons were grown men, the apartment was sold, and he was absent from my life. We needed to organize a reasonable and definite conclusion. One day there was some sort of disagreement and it escalated. In anger, he took a knife and plunged it into a breadboard. I picked up my keys and purse, got in my car, and thought I would not see him again. I went to an attorney the next day. He advised me to stay out of reach and out of sight. A friend offered me a cabin he had in Red River and I was about to go there.

I dropped by the school to say good-bye to RD. He was temporarily returning to Ohio to work on a sculpture commission. He reached in his pocket and put his keys in my hand. He was going to be away until school started in the fall. I should use his place as long as I wanted. He drew me a map so that I could find my way through the maze of tiny dirt tracks. I said good-bye, very unsure what was to happen next.

I went to La Mesilla immediately and stayed in RD's house. I could hardly bear to leave it at all. A few Santa Fe friends came to visit. Kate painted a green-and-red Black Mesa. Terry made a still life of the water kettle. Mostly I was there alone, relishing the solitude. I was writing every day and painting. Melinda, who I knew through the bilingual education department, lived at Santa Clara Pueblo. I saw her there and went to the summer buffalo dances.

ARROYO HONDO • *In the summer I moved into a guesthouse in Arroyo* Hondo, south of Santa Fe. I left RD a note and a map, planted some flowers at his house as a thank-you, and hoped he would call when he came back.

My little house was charming. It was surrounded by horse farms and houses on five-to-ten-acre lots, with fields of wild flowers, crooked fences, and red skies at sunset. I used the living room as my studio and a little glassed-in side porch as a sitting room. I had a nice-size bedroom with a kiva fireplace, a big kitchen, a tub in the bathroom, and a washing machine. Paula came in her small white pick-up truck. We moved whatever I was taking: books, a few pots and dishes, clothes, art materials, my beautiful easel, and the drawing table. Steve had moved to Jakarta by then, and I had his cat. The rest I left for Edwin.

New Mexico has modern domestic laws and treats marriage as a contract between consenting parties, with provision for the contract to be dissolved. It's a community property state, which means that whatever is accumulated in the course of a marriage belongs to both parties, and must be shared equitably if the marriage is dissolved, regardless of who earned which part of the family income. The lawyer called me and said that the judge rejected my petition for dissolution because she did not find that the division of community property met this standard. I was to make a list of the property retained by each of us and, in my own handwriting, provide some information about my education and financial situation. As a result of the work of the Forum Committee several years before, the Department of State had revised its policies. Spouses now had a vested right to half the annuity earned for each year of service, in recognition of their contributions. That was also part of the community property. We each would keep whatever was in our separate names alone, without further inquiry. I took part of the household goods, like linens and kitchenware, and carefully inventoried it as best I could under the circumstances. All this paperwork took time and was very uncomfortable. The lawyer spoke to Edwin and at last he signed the property settlement. A little while later I had the final decree. It took time to make the mess and time to clean it up.

Those first weeks in Arroyo Hondo were wonderful. I walked the narrow unpaved roads and admired the waves of Pecos sunflowers and asters that were starting to bloom. I occasionally met a neighbor on horseback or out walking. My landlord's dog, a huge black lab, liked to trot alongside me and the landlord was happy that someone wanted to take him on a walk. I met some neighbors and began to have a few visitors. RD came back for the start of the school year, and I was happy that he wanted to pick up where we had left it in the summer. He continued to live in La Mesilla and came to see me often. I was not ready for anything more.

I moved into the guesthouse with very little by way of furniture: a small loveseat, an old table, and two straight chairs. I slept on the floor on an air mattress from Kmart. The corner of Old Pecos Trail and Old Las Vegas Highway has now become a semi-official market, but then it was a few guys with pickups selling firewood. I bought a load of wood for the coming winter and about twenty aspen trees. RD came over and asked what I was doing with all those poles. I needed a bed, I told him, and planned to make one. I had a very rudimentary toolbox and almost no knowledge of carpentry, but I would know more by the time I was finished. RD said he would help. He knew a lot about carpentry but he had never made a bed, either. We worked on it for much of the fall.

I had a little hand plane and stripped the bark inch by inch, a satisfying job but very slow. I made a picture of a bed. RD said, "It will look pretty but it will never hold up." We drew up plans, with almost straight posts at the corners and long trees as rails on the sides, head and foot holding it all together. I sanded and polished the tree trunks, smoothed away the knots, although even now they have the shadows, the memories of the branches. In the hot September air the sawdust sprayed out of the saw and caught in our skin and hair and eyelashes.

We had a lot of fun making that bed. It has aged pretty well, although it does have a few idiosyncrasies. But then, so do we, so it's a good fit for the two of us.

Glowing in the morning
    As early sun sends a knife of light into the room
Glowing at midnight
    As the moon changes from evening gold to night white

Still holding together for now.

I was painting and doing photography. I walked every day, in snow, rain, and sun, and almost always the landlord's black Lab, Jonathan, came along. He was good company. I had simplified my life down to essentials. It felt very good.

I showed my work to various galleries around Santa Fe. Most of the owners were not at all interested in the kind of work I was doing. A few were kind and generous and sat down with me to explain the Santa Fe gallery world, and offer observations and suggestions. Richard W. had opened a lovely gallery, and when he moved downtown he invited me to show my work. His biggest problem was that people wandered in thinking it was a small museum, not a gallery with things for sale. He took me to lunch once in a while, and we talked about Japan and many other things. He was wonderful company, and I often think of him when I pass the First Interstate Bank corner. I kept working and walking and getting used to having RD in my life.

In Española one afternoon in late fall, the light fell onto the loft in square shafts. The sheets were tangled around us. We soaked up the warm sun for a while and realized we were hungry. Cooking was not RD's strong suit. Given the alternative of getting dressed, driving a few miles, and eating in Española, we decided to cook. He had a hot plate, one saucepan, one small skillet, and a microwave oven. He found a package of spaghetti and a jar of tomato sauce, sequestered for emergencies. Some greens and other miscellany lurked in his tiny cube of a fridge. There was salad, sort of. We put the sauce in the pan on the hot plate. A creative solution was needed. He had an enormous bowl that he filled with water and put in the microwave to boil so that we could cook the spaghetti.

If two people did anything in the space called the kitchen they would have to be in constant physical contact. When we reached for a fork or the salt, a body was right there to reach across. There was plenty of distraction while we waited for the water to boil. A glass of red wine, a taste of the sauce. Still waiting. He rummaged around and found some ancient crackers and the remainder of a chunk of cheese. Twilight turned to dark. The water had heated up to tepid. Did the water really have to be at a rolling boil to cook the spaghetti? The whole package went into the water and back in the microwave. Many cycles later the spaghetti was not anywhere close to al dente. A little more red wine and the time had come. The entire contents of the bowl were glued together in a solid tangle of sticky spaghetti lines. We could hardly cut it with a knife. More like chewing gum than food. When we turned over the bowl the whole jumble bounced in the sink. We tried to eat it but we laughed so much that finally we gave up, put on our clothes, and went to Española to the one and only place, near the highway, that served spaghetti.

RD loves to build things, anything at all. His solution to any problem is to draw it up, with a sharp, 2H green pencil on white tracing paper. He saw my paintings sitting on the floor and designed and built a storage rack. He made bookcases and I unpacked the book boxes. When it started to be chilly, he helped to put plastic sheeting over the old-fashioned steel windows. I had very few appliances and wanted to get a blender to make the smoothies we liked. We went together to a store and he picked up a couple of small appliances, too. At the checkout he took out his wallet to pay for everything. I nervously asked him if we were setting up housekeeping. He reminds me that I was visibly shocked at the idea. We paid separately and went back together to my house.

One weekend RD brought extra jeans and hung them in an empty closet. I had to ask him to take them home again. He was growing to be very important to me; I did not want to lose that but I could not imagine, then, living with anyone. Or, rather, I could imagine it and knew I was not ready to take on that level of commitment. He knew it, too, and put his jeans back in his car.

I went to New York to visit my family for a few days. I hadn't seen them since I had come to New Mexico. My parents were just the same, together at war, and I tried to have time with them separately. I saw my brother once or twice. I was glad to have seen them and glad to be returning to New Mexico.

I came back to a very cold house. The cat was nearly crazed. The boy next door was supposed to have fed her and forgot. She survived by eating the plants and was very agitated for many days afterward.

It was very cold and the cat wanted to sleep with me, curled around my feet under the comforter. The house had electric baseboard heaters, but they put out very little heat. After much complaining, the landlord bought a little wood stove for the living room fireplace. I warmed bricks on it every night, wrapped them in towels, and put them in the icy bed.

The kiva fireplace in the bedroom was pretty and romantic and provided a little warmth, but as it burned down it sucked more heat out of the house than it added. I slept in hiking socks and long underwear, and I still froze. First thing every morning I put on layers of clothing, carried in firewood, and relit the stove. I stoked it at night but it was small and needed new wood every hour.

The cat didn't approve of RD usurping her place in bed. She was very out of sorts when he stayed over. We had to push her out into the living room and close the bedroom door for the night. We slept wrapped together, not a finger or toe outside the comforter. We were so cold that everything was funny. We laughed and laughed and warmed ourselves with nonsense. By morning, ice had formed on the plastic over the windows from our condensing breath. Time after time, an image like a smiling whale formed on one pane. It was a talisman of sorts, without intrinsic meaning but always welcome.

That winter I met RD's mother, Marian, and her boyfriend, Phil. One afternoon they arrived unexpectedly from Ohio on their annual driving trip. RD called to say he was coming to pick me up so I could meet her. We had a nice evening and I invited them back to my house at Arroyo Hondo. I still have the snapshot Phil took of us.

I developed the habit of walking meditation. The straw of summer flowers stuck up through the snow, bright and clear, each fiber visible and distinct. In the cold road the dirt tracks froze for days and then became a river of mud before refreezing with ruts half a foot deep. The fence posts leaned every which way and pulled the wire strands into patterns of crossing lines. The juniper trees were weighed down with the profusion of blueberries that comes with a cold winter. My boots joined the tracks of deer, rabbits, a small bear, the first beings crossing a field in the morning.

One Path Home
Kikyo Ichi Ro

Alone the old crane stands
In the morning stillness
Long feathers rustling amidst brittle stems
Eyes sweeping the sky

Considering the path home

I spent that winter painting, falling in love, walking, and separating the here and now from wistful glances at what might be or might have been.

The little guesthouse was cold and colder. I kept a kettle on the woodstove and a pot of soup on the kitchen stove. I baked just to warm up. One morning I opened the closet and found that my clothes had frozen stiff. I fired up the woodstove in the living room and hung clothes everywhere, with newspapers on the floor to catch the melting ice. I pulled out shoes and everything else that was on the frozen floor of the closet. The walls were soaked. No wonder it was so cold. It took a few chilly days for everything to defrost, become wet, and then turn moldy. Most of the clothes were ruined. The landlord came over and said that he would think of something when the weather improved in the spring. I didn't have a lease and started to look for a place to move.

THE FIRST WRECK • *I had very little savings left. I spoke with some mortgage* brokers and decided to try to buy a small house. We looked in all the modest neighborhoods. I had a contract for a nice little place, and just as it was ready for the last signatures, the agent received an offer over the asking price. She suggested I raise my offer. I didn't want to start down that path and walked away. I had a commitment for a mortgage, good for only a few more weeks, and no house to buy. I was supposed to meet RD for lunch at The Natural Cafe on Cerillos Road. I drove down a little street to look for a parking place. Near a small park there was a huge sign on the wall, "FOR SALE BY OWNER," with a phone number. Two ferocious attack dogs were in the front yard so I didn't dare open the gate, but I called right away from a pay phone nearby. The owner made an appointment with me for five minutes later. She showed me around and the two of us came to an understanding right then. Her husband brought a contract form and we signed it that afternoon. I thought I could live there, possibly for the rest of my life.

All went well at the closing a few weeks later. With only a little trepidation, I signed the piles of forms and walked away with the keys. I owned a house. I arranged to meet RD there. As I opened the door, the neighbor looked over from her garden and said hello. We chatted for a minute or two when we were interrupted by an enormous crash from inside the house. Quickly I said good-bye to Mary and went inside.

RD and I had talked about some improvements. The water heater, for example, was in the dining room. There were some other oddities that I supposed would be addressed in time. RD had brought his tools and, as I was saying hello to the neighbor, without any further ado, he began the destruction. RD is a very forthright person when it comes to demolition. I never slept without dust and rubble somewhere in that house.

Remodeling is a world unto itself. I had never been around a construction site, had never done anything more extensive than hiring that Chinese carpenter to enclose a little section of the furnace room back in Fairfax.

I was an absolute innocent as to the meaning of taking on the renewal of a thirties house. By 1992 many owners had modified the original house, with varying degrees of knowledge, planning, and success. For example, the hot water tank in the dining room. I was unprepared for the volume of omnipresent debris and had no idea of the tools necessary, nor the time, the most expensive commodity there is.

Remodeling is like Monopoly. You land at some necessity and must pay for it. It is about having a clear goal, a carefully made plan, following it meticulously, and modifying it every day in the light of new discoveries and changing circumstances. In other words, it is just like your regular life but much more expensive.

RD had designed, built, and remodeled houses for many years in Ohio. His vocabulary included jacks, studs, headers, lag screws, hanger bolts, joists, trusses. He had four kinds of hammers, a dozen different screwdrivers, eight different saws (cross cut, rip, miter, reciprocating, circular, on and on), sets of more beautiful tool parts than I could imagine a use for.

I met John Manion at the tool rental shop. I had gone there for something but didn't know enough to know what I needed. John was concluding his business and offered his advice, very expert advice as it turned out. He came to the house that afternoon. By the time he left, the three of us had started a rewarding and loving friendship. John was to help us through two years of travail and accomplishment, contributing laughter, sweetness, good ideas, and hard work.

The original main bedroom was in the front, exposed to the street. We wanted to sleep in the back bedroom, overlooking the garden I was starting. The whole back of the house was miscellaneous add-ons, none of them making much sense. RD said we'd just take down a few walls and reconfigure the space. So we did.

He was immediately busy with his sledgehammer again. It turned out that the interior walls were all made of concrete block. The dust drifted through the house in gray clouds. RD showed me how to swing the sledge against the block and not against myself. At a certain point, as instructed, I raised my leg high, hit the weakened block with the sole of my shoe, and the wall came tumbling down. One of life's great experiences, not to be missed by any woman of my generation, is to use a sledgehammer. RD rebuilt the walls leading into the bedroom with a soft curve, which we hand plastered. He modeled the radius after the curve of my hip.

And so it went, the house gradually being reshaped. We replaced the old leaky steel casement windows, opened a few more walls, redid the bathrooms, put an efficient wood-burning fireplace, and painted everything. An electrician replaced the old wiring and thirties fuses. The walls were plastered inside and stuccoed outside. We had a new water heater, no longer in the dining room, a nice utility room with a washer and dryer, and a large sun room, intended as studio space for me. RD built a wooden tree, like a sculpture, for drying clothes outside. I painted all the branches in blooming colors. When the city inspector came he admired our handiwork.

The house had a nice, big kitchen. I cleaned the old appliances, took off the pantry doors, and painted the edge of each shelf with a different color. Despite the dust and commotion, I closed the kitchen doors and began to cook again. RD appears to have an infinite appetite for baked goods. Breads, cookies, tea cakes, lizzies, muffins, pies...he will eat whatever emerges from my oven. And he washes the pans. Ever since then we have made it a custom to stop every day with a cup of tea and a sweet thing, and admire the view and each other.

The garden was another renovation project. The previous owner had dumped truckloads of gravel to make a parking lot of the backyard. Except for a huge apricot tree there was no garden left. I started the job of screening gravel from the soil. Bit by bit, I used it for the carport and garden paths. I planted a little orchard at the back and as many irises as possible. The neighbors on each side had pretty gardens, and they were glad when my eyesore lot became a member of the neighborhood. Each of them gave me something to transplant.

Over the back wall, my neighbor was Eloisa. She was about eighty then, very lively and funny. Eloisa had grown up in Velarde and gone to high school in Albuquerque. She worked in a hotel in New York for a year or two before returning to marry a man from Santa Fe. We chatted over the wall or I walked the two blocks around to her house. She suggested that I put up a short ladder and save myself the walk. About a year after I moved there, I was having lunch with her and she took out her old high school yearbook. There was a photo of the whole school, including RD's father and his three uncles, a blond stair-step family of four tall boys. Eloisa remembered them, said you couldn't have missed them with their looks and high spirits. Funny how unexpectedly loose threads can be tied together.

We bought a second-hand set of large windows and sliding doors that fit the back porch exactly. We laid a brick floor and set up my drawing table once more. In my glass studio, overlooking my new garden, I started to work.

MEMORY FOR STEPHEN • *Stephen called me one day. Very tentatively, he* said he had something to ask me, but I should say no if it was too difficult. Was there any way I could draw a likeness of Aileen? What a shock. We had been conditioned by Edwin's rule of not speaking her name. I had spoken of her briefly now and then to one son or the other over the years. Here was Stephen, bravely crossing this invisible but solid line. Yes, I would try. I started that day and in the first picture Aileen looked as she had at the end, drawn thin and in pain. Through a long series, I went all the way back to the beginning. I gave Stephen a likeness that seemed to capture her. And I found, with that gift, my son had freed me from the need to carry Aileen's image so closely. By the time I was finished, I was gradually able to let go of my ferocious hold and ease into a gentler memory. She resides in my heart as a loved member of my family. I think of her from time to time. She would have been middle-aged by now. I have loved her every day.

PASSING THROUGH THE TAOS BOX • *Our house was finished and could* serve us well. I liked the neighborhood, the neighbors even more. But both of us missed the open landscape, the peace of walking over open country, and especially we missed seeing the mountains. We thought about buying a piece of land for the future, a place to build the home of our dreams.

We took a day off. We liked Taos and from time to time drove up past the dramatic red hills of Abiquiu. We often stopped in at Blumenschein House — the home of a pair of artists about ninety years before — took in a few galleries and stopped for hot chocolate. Feeling mellow and happy, we headed for Santa Fe.

The road passes through the Taos box, the high walled canyon that encloses the Río Grande. The road curves around and on the return, south bound, for one or two minutes the hills form a perfect V framing the sky. Early on that evening the hills were silhouetted in a complete, uninflected black and the last sun turned the sky perfect red.

Around that point on the road, RD said to me that we should go ahead and find the land, and by the time we built a house there, we would know that we wanted to live in it and make our lives together. He made that statement as a prediction. I heard that we had not yet reached a conclusion about our future. I took a step back.

Nevertheless, early in 1994 we looked at land all around Santa Fe, a quarter acre, twelve acres, open fields, wooded hillsides. We saw a piece out toward Pecos, with a rustic house already on it, part of a five-parcel group, with a shared well. The water was so poisoned by arsenic from the gold mines, shut down decades before, that the people had to purchase water even for showering. We were introduced to a parcel on Rowe Mesa where both owners had recently died of AIDS. They had bought it to have a private place to spend their last days together. They were in their twenties. We saw new subdivisions along Highway 285 crowding around Eldorado, parcels sitting on solid rock where you would have to blast with dynamite. Off Old Las Vegas Highway, above Bobcat Bite café, we went to see a lot on a heart-stopping driveway cut into a hillside over a deep arroyo. The snow was churned with melting mud and the Jeep had no traction at all. We slid and slid, finally coming to rest a few inches from the precipice. We saw land without water, and land without anything at all except the mountains and the blue New Mexico sky. That's the piece we finally bought. West of Tano Road, we turned off a quiet dirt track—you couldn't call it a road at all—and stopped at a wide arroyo. We went the rest of the way on foot, through the late snow, and climbed a steep hillside through a forest of juniper and piñons. We turned around, took in the view, and knew we had found our spot. We told the real estate agent to draw up a contract.

On that late winter day, you could not have imagined a better place. The land looked east to a long leisurely view of the Sangre de Cristo Mountains, the ski basin, and Truchas Peak in the northeast. To the west the Ortiz seemed like a stage for the Jemez range and as you looked to the northwest, there was Chicoma, the place the Santa Clara people consider the center of their world. Chicoma is an old volcano on the northeast edge of the Valles Caldera, with a summit near twelve thousand feet. From Santa Fe it has a triangular face covered in snow all winter. The mountain gives the impression of standing guard over the peace of all who live in its view. Of course, the land is just itself, neutral, an existential fact. It is the minds of people who give it meaning, turn the land into landscape, and in turn are influenced by both the terrain and the meaning.

Our five acres were more than a half-hour drive from Santa Fe, over hill and dale and more hills. From there, we had to build a road to get all the equipment to the site to build the utility infrastructure. Electric and telephone lines ended about half a mile back. A well was needed. There was no mail service. Permits and paperwork were necessary for everything. And that's before we drew a single sketchy line of a future plan. Meanwhile, we had to negotiate the contract.

The seller of this land owned four parcels. He had bought the land many years before, and he was the last purchaser in a daisy chain of speculation. He had been trying to sell it ever since. He didn't want to improve it, had never seen it, and had neither affection nor respect for it. It was the same to him as buying shares of speculative stock. Except that land is not liquid. It cannot easily be turned into money. We came along after he had been seeking a buyer for twelve years. As part of my offer, I suggested that we share the costs of the absent infrastructure. RD and I would do all the work and then have what we needed for the future. The owner could make a small profit on our lot, and have three vastly improved and more saleable parcels on which he had a chance of making a large profit. One of his requirements was that I finance the purchase through him so that he could receive the interest. We decided on a five-year contract. At every step his lawyer laid down an impediment. It took seven contracts and almost six months. Several times I wanted to turn away but RD kept reassuring me. Even at the closing, though, the lawyer had one more word. When the settlement officer at the title company phoned to discuss an error they had made, the lawyer said that "you girls" — the settlement officer and I— should just do as he said. With a look of agreement over the table, Gloria and I gave them until ten o'clock the next morning to fix the problem. They did, and the land off Tano Road was ours. Bob sold the other three lots within a very short time.

WEST OF SANTA FE • *The more we went out there the more we loved it.* We walked for miles over the countryside. RD was always busy on Fridays and I made it my habit to walk on Friday afternoons. I made my way along the arroyo, which ultimately fed into Diablo Canyon or up over the mesas and plateaus, encountering only hawks, rabbits, and an eagle once in a while. I quietly passed rattlesnakes and king snakes resting in the rocks. The only sounds were my boots on the grass and stony slopes, and the wind in the piñons. I found myself renewed, considering the questions I had studied earlier: pointing directly, learning to recognize the authenticity, the reality, and individuality of each thing, each one, I encountered.

    Meanwhile, the renovation of the house in the city was finished. The debris was gone, the garden bloomed, and we had something like a normal life. RD and I were feeling our way, trying to know each other and build a life that would nurture and sustain us both. I was still a little wary but RD had eased himself into a belief in our comfortable future together. I laugh at how earnest I am, although less so than when I was younger. I am the original Ernestina. RD gave me his concept of "should-ectomy"— cut out the received "shoulds" and do what seems best right now. Choose to be happy. Choose your life. He is a free person.

The land had no exact address. On the deed it was "Off Tano Road." We went there often. We decided that, with the utilities in place, and the heart-stopping process of drilling an eight-hundred-foot-deep well successfully concluded, we wanted to live out there. We put a "for sale by owner" ad in the paper. On that first Sunday, we had three potential buyers for our little city house, two of them offering contracts. About forty days later, the sale — to an architect — was completed. We cleaned maniacally, toted our spare material to the new site, rented an apartment for three months, and prepared to build a house. RD went to Ohio again for a sculpture project, and we spent a month faxing plans back and forth. I took out a building permit, engaged a contractor to build the shell, and camped out in the apartment. Who, in their right mind, would have expected to build a house from absolute scratch in three months? We were in love with each other and in love with the land, occasionally out of our minds on both counts. We went ahead and started the project.

Building a house requires more than ten thousand decisions, many of them made under pressure of time or unexpected circumstances. All the differences in expectations and hopes are revealed, often in the company of total strangers.

We walked over the lot many times, weighing the advantages of various possible house sites, trying especially to maximize solar gain in the winter and keep the house cool in the summer. My vocabulary expanded quickly, like a child's. I did at least a little of everything. I learned to pick a two by four at the lumberyard, to carry my end of a sheet of drywall, and an eighty-pound bag of concrete. We needed a trench for the propane gas line, which was not included in the main contract. The trench had to be dug by hand, tight in between the trees. Neither the contractor nor the crew wanted to do it, not even for extra overtime pay. RD was not available. I called Rachel, the teenage daughter of my former neighbor, and asked if she wanted to help. She and I dug that trench, four feet deep, a foot wide, fifty feet long, in the hard caliche soil. The construction workers watched us on their breaks.

The previous year RD had had an office at the College of Santa Fe. The buildings then occupied by the college had been built during WWII as a complex for the army units guarding the Japanese internment camp in Santa Fe. One hot June day, RD had noticed that the old army post office was going to be demolished. All the shelving, held rigidly in place for decades, was going to the landfill. Instead, we did quick salvage work and stored the boards. After sanding off fifty years of paint, that old, clear, number-one New Mexico pine was turned into handsome cabinets for our new kitchen. For bathroom tile I took one of my watercolor paintings to a tile maker, and he matched the colors.

For a while, we slept in the living room in front of the big fireplace. RD built a temporary wooden ladder to the upstairs. (We've had more than a few of those.) After the pine floors were down we dragged our queen-size mattress up over the ladder and began to sleep there, waking every day to the sun rising over the mountains and illuminating the meadow below us. RD built the stairs and I shaped and planed narrow aspen balusters with a hand plane. I believe it is among the handsomest of staircases — easy to climb and descend, and beautiful to look at.

During the house construction, I had prepared meals on a little hibachi or in an electric skillet. We ate out often. As soon as I had a functioning kitchen (at least a year before it was completely finished), I started to cook again. RD can put cereal in a bowl and he makes great cocoa. Otherwise, his cooking is almost nonexistent. He has two wonderful kitchen skills: He is a terrific chopper of fresh herbs, and he actually likes to wash dishes. I cook and he cleans up. While I sauté, he leans on the counter behind the cooktop and watches and smiles and chats.

Managing a project is harder than the physical work. There are a lot of personalities: contractors, subs, workers, suppliers, inspectors, delivery people, and neighbors all have to be taken into account. When the builder is the homeowner, it compounds the complexity. I struggled to control the expenses, keep records, and organize cash flow. The project was afflicted with a serious case of "while-we're-at-it-anyway-itis," a common construction disease. The house grew from a sensibly restrained plan to a beautiful house worthy of its site. In the process, we committed our financial and physical resources to their limits.

From the time the house was just barely habitable, we had company. Daniel was working on his doctorate and continued to come on his breaks and in the summer after his teaching was finished. My friend Perla came from Mexico. A little later on Stephen brought his future wife, Melissa, to meet us. They were newly in love and beamed at each other steadily. My mother came once or twice. She hated the quiet and said it gave her the "heebee jeebies."

Our nearest neighbors were about a quarter of a mile away. Past their corner, Tano Road was more inhabited, with a total of about one hundred and fifty houses along about five miles of unpaved road, then about another mile to downtown Santa Fe. Sometimes we drove from town over a barely passable farm road from Camino La Tierra. In half an hour we were in our own world.

One of life's great pleasures is making a garden. You break your spade on the caliche, wait for the rain, which may never come until some tempest washes away all the infant plants. The rabbits get whatever the moles left behind. Your friends send over cuttings and divisions of their favorites. And then one fine day it is there.

June Garden

Hardy perennial lilies
Do not need lifting.
Tall and graceful,
They like the sun.
They are dependable year after year.

Peonies are slow to take hold
But once established
Live in their beds
For centuries.

Iris quite quickly
Have great masses of beauty
But must be uprooted from time to time
Or die of exuberance.

To keep out the voracious rabbits, RD built fences and then reinforced the fences. I planted trees and iris, which, ten years later, turned into a river of color. We wanted a pond, dug out the hole, installed the filters and pumps, put in water lilies. A sweet toad took up residence and reappeared every spring. The pond was ethereal in the winter, with a skim of snow on the rocks.

I kept adding native and near-native plants to the garden, relishing their musical names: artemesia, forestiera, mountain mahogany, slender wheatgrass, love grass, penstemon, verbena, achillea, aquilegia, rudbeckia, centaurea, gaillardia, dianthus. RD walked through the emerging gardens and had me say the flower names just for the sound.

I don't think we ever considered just sitting down.

When we built the house we had debated between two sites. We sited the house high on the lot. We planned to build a guesthouse someday in the meadow, a site with a long eastern view of the Sangres. It was a more intimate site, very cozy and protected. We drew up a plan, did the paperwork, and in a few months repeated the house-building process in miniature. The guesthouse was just right. We thought one of us might use it for a studio someday but for the moment we decided to rent it. The first couple to see it moved in.

All went well for a while. They were people in their forties, newly together and they seemed happy there. They subscribed to a political theory that participation in the legalities of federal and state law was voluntary, and they could simply opt out. He had been working in construction, but when he told his employer that he would not allow payroll deductions for taxes, he lost his job. They fell behind in the rent, of course. After a couple of months, I told her they had to pay the rent. Her response was that I was very greedy, a capitalist exploiter, and she felt like punching me out. Since then we have had many tenants in various houses, all of them with a story. A few became our friends.

Having tenants means accepting the responsibility for part of someone else's life. Our property becomes their home. It must give them privacy, security, safety, and comfort. It is rare that rent even covers the expenses. Over time rental properties will probably appreciate and ultimately be profitable. Meanwhile, a lot of people come and go in our life.

REAL LIFE • *For several years, our activities continued at hurricane force.* Between the isobars of the many pressure systems — business, building, establishing a new life and a new household — I unpacked my art materials and started to re-acclimate myself to studio work. I began to keep my poetry journal again, at least intermittently. I came back to painting with a fresh eye. The new work was on stretched linen, colors sweeping across the whole canvas. I used traditional linen, good oils, prepared the grounds myself. I relished the return of the scents, the sound of the brush, and the tactile pleasure of painting that had been absent for a long time. These works changed perspective, coming closer to the physical source, becoming abstractions of light. One summer I made a portrait of RD while he was away working on a sculpture. It is a good likeness, I think, somewhat minimal. The line of his jaw, the blue of his eyes come directly out of the brown linen.

I roamed the nearby mesas and arroyos, walking and looking at the landscape with attention. I took my camera more often and sought the same shift in perspective, trying to see more definitively whatever was right in front of me. It was a time of discovery.

On my rambles I noticed that new roads were being cut here and there. We had a few new neighboring houses, and large new houses were being built on all sides but still at some distance from us.

In the summer of 1997 we made another trip west. I had an exhibition in Ashland, Oregon. The Dankook Cultural Center there had invited me to do an exhibition of photography and give a talk. It was my first photography show and the first solo exhibition I had done in twelve years. I prepared thirty-five pieces. We had had a lot of correspondence over many months, but when I arrived the gallery was in a shambles. The partitions were all askew and leaning over, the walls dirty, and the carpet filthy and covered with trash. They didn't even have a broom. I was supposed to be hanging the show for the opening the next day.

RD got into his director-of-the-organization mode, commandeered a vacuum cleaner, broom, paint and a brush. He always had a few tools with him and pulled his cordless drill from the car. We cleaned, bundled trash, touched up the paint, and set up the partitions. The president of the center was hosting us at his house and pitched in. I never found out what the employees did. By the next afternoon RD and I had installed the show. We took a shower and rushed back for the opening reception. I was prepared for a dud, but almost two hundred people came. They walked through the exhibition, and many sat down for the gallery talk, followed by two hours of questions and comments. The reviews were few but excellent. It was an amazing reversal from the chaos and disappointment of the previous day.

THE VIOLA • *Almost all my adult life I wanted to play the viola. I love the sound of it. For my fifty-fifth birthday, RD arranged to have it happen. In the kitchen he handed me the case, the unmistakable shape. I was flabbergasted. How could he have remembered what I might have said in passing some time before? There was an instrument, snug in its red-velvet wrapping. I think he was almost as happy to give it as I was to have it. It is not often you can make a person's dream come true in front of your eyes.*

Playing the Viola

A body wrapped around the sinuous space
  Taut, shining
  Full of air

Another muscle and bone, air and water
  Roused
  Awake

One more, supple, stretched, reaching
  Lifted high in expectation
  Arching forward

 In the last moment
 Poised over the voluptuous void, breathless
 They tremble, touch,
  Breaths coming together
  Become a single instrument

They make music.

We were happy out there west of Santa Fe. The quiet and peace of our house was one of our greatest pleasures. One summer night RD woke me at three o'clock in the morning. We put on nothing but our shoes and walked through our meadow in the moonlight under the stars. On winter mornings, a few times a year, there is a whiteout. The clouds tumble down over the Sangres' peaks and flow over the lower elevations. The inside of a cloud is white, with visibility only a few feet at most. You hear, and feel on your freezing skin, the sound of the silence.

Whiteout: Twenty perfect minutes

All night we lay under our white comforter
in the comfort of our white bed
while the snow slid over the mountain and lay down over everything

In the morning
the feeble sun glimmers down
until the cloud-blanket begins to evaporate
in great sheets of silence

THE WEDDING • *We had been together more than six years.* We had traveled to see our children in Austin, Columbus, Ohio, Chicago, Seattle, and the San Juan Islands of Washington State. We had added more grandchildren and more in-law children. We don't remember how the subject came up, but we do remember that one fine day RD said, "We could get married." I asked him, "Why? Since nothing is broken, we don't need to fix it." He answered and his reason was the right one for us. With my face red, I said yes. I think we were both surprised. For a few days we walked around with sudden blushes appearing inexplicably on our faces. Both of us knew that when we finished building the house we had come to know we wanted to spend our lives together, just as he had said on that afternoon drive home from Taos.

We set May 18, 1997 as the date for the wedding. We invited twenty-five friends to join us in celebrating the day. Several of them had thought we had been married long since.

We had so much fun being an engaged couple! It was a completely novel experience for both of us to be so lighthearted. We shopped for rings. We shopped for clothes. I helped him buy a very elegant white linen shirt. He helped me find a long skirt and a white lace top. We ordered flowers, an armful for the house, flowers for my hair and to pin on his shirt.

We decided to have a simple ceremony, in our own words, in the garden next to the lily pond. We asked Lynn Pickard, a judge of the New Mexico Court of Appeals, to officiate. She did so with charm and good cheer. When we asked about her fee, she told us that it was her pleasure and her honor to be able to give such services and she would not accept any remuneration from us. We sent a donation to St. Elizabeth's Shelter in her name.

Steve and Melissa had married the year before in Austin. Daniel was in Chicago at an advanced stage of his doctorate in mathematics. He was on a very tight budget, and his gift was to make the wedding cake and manage the preparations. Melissa and Steve joined in. He made long tapes of music and took most of the photos. They were our witnesses. The other kids couldn't come but we saw all of them in the course of the next few months.

On the great day, we all went to Bishop's Lodge to have a fancy Sunday brunch. The ceremony was at five in the afternoon. Melissa sewed a little gold charm into the seam of my skirt and I have never cut it off. RD and I stumbled breathlessly through our promises to help each other and have adventures together. We planted a plum tree near the lily pond. We could do nothing more but look at each other in amazement.

At dusk, candles burned in glass holders around the garden. Music played. RD and I cut the cake and danced in the moonlight. Our friends went home. The kids kissed us goodnight. Upstairs, we stepped out onto the roof deck and looked at the stars.

A week or two later, we packed up the car and set out again on a long driving trip to the west coast. We went west on I-40, camped at the Grand Canyon in our new blue dome tent, and from Los Angeles camped our way north up the coastal highway. In San Francisco we stayed in a hotel, renewed our acquaintance with the city, and ate some memorable meals. We admired the Oregon coastal rock formations and went on to Seattle. We stayed a while with RD's Joel and Susan and their children. Then we headed home.

POETRY DEBUT • *I was invited to do a photography exhibition at St. John's College in Santa Fe in 1998. The gallery is very large. I suggested to the curator, Ginger, that RD also show his sculpture in the space and she agreed. He wasn't sure how many pieces he could have ready in the months ahead. I asked a friend, Laura Wilson, to join us. Both of them presented work that is entirely abstract. Laura's welded steel and RD's found-wood pieces were a good combination and a fine counterpoint to my photography. Our combined work was well balanced. The opening reception, enlivened by a string quartet, was a great success.*

I wanted to try something new. I had been keeping my poetry journal off and on, writing because I love the words, the rhythm of exploration, and then not writing because there was so much to do. Instead of the regular wall text telling the viewers what they were seeing, I decided to link the photographs with short poems. Ginger liked the work and the concept and suggested that St. John's College publish a small edition chapbook titled *Intimate Landscapes*.

Paper and Ink

Ink: blackest love
Paper: whitest host

Trees: living breathing green
   home for birds' songs
      worms' love

Cut blasted burned charred
Ready to accept the embrace of our words.

Paper: whitest host
Ink: blackest love

Architecture and building are interesting, sometimes exciting and satisfying work but very consuming of time as well as energy and money. I have found that successful building requires interaction with a great number and huge variety of people. Poetry requires quiet focus, solitude, and my whole attention. They don't mix well. Notes in my journal may stay there for years out of my line of sight, waiting for me to look right there, waiting for me to notice them. Now, suddenly and unexpectedly these cloistered words went out in the world.

DAD • *My parents liked to go to Florida in the winter. They stayed at the same* apartment-hotel, in the same suite, and went to the same places each year. They loved the ice show and the Miami City Ballet and looking at the ocean from the patio outside their living room. Dad was having a lot of trouble with his shoulder. In 1998 when they returned to New York, he went to a chiropractor, who immediately sent him to a physician. He was hospitalized within a few days for tests. RD and I went to New York to see him and await the results.

The test results showed that he had advanced bone cancer. He did not seem very surprised. Apparently he had suspected a serious problem since November or December but had wanted to deal with it in his own way. He was definite that he did not want any treatment other than alleviation of pain. He wanted to go home. Mother began a campaign to put him in a nursing facility. She went to all the hospital resource personnel and made it clear she did not plan to care for him at home. I don't remember what I said but she calmed down. The doctor was very helpful and put Dad into home hospice care. I did the phoning to find out the financial details, dealt with Medicare, and attended to a few other things. Someone recommended a practical nurse. Monique was hired and she stayed with them in their apartment six days a week, taking care of Dad and assisting with Mother. Monique was a natural caregiver and a very empathetic person. Her kindness went far beyond professional necessity. Hospice regularly sent nurses, an excellent social worker, and supported the family in many ways. RD and I went back to New York a couple of times during those months. In between, Dad and I talked on the phone frequently, every morning toward the end.

Dad had an agenda to complete and he chose to do it with me. We had had some difficult times between us, but our several-months-long conversation put those times in a new perspective. We shared a closeness that came to us naturally, unforced, unexpected, and redeeming. He was suffering greatly and needed his life to draw to an end. One morning he talked again about his father, then his mother. He said that his situation was insupportable. He was aware of what he needed to do but could not reach or open the bottle of painkillers, within his sight and sufficient to cause his death. He asked me to come back to New York to help him. After a few seconds stunned pause, I said that, of course, I would come. We set a date for the following week. The next day when I phoned, he said that he just wanted to listen, he was too tired to do any talking himself. I told him about the morning in Santa Fe, the irises blooming in my garden, what I was going to do for the day. He interrupted me and, calling me by my childish nickname, said that he thought it was time to say goodbye. I said I would phone the next morning. No, he said, it was time to say good-bye. And I did. He died that afternoon.

RD and I went back to New York immediately. On the previous trip, we had made the arrangements with a funeral home nearby. My brother thought it was morbid but I was very glad that at least those necessities had been decided. It fell to me to do the mandatory identification of the body. RD stood beside me with his arm around my shoulder. Dad looked so much smaller than he had in life. There was no illusion that this was peaceful sleep. The person he had been was absent. At the cemetery, Mother did not allow anyone to make any remarks at all. I wanted to say something to my niece and nephew, Bobby's children, and to Stephen and Daniel, and later in the day I found a little time with each of them. My father died with dignity and grace in the uncompromising awareness of his own mortality. The past cannot be changed, but our future is understood in the context of our evolving and malleable perception of it.

TRAVELING • *All this time our family was increasing. We had several new* grandchildren in the northwest, and combined visits to them with the long driving trips we loved. With all we were doing in the nineties, RD and I also were traveling. We camped in Colorado and took several cross-country trips. One summer day we saw the motorcycle rally in Sturgis, SD, drove past the mammoth wheat fields, stopped at the Little Big Horn in Montana.

The battle, also called the Battle of Greasy Grass Creek, was between the Lakota and the U.S. Army in June 1876. The Lakota and Cheyenne families camped under the trees for the summer powwow. George Custer led the U.S. Army there. He and his commanders made a hash of everything. In one sense, it was the strongest victory the Lakota had against the Army, a high water mark in their determination to retain their homelands. On the other hand, the American military defeat stimulated ferocious warmongering and led to the campaign of annihilation against the Lakota and most of the other people of the Great Plains. It is one thing to recite the story. It is another to see the river under the trees in summer, walk along the battle lines, and contemplate the enormous grasslands. There are small signs low to the ground: a glove was found here, a person fell there. The Little Big Horn is a place that moves you to wonder, for what happened there and for the land itself.

We stayed in a ramshackle but friendly motel in Livingston, Montana. The town was getting ready for the annual fly-fishing convention. We found what must have been the last room anywhere around. Early the next morning, we bought corn flakes in a grocery store and then parked along the Yellowstone River. The river falls through the mountains there in the northern Rockies. The sharp jagged peaks and deep green pines are very different from our ponderosa forest in New Mexico. We saw the sun come over the eastern rims. The sound of the slow wind and radiant water followed the curved line of the river. We ate our cornflakes together in the most perfect peace.

On another trip west, we stopped in Santa Nella, California, in the middle of the desert between San Jose and Bakersfield. It is devoted to putting gas in the cars and trucks, providing a place to sleep, and, above all, serving pea soup to travelers. There were about half a dozen motels and three or four restaurants the first time we stopped there. A couple of years later we saw at least five times that many.

My Great Uncle Harry, my grandmother's youngest brother, left home in his teens and went to California. He earned his living as a newspaper reporter but his true work was as a pioneer photographer. For decades he photographed the desert. In the very late eighteen nineties and early nineteen hundreds, he packed up his gear, heavy wooden tripods, bellows camera, plates, and all the equipment needed to make photographs in the field. He set out, originally in a wagon, later in his car, for the desert. When the road ended he hiked in to whatever spot he was seeking and set up camp and his camera. Then he waited for the rain. With moisture, the desert suddenly exploded with flowers and wildlife for a few days. When the light was right he exposed his plates. I thought of him and his adventures when we stopped in Santa Nella. Uncle Harry said he thought California had experienced two tragic mistakes. The first was to bring water and replace the desert with orange groves. The second was to cut down the groves for highways and subdivisions. His wife, Aunt Rhoda, made ceramics for a living but her true passion was stock cars and in her seventies she still drove in cross-country races.

IN THE STUDIO • *In my experience, as Uncle Harry said long ago, making art* in whatever form or media requires not just the hours literally holding a brush or writing away, but focused, sustained attention. Through the nineties, I was working in the studio, trying new tools and new media to investigate my ideas about the landscape. I used a camera more often and more purposefully. I kept writing poetry. By the end of the decade, I had drawers full of poems, both completed and in process. Most of all I painted. By the late nineties, I had done some large solo exhibitions and put paintings in a few group shows as well. My life continued on several tracks at once. House building, traveling with RD, and working in the studio were not mutually exclusive, but it was difficult to make those lines converge.

I asked my friend, Ford, if he wanted to do a joint project. We decided on a collaborative photography exhibition. We started out to do serious, normal art, but soon the whole thing became a satirical and surreal send up of the art world. A tiny, black-and-white, plastic pig was our mascot. Porcine Productions published the art books. The entire extravaganza, called *Playing Around*, was more than one hundred pieces. It was installed in the upstairs gallery of the Harwood Museum in Taos. A few publications took us seriously and answered our nonsensical, multisyllabic, argle-bargle art-speak and Dada photographs as if they were some deconstructionist manifesto, but most people laughed along with us.

Playing Around was a one-time game. Most of the time, I was painting in oils or doing photography, with poetry providing the running commentary. I was painting larger, more abstract works, finding a format of about forty-eight by fifty-four inches to be very comfortable. I like traditional materials. Real linen and good oil paints applied with natural brushes, rags, and palette knives. RD's mother, Marian, gave me a set of palette knives that had belonged to RD's father. I was using them more freely than I had in the past. Over two years, I did an abstract series based on the story of Othello, from Desdemona's point of view.

A few times I entered paintings in juried competitions meant to benefit charities. I was occasionally accepted but mostly not. Twice I was a volunteer as well as an entrant and saw the process from a close vantage. I had been away from the art market for a long time. After one particular rejection, I invited the judge of that competition to the studio with the understanding that she critique my work professionally. She was a moderately recognized independent curator, and I thought her opinion could be worth hearing. She tore the work to shreds. She told me that I needed to study for at least five years and learn how to paint. She recommended that I go to the galleries, see what was current, and attempt to create something that was more "with it."

It was a breathtaking performance. On her way out the door, she passed a painting in the hall. She stopped, looked at it very intently, and said it was a wonderful piece, exactly the sort of thing I should be doing. It was the very painting she had rejected for the show a few weeks before.

In Santa Fe, Arlene LewAllen, the owner of a major downtown gallery, had encouraged me for several years. She appreciated my work, although it didn't fit the mission of her gallery. She suggested I see some gallery and museum curators that she knew and called to facilitate the appointments. I made the contacts and went to see the chief curator of a major Midwestern museum. She had slides of my work for a few days before we met in the sculpture garden of the museum. The painting is beautiful, she said, finely executed, and completely irrelevant. Beautiful painting has nothing to offer in contemporary life. She insisted that neither beauty nor virtuosity have a place in the modern world of art. My friend Nick Livaich, a very sensitive artist, said that it was too late for us to give up either beauty or virtuosity, although he thought there really was no room anymore for beautiful surfaces or aesthetics.

Of course, I kept working.

2000 • *Leading up to the millennial celebrations of 2000, the infamous Y2K, there* was a lot of hype about pretty much everything. Along with party favors and dot-com technology stocks, people were stocking up on staple foods and candles in case the electric grid collapsed. The world was going to come to an end. All the computers were going to crash and time might be erased. Depending on the prophet, either Armageddon or the Second Coming was imminent, possibly both.

Three aspects of life changed for us that year. RD was going to be sixty-five, and I wanted to celebrate the milestone in some significant way. I offered him the choice of a special kind of fancy radial arm saw or a trip to France. The man actually stopped to think about it. After a minute he said that maybe he preferred France.

The second was that I was granted a residency at an artist colony. I went for a month and nothing has been the same since.

The third was that we decided to try living in a smaller space. We rented the main house and moved into the one-bedroom guesthouse for a year or so. All three of these experiments were a great success.

The guesthouse was less than eight hundred square feet, but it was a complete little home. When we built it we thought about the awful guesthouses we had each lived in and made sure there was a nice kitchen and bath, plenty of heat, skylights, closets, and a garden. It even had a washer and dryer. In Santa Fe guesthouses, none of those items can be taken for granted. We loved living in the intimate, cozy house with little housekeeping and big views. It was more than a little frustrating not to have a good workspace or storage for my materials, but otherwise it was terrific. We considered adding a studio. When we left for France, we simply locked the door, with no worries at all.

I have lived a life in motion, but RD was born in Ohio and stayed there for more than fifty years until he moved to Santa Fe. In 2000, we went to France for a month and rented an apartment. April in Paris is rainy and often cold. The gray winter skies dissipate very slowly. We walked many damp miles, joyful when the sun came out. RD was swept away by the architecture, the sights and smells of Paris, which he was experiencing for the first time. We loved the little stands selling crepes on the street, every inch of the embankments along the Seine, the kids with their boats in the Tuileries, the third-floor walk-up apartment with its eighteen-inch shower stall and blue tablecloth, the buses and especially the bus maps, all of it. By the end of the month the spring was in full bloom. The cherry trees

By the end of the month the spring was in full bloom. The cherry trees along the Arsenal at the foot of the Canal Saint Martin were as pretty as spring can be.

In 2000 I was granted an artist residency at Anderson Center in Red Wing, Minnesota. The founder, Robert Hedin, is a poet. The center is a lovely old house, originally built by his grandfather, an inventor. Robert and his wife, Caroline, have created a place for artists to work in comfort and quiet. The property has disparate uses but they all work together. It was a very productive and dynamic experience for me.

Previously I had not spent any time in the prairie grasslands. Like so many before me, I was greatly moved by the landscape of Minnesota, the rolling openness of it, the solitary farmsteads, the austerity, and the grandeur of it. The Mississippi River runs along the edge of Anderson Center and through Red Wing. The grain elevators are a massive presence across from the bluffs above the river. I took photographs, worked in the darkroom, and changed the way I looked at the landscape.

The artists each took a turn inviting the other residents to our studios and sharing our work in progress. One evening, they came to look at my photographs. I read some of the new poems as well. The group, all writers, saw the poetry and photography as a united body of work and had useful suggestions. This was the first occasion when I had the benefit of critiques from writers.

An Israeli artist was there, translating his memoir into English. During the residency, I worked with Ephraim almost every evening on the translation. We became well acquainted in the process and stayed in communication until his death in 2009.

Driving home around the first of October, I started out early in the mornings. Along I-70, shallow excavations were left after the soil was used for the highway construction. The water table is so high that those excavations have become ponds and wetlands supporting a healthy prairie ecology. I stopped several times along the shoulder to set the sight in memory.

Ever since the experience at Anderson Center, I have periodically gone to residencies. The combination of time, voluntary solitude, and fellowship is a powerful one, and I am very grateful for each opportunity. Every time the work has changed with new insights and perspectives.

rainy London long enough to get library cards at the Islington library. I noticed a curled up leaf on the floor of a Kew Gardens conservatory and photographed it from several points of view. Since I liked it so well, RD made a little cardboard crate and carried it home. It is in my studio where very slowly it is turning to dust. We went on again to Paris in May. We enjoyed the feeling of familiarity and the ease of reconnecting with our favorite spots.

By this time we had the travel bug in earnest. The next year we made a long trip to Italy, with a week or two in Florence, a little time in Siena, and a month in Rome. Walking from morning until evening, we ate gelato in every neighborhood we passed through. We drank local wine, and looked at art wherever we went. In Siena on a rainy afternoon, we ate the tiny traditional pastries in a café with geraniums in the window. It may be the single best coffee break we have ever had — so far.

We used to camp a few times every summer in the Santa Fe National Forest above the city on the Ski Basin Road. For several years we went to Colorado. Our backs get crabbier now in the damp mornings. The tent seems to be lodged more permanently in the garage. We still like to spend some summer evenings in the forest. The night sky is vivid and close at these altitudes. We bundle up in our sweatshirts, wrap our hands around a tin camping mug of tea, and sit silently as the fire burns down. The wind in the ponderosas carries the vanilla scent of the bark.

MORE BUILDING • *Things had been changing around our neighborhood.* A very large number of houses had been built all around us and hundreds of acres had been subdivided for more. We didn't like the profusion of stylish, cookie-cutter houses — very big, very expensive tract houses. The peace and privacy and connection to the land that had first attracted us were disappearing.

We decided to sell the property and listed it with a real estate agent. There were few showings and a lot of wasted effort. Eventually we decided to rent the house, travel, and try again later. The first person that came to see it as a rental said it was like his dream house. He had been looking in our area for months. He loved the site and the individuality of the house. Would we consider selling it? Yes, definitely. The three of us sat down together and had the basics worked out in an hour. Everything was completed in a few weeks. It happened that he owned a house in the city he wanted to sell. We thought it was a good candidate for renovation and as an investment. We bought that house, did the renovation work, and it was rented by 2005.

Meanwhile, in the midst of all this activity, in 2003 I attended a residency in Vallauris, on the Riviera in the south of France. It was the hottest, driest summer in modern European history. Forest fires were burning all over the continent and the odor of smoke was in Vallauris, hundreds of kilometers from the nearest fire. Officially, thirty-seven thousand and four hundred fifty-one Europeans died as a result of the heat, about ten thousand in France alone. The Mediterranean Sea heated up, crops failed and the major currents in the Atlantic were altered in their course and volume. Newspaper headlines daily recounted the death tolls and showed maps of burning forests across the continent. The drought affected fishing, winemaking, river navigation, every aspect of life all over Europe.

Vallauris is famous for being the place where Picasso made ceramics and as a summer resort. It is about three kilometers straight down to the Mediterranean. Unfortunately, it is also three kilometers straight up again. In the ferocious heat, at the end of most days I walked to the beach and back.

The residence was in an old vertical house on a square in the old city. The facilities were austere: a mattress on the floor, a rickety pressboard armoire for clothing, and a folding chair and table as a desk. The stone house heated up every day. It was difficult to sleep. I worked on a series I called *Les Lumières*, inspired by the patterns of the streetlights coming through the shutters on those hot nights. By six in the morning, I was at the studio to have a few cooler hours for painting. Some calligraphy and watercolors became the basis for prints I did later in Santa Fe. I met several artists in town and formed a habit of coffee in the café on the Place Lisnard. Some of the artists invited me to their homes nearby and for an excursion down the coast.

I had a small show in the gallery just before I left. The mayor invited me to have an exhibition in the city museum. After I returned to Santa Fe, I printed photographs, made small editions of several art prints, and sent them back to Vallauris where they were shown for several months.

In 2004 Can Serrat offered me a residency in Catalunya. The tiny hamlet of El Bruc is adjacent to a national park, about forty minutes bus ride from Barcelona. I was in a large studio divided by an arch, with a Norwegian artist, Grete. We had the good luck to have very similar needs in the studio — no music, about the same degree of heat — and we found ourselves enjoying each other's company. I painted on fabric and made a few artist books, did a huge amount of photography, and composed a lot of poetry, the first Spanish-language writing I had done since leaving Mexico. We were an intimate group of six artists and ate midday dinner together. We gathered again informally in the evening around nine or ten for supper and conversation. Grete urged me to read some of my new work and then other colleagues asked me to read on several more evenings. Bjorn, a filmmaker and poet himself, was particularly strong in his response to the poems.

The residency at Can Serrat was important in another way: it was my first opportunity to be in Spain. Grete and I took a day off and went to Barcelona, with its marvelous architecture and geography. I went a few more times and thought the combination of mountains and Mediterranean Sea just about perfect.

After the residency in El Bruc near Barcelona, RD met me and we went to Sevilla for a month. The city's history is everywhere. The Islamic Mezquita surrounds the renaissance cathedral. Romans, Goths, Arabs, French, Catholics, Jews, and Muslims, have all left their marks on Spain, evident in Sevilla as you walk anywhere in the city. Sevilla has another aspect, too: it smells delicious. In the eighth century, an Arab ruler wrote home to Damascus that Sevilla was full of the smell of orange blossoms. In winter the modern streets are full of orange trees in fruit, and the aroma of oranges is mixed with night jasmine, flowers, and the Río Guadal-quivir. We made excursions to Granada and Córdoba. The beauty of the landscape and the beauty of the physical cities are influenced by the historical mix of cultures and aesthetic choices made over centuries.

When we returned home, RD and I began looking for a house for ourselves. We liked the north side of Santa Fe for the convenience of being five or ten minutes from the movies and it had open space and long views of the mountains. We found a beautiful location. The house itself was probably one of the worst in Santa Fe. When it rained outside, it rained inside as well. The aluminum windows did not meet the frames, and we could imagine the wind in winter coming through. The site is splendid but the original builder did not let the views be visible from inside the house. The plumbing was rotten and had rotted out some of the floors. The floor plan was irrational and the ceilings were a little over seven feet. It has turned into our best house, our dream house. I have the studio of my dreams as well, that is, the studio is the place to dream.

We worked on the house for most of a year and transformed it into a comfortable, elegant home. It was heavy labor. I again did the staining of all the windows and doors, planted new landscaping, hauled trash. We were out in all weather — cold, snowy slush, hot sun — and, as usual, I was entirely occupied with budgets, scheduling, coordinating the trades, and purchasing materials. My hands were torn up, and I was marooned on the island of the construction job. The financial management for our endeavors falls to me. I don't like this aspect of house building. When we began to build, I didn't know anything about any part of it, including the finances. I do now.

In 2006, urgently needing a change from construction, on the spur of the moment, I went to Massachusetts for a few weeks. A retired couple, poets, used their home as an artist residency. I took out my camera and walked around for days, looking for the details that revealed the place, finding blue granite, beautiful wild fungi, cemetery stones covered with lichens and stringy vines. Nights I wrote intensively. The hosts announced an evening when everyone was to meet in the living room and share their current work. I read some poetry. I wound up being asked to read more than I had planned. The owner, a former professor, commented on the work and the impact the pieces made. It was a bit strange to have him lecture on my poetry while I was sitting right there. Nevertheless, I was very gratified by their response to it.

I returned to Santa Fe with a backlog of photographs to work on, new poems to think about, and a house to finish.

HOUSES • *Houses seem to be static, rigid things, made of heavy materials,* permanent, and resistant to change. I have come to see that the building itself is constantly changing. It shifts, settles, mysteriously and suddenly leaks. Electrical and plumbing parts that have worked well for years fail just by getting older. The sun and snow eat away at the most impermeable roof. The occupants, even the most conscientious, do violence to the finishes, and sometimes even the structure, just by using it, breathing in it. The users add history that is retained in the house and the house, in turn, makes each successive occupant part of its life. Each resident also contributes to the inevitable decline. A house is malleable and responsive to the changing occupants' lives as well as changing times. Living in a house changes the people in it. It is possible to accept responsibility to the environment without sacrificing comfort or beauty. Vitruvius used passive energy two millennia ago in Rome. His description of successful architecture is a building that is sound, fitting, and beautiful. I haven't heard an improvement on that formula.

I did not make any new poems or paintings during this project and felt myself again sliding down the slippery slope. We invest our financial resources and ourselves in building projects in the hope and belief that we can make ourselves independent and financially secure in the future. We have both pleasure and pride in our work, but the future becomes the present. I have become very ruthless in excluding extraneous elements to have the luxury of working in my studio.

ROCHEFORT-EN-TERRE • *A wonderful opportunity came along in 2007* when I was awarded a residency in France. The chateau of an American artist had been given to the Department of Morbihan, which includes Bretagne, in western France. It could accommodate three or four artists at a time. The village, Rochefort-en-Terre, is very small and compact, with medieval and later buildings, all stone and roofed in dark slate. The rolling fields in April were newly tilled and filling with yellow mustard flowers and vegetable crops. It is an evocative location, with romantic ruins, hills to climb for long views, and crepes. The villagers insist, in fact, that this is the origin of crepes and crepes are served everywhere for every kind of meal.

The grant encouraged the artists to explore and enjoy French culture. That was not hard at all. We were just three artists at that time, and we often worked through the day and set off together around three or four in the afternoon to see some nearby town or landmark. We went to Questembert on Tuesdays to buy our groceries at the weekly market. Each week we went to at least one place farther afield: Rennes, Nantes, the megaliths at Carnac, Quiberon and Vannes on the Atlantic coast. I made a lot of poetry and a series of watercolors. Later, I sent some photography for the annual exhibition at the gallery in the chateau and a gallery in the village did a solo show as well.

The residency at Artscape in Toronto is a different model. It is in an old school building on a car-free island in Lake Ontario. The ferry ride from Toronto is enough to let you leave everything else behind. The accommodations are very simple and there are no distractions. The quiet and peace are disturbed only by the sound of the lake tides and the wind in the trees.

Audacious claimant

The lake pretender
aspires to be the ocean.
The wind is bringing a storm
    and the lake-sea is its leader.
What a splendid color!

The waves are just wannabes,
The beach trees have bowed well over
    and the backs of their leaves are greeting
the slanting stinging not-yet-wet air

Several artists live at Artscape full time and the rest come and go for days or months. The bedrooms for temporary artists are small rooms that were once teachers' offices and the studios are the high-ceilinged former dormitories and classrooms. The staff is wonderfully supportive. I have done some presentations and installed a photography exhibition for the celebration of the hundredth anniversary of the building.

Making art is a solitary activity with long hours alone in the studio. A residency offers the absence of daily responsibilities, the stimulation of new surroundings, solitude when you need it, and fellowship if you want it. The change of scene presents an opportunity to be released from intellectual constraints and think anew. I like the mixture of nationalities, disciplines, and ages. I have been the recipient of very useful critiques and commentaries and been challenged by the interesting points of view I've encountered over the years.

Each time I return from a residency, I am full of optimism about the work, overflowing with ideas and projects underway or in mind. And equally, on my return I am immediately inundated with home responsibilities. I have not yet found the formula that balances these conflicting necessities but I keep searching.

BARCELONA • *Since our first acquaintance with Barcelona, RD and I have* gone there as long and as often as we can, usually a few months a year. The city is most famous for its architecture, buildings from ancient Roman times, from the Middle Ages, from every period of time to right now. At the turn of the twentieth century, a group of architects invented the style called Modernist. Many of the buildings have sensual, curved walls, Art Nouveau ironwork, and are decorated with colors and ceramics. The city's architecture and history, the colors and stories, the mixture of ancient and contemporary, are profoundly moving and full of energy.

Over the city on the east, above the harbor, is the mountain Montjuic, "Jew's Mountain." From the top you can see the whole city, the marina with thousands of ships and boats, and out over the Mediterranean Sea. The mountain is mostly a park, with hiking and walking paths, and sports buildings constructed for the 1992 Olympics. There are many museums in this mountain park and at the bottom is the Mies Van Der Rohe pavilion and the fabulous Fundación Caixa. It is one of our favorite places. We go often to Gaudi's Park Guell with its strange curvilinear forms, broken-ceramic designs, and musicians playing music that drifts through the trees and arched walkways.

And then there is the central park, La Ciutatdella. Every Sunday a club meets for swing dancing on the bandstand, and little kids dance on the paving below. Rowboats make their way around the small lake. Every sort of person is in the park — families, young lovers, children with tricycles, teenage boys with skateboards, lots of dogs and baby carriages, lots of people past middle-age enjoying the sun and the sights. The mix is the huge variety of people who live around the Mediterranean, complexions from ebony to Nordic.

And, of course, there is the beach, a long, wide, fine-sand beach facing south toward Africa. Sand sculptors, gymnasts, men playing checkers, sun worshippers, kids with kites, musicians along the boardwalk, picnickers and café sitters, jugglers, cyclists, skaters, walkers, runners — all are there, with room for everyone.

Most of all, Barcelona is epitomized by the energy on the streets. It is a major city where almost everything closes for a few afternoon hours except restaurants, which are jammed with people. Design and renovation are the way of life in this city, and so is friendliness and calm, and busy streets. If we could, we would live there.

A NEW BOOK • *Almost no one lives hermetically sealed off from the world.* There are inherent conflicts between what is required to make art and what is needed and wanted in the rest of life. Time doesn't usually come with two-way stretch. The freedom from imperatives and from everyday preoccupations is the most valuable thing an artist, or anyone else, can have.

With the accumulation of poetry over several decades and the encouragement of the residency experiences, I was thinking about the possibility of publishing a small book similar to the one that had been done by St. John's College in 1998. The project grew exponentially and became a retrospective between covers, a sampling of the visual art and poetry of three decades. In creating *Stone Music*, I learned about the mechanics of making a book: choosing the poetry and visual images, working with the book designer, approving the digital scans for the images, writing some text, going to the printer in Canada to approve the colors and print quality before the book was run. Making a book involves dozens of people. I could not have imagined it before I did it. I also learned something about my own work. There is a permanence and validation in sending the work out into the world, and seeing where it — and I — had arrived. One day I was in the downtown Santa Fe library. In the catalogue, almost accidentally, I saw *Stone Music*. Forgetting my original purpose, I went to the shelf and there it was! Dinged at the corner because someone had taken it out and read it. I smiled with the pleasure of knowing that my work had reached the mind of another, anonymous, person.

Making A Poem

Words heard before
Sounds spoken in another time
Nothing at all becomes something
Mystery upon magic
Someone is listening

Once *Stone Music* was finished, I was hard at work again in the studio. Along with making a great deal of photography, I was composing poetry at a very fast rate, pent-up ideas that had been cooking for a long time. It seemed that at least one more book was in the offing and it became *Box of Light – Caja de Luz*. The poems are written in Spanish and English, on facing pages, and I included some ink drawings. The cover is a detail of a blue window in Nantes Cathedral in France. Exact translation of the poems didn't work well. Instead I tried to be faithful to the ideas, rhythms, and meanings in each one. I said in the preface that they were more like cousins than twins. I have heard from people from many places. It is a terrifically good feeling to realize that my ideas and art travel in this lovely vehicle and arrive intact in another person's hands.

MOTHER • *In 2009 we were in Paris for two weeks, on our way to Barcelona. I* had an urgent message from Steve to call him. My mother had died. We scrambled to find flights to New Mexico. With the help of Daniel and Steve and my brother, Bobby, we arranged the funeral long distance and met Steve and Dan in Albuquerque. We had the funeral there, as she wanted it, with no one else present, her ashes under a yellow rose tree.

Duty is a strange and difficult concept. I accepted this duty of care for my mother. She was not able to look at her own life, and, even in her last years, only rarely could look directly at me. I saw and spoke to her often, but I know she did not hear me. True to her own life, she had no idea of how to love anyone. When my own sons counseled me that I did not have to accept her mean-spiritedness — mean enough to bring tears to my face —they could not imagine the pity I felt for this lonely mountain of a woman insulated by her fat and her fear.

She rarely had peace of mind or heart. I believe that was the source of her harshness and cruelty to us, her children. She was a very fearful person, afraid of the dark and afraid of being alone. Her furies were present every day and especially every night. Her decisions were dominated by her fears and so she was never free. I always hoped, perhaps irrationally, that she could find some solace. I never saw any sign that she did.

DOUBLE LIFE • *When I returned to Barcelona after Mother's funeral, I* wanted to take up this book again. I had been thinking about it for a while. It started out as a look at the nature of making art and life as an artist. That beginning has become something else. The winter was colder and rainier than usual in Spain. The sea and the mirador at the top of Montjuic tempted me less to enjoy their pleasures. The story was written, almost complete, in the three winter months. I have never tried a long narrative before. It is another experiment. I learned more than I could ever have imagined from this process. As I typed away at all hours of the day and night, the book evolved into the one you have in your hand.

Back in Santa Fe, once more we have been engaged in another building project... for the last time perhaps. That house, called *Mañana*, is our retirement plan. We hope that the year and a half of intense work will help to support us decades from now. Meanwhile, it is rented to nice people and we accept the responsibility that goes with that relationship.

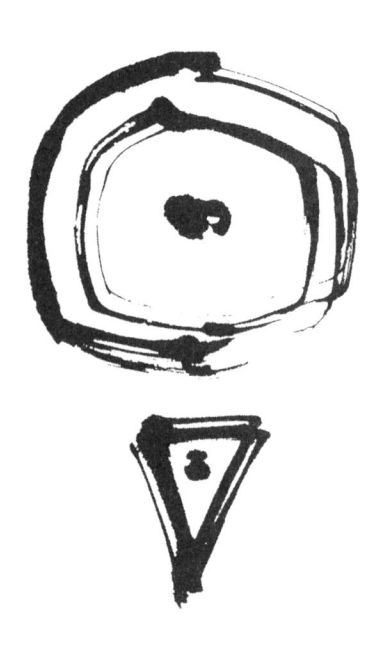

TWELVE

In Transit

I HAVE THOUGHT ABOUT THE INTERSECTIONS of desire, luck, opportunity, travail, and temperament. From my earliest childhood, atonement and redemption have been constant themes. I thought that if I tried harder, did better, became better, no one would need to be angry. I did not recognize the power implied in this dictum, but I did understand its imperative force. The two faces: because I could, I must, and also, because I must, I had to be able — no matter what the cost.

I understood and continue to believe that my existence was the ruin of my mother's dreams for herself. Or perhaps I was just the ever-present excuse, over and over, for her not to follow those dreams. My brother and I were also the excuse for my father not to follow his heart's desire and make his life with Cammy, and when that excuse ran out so did he. After twenty years he turned his back on her. For as long as they lived, my parents told me that they gave up their chances for happiness to suffer for me. I knew that I had better prove myself worthy of their sacrifice. No one ever could.

My father, in the last months of his life, talked to me very openly. He had made mistakes. My brother and I were two of those mistakes. He thought he should never have had children with a woman so unsuited to him and to the life he hoped for. He was past apology. Knowing he was dying soon, he wanted to examine and wash away the obscuring clutter and leave only a brave, austere understanding. For months we spoke often, and at the end, daily, early in the morning when he was less tired. Then he wanted nothing.

Why did I enter and stay in a marriage when so early on I recognized that it was not the right thing? I was certainly not the right wife for Edwin. Why did I agree to become pregnant so soon? Why did I not leave from Kwangju, or in 1967, or in 1970? Instead, I agreed to buy a house in a place I did not like and live in a style that was more foreign to me than a foreign country. Why did I not leave in Fairfax, where only my husband's absence gave me the solace and space to continue my life? Why did I say no in bed, only to accept that my refusal was meaningless and then do what was physically and psychologically repellant to me? And why did I think that changing the external circumstances — the next country, the next house — was going to make any difference? His often renewed and rebroken promises were only part of the puzzle.

Perhaps I absorbed the model of my early years that led me to believe I was not worthy of happiness and that I could only fix what was wrong by doing better and being better. Did I choose a husband who would control circumstances so that I dared not follow my own way? I had so little experience with choosing happiness that I did not look for it. How, one day, was I able to discover its possibility?

As a child I made so many families of dolls and drawings of houses. It was not as a game but a way of imaging an alternative to the disorder and sorrow of my family. Through those drawings of houses, I imagined a place for a happy life. As an adolescent, I drew, almost obsessively, architectural plans and renderings of homes where people could live in harmony and where I had some control over the contours of life. Yet I did not have the will to refuse the paths that led away from my work and allowed, even forced me, to forsake it when I apparently needed it most.

You can do only what you think is possible. If you don't imagine something to be possible, it is not available as a choice.

For as long as I can remember, I have made art in some form. I was never without a pencil, colors, paper, most especially, thoughts in my head. I have always been able to carry on the necessary business in the outer world and have ongoing, interior strata of activity, completely separate and simultaneous. Being an artist was not a label I sought or understood. It is my identity, not a job. That identity was often almost invisible to me, buried under the masses of other obligations I thought I had to fulfill, swamped by doubt, overrun by my inability to put first things first.

An artist's task necessitates strange paradoxes. A painter starts with the perfect white field of linen or paper and deliberately ruptures that perfection in search of something more valuable. In composing poetry, the poet assembles the familiar words into something unique. An artist's job demands making something out of nothing — out of nothing but yourself and what you can learn about the world around you.

The intractable contradiction continues to arise between the demands of my artist life and the needs and pleasures of married life and family. The intense desire for the work of making art is a yearning necessity, as irresistible as the most attractive and jealous lover.

There are only about six basic stories to tell. Part of the artist's task is to cast what light we can on the human condition. It is fashionable right now to say that beauty and harmony have no meaning, that all we need is some adrenaline-pumping, eye-popping hugeness to be satisfied. I believe that humans are hardwired to desire and recognize beauty in all its forms. It is the human mind that transforms facts into truth, stone into sculpture, empty sounds into poetry and music. Each of us is alone, an anonymous, separate being. Art lets us see who we are; it is the bridge from one mind to another. It lets us hold a transforming mirror to our human qualities and remember who we can be. It is the ultimate freedom.

I try to be agile and flexible, doing what has to be done, never knowing with certainty what the outcome will be. As I leave the rigors of house building, I know only that I will continue to work, using the art of words and images to explore the world I hope for. I cannot retire from being an artist any more than I can retire from being a person.

I have a sense that time is not as expansive as it once was. There is a lot of the world yet to see and favorite places to savor again while it's feasible to do so. I cram a lot into the days. Maybe I am trying to have a whole lifetime in the fraction of time I have with RD. Limerence, an overwhelming, intimate joy, prevailed intensely for a while and, with luck, makes its reappearance again and again. Out on the Internet, I find that limerence is treated as a problem to be cured, like alcoholism. RD and I consider it a gift we create for ourselves by our awareness of loving one another. It is the shimmering, focused sense of being together, of being joined in mind and breath, by hands and work. We can stand in the kitchen making breakfast and suddenly be swept away by the knowledge of our good fortune.

There is nothing between us

Not a molecule struck by lightning
not a breath inhaled
and released into the planetary atmosphere,

Not the thickness of a thread
is between us

Only the length of that thread
twisting, stretching, lengthening
to whatever is the necessary infinity.

Nothing is between us
but this hour.

I have spent my life as a foreigner, geographically and in my own life. From childhood in New York, through my life in Asia, Mexico, and America, I lived in over thirty different dwellings in more than a dozen different cities. Always, I search for home, moving toward it, or its illusion. I suppose the ache for constancy, for steadfast permanence, will never abate. I think that Heraclites had it right: It is not possible to step in the same stream twice. Even the Rocky Mountains seen from my window are in flux, uplifting themselves, eroding away, their shadows and colors changing every minute under the high-altitude light. I find myself astonished every day by the sights on this expedition, the new, unruly landscape to be negotiated.

My line of travel has been serpentine, calligraphic, curving with deliberate and inadvertent turnings, the thickness varying with the pressure applied. The ink is formless and full of possibility. It can become anything — a poem, a book, a beautiful drawing, a letter of good-bye, a stain on the table. The act of relinquishing, of setting free the ink carried in the brush, releases its possibilities and allows the ink to settle into its future. It fulfills a potential that becomes its destiny, made possible by enacting a choice. It is the opposite of fatalism. This deliberate act of will creates the circumstances in which new possibilities are realized. Destiny in this sense is the future.

I wonder why I cannot be satisfied with this life where I have finally arrived against all odds. The search for and discovery of harmony is the counterpoint to my experience of violence in its many forms. There seems to be a fugue-like quality to the pursuit, approach, and distancing of both harmony and home. I wonder if they are the same thing. I wonder how I will find out.

Right: *Kikyo Ichi Ro (One Path Leads Home)*, ink on paper, 1974

> *Alone the old crane stands*
> *In the morning stillness*
> > *Long feathers rustling amidst brittle stems*
> > *Eyes sweeping the sky*
>
> *Considering the path home*

归乡一路

雪溪

AFTERWORD • *I have thought about how to tell this story, to protect the sensibilities of other people and still tell the story as I have lived it. I have generally not used full names and in a few cases I have changed names.*

All my life and around the world, I have been the beneficiary of kindness and thoughtful guidance. Strangers pointed out the customs and signposts of a new country. Some became friends. As a foreigner, perspective is altered. I stand outside my expectations and see myself in an untried, sometimes unexpected context.

I have made paintings and photographs, composed poetry, fallen in love, grown old enough to be a grandmother. I have experienced and witnessed the anger, frustration, and aggression that spill out almost at random, often toward any available target. Whether political, military, parental, spousal, or just ordinary criminal, I have not yet come to understand the ubiquitous violence or to accept that we must live with it. As an artist, I have thought it possible to create a suggestion that might serve as an alternative reality.

Memory is notoriously unreliable. I have asked some people to clarify one point or another, but their memories are just as capricious as mine. We all modify our past by its successor. I am deeply grateful that they remembered our times together and were willing to share them with me. I hope I have been faithful to our experience. Things may not have happened exactly the way I have described, but the story is all true.

My thanks to Susan Vander Mast for friendship, the suggestion that led to this book, and being its first reader and constant critic. My gratitude to Michael Clarke for his vision and encouragement. To my friend Michael Motley for his beautiful design and his words at just the right time.

Most of all, to RD, for relentless intelligent criticism, for patient encouragement, for ruthlessly insisting on the truth.

Barcelona 2011

CHAPTER ILLUSTRATIONS

Frontispiece: *Persimmon*, ink on paper, 1975

Chapter 1: *La Falda de La Sierra, Tepoztlan*, ink on paper, 1984

Chapter 2: *Hikari (Shining Light)*, ink on paper, 1975

Chapter 3: *Trio*, ink on paper, 1976

Chapter 4: *Toksu-Gung (Toksu Palace)*, ink on paper, 1984

Chapter 5: *Nameless One*, ink on paper, 1986

Chapter 6: *Ghost House*, ink on paper, 1986

Chapter 7: *Second Serpent*, ink on paper, 1986

Chapter 8: *Mountains and Valleys*, monoprint, 1975

Chapter 9: *Wild Orchid*, ink on paper, 1974

Chapter 10: *Night Blooms*, ink on paper, 2001

Chapter 11: *Sun*, ink on paper, 1985

Chapter 12: *Light*, ink on paper, 1974

Afterword: *Pine Branch*, ink on paper, 1973